The Motley Fool

INVESTMENT GUIDE

— THIRD EDITION —

HOW THE FOOLS BEAT WALL STREET'S WISE MEN AND HOW YOU CAN TOO

DAVID & TOM GARDNER

AND THE MOTLEY FOOL TEAM

SIMON & SCHUSTER PAPERBACKS

NEW YORK · LONDON · TORONTO · SYDNEY · NEW DELHI

Simon & Schuster Paperbacks
An Imprint of Simon & Schuster, Inc.
1230 Avenue of the Americas
New York, NY 10020

Copyright © 1996, 2017 by David Gardner and Tom Gardner

First Simon & Schuster trade paperback edition September 2017

SIMON & SCHUSTER Paperbacks and colophon are
registered trademarks of Simon & Schuster, Inc.

For information about special discounts for bulk purchases, please contact
Simon & Schuster Special Sales at 1-866-506-1949
or business@simonandschuster.com.

The Simon & Schuster Speakers Bureau can bring authors to your live event.
For more information, or to book an event, contact the
Simon & Schuster Speakers Bureau at 1-866-248-3049
or visit our website at www.simonspeakers.com.

Interior design by Ruth Lee-Mui

Manufactured in the United States of America

3   5   7   9   10   8   6   4   2

Library of Congress Cataloging-in-Publication Data has been applied for.

ISBN 978-1-5011-5555-0
ISBN 978-1-5011-5876-6 (ebook)

CONTENTS

PART I

WHO, WHAT, WHY, AND HOW

1

"FOOL"?

Take heed . . . The wise may be instructed by a fool . . . You know how by the advice and counsel and prediction of fools, many kings, princes, states, and commonwealths have been preserved, several battles gained, and divers doubts of a most perplexed intricacy resolved.

—Rabelais

The world has changed dramatically since The Motley Fool began its quest to help the world invest better in 1993. Today's individual investor is armed with more information and greater—and cheaper!—access to the markets than ever before. Today, we can find a stock idea, research it online, and buy shares, all in a matter of mere moments . . . not that we think you should.

But much remains the same. Investing in individual equities remains the truest path to lasting wealth. Many Wall Street brokers will argue to their last breath that you can't do it on your own. But we have clear evidence— now with a track record that spans more than twenty years—that individual investors *can* beat the market . . . so long as they can overcome a few key behavioral barriers.

And yes, we're still answering questions about the name we chose for our company. So let's start there.

Fool?

That's certainly not a very *wise* choice for a name when you're trying to ply your trade in the investment world. For decades, financial professionals have done their best to sell customers on their Wisdom. Whether it's the pinstripe suit, the knowing smile, or the self-satisfied advertising slogan (one company referred to itself as "Rock Solid, Market Wise"), your typical broker, money manager, or financial planner has striven for an image of success, intelligence, experience, respectability—in a word, Wisdom.

And for decades, they've been making a fair amount of money off of fools. You know about fools. You might even have been one yourself at some point. Ever bought a stock on your dentist's recommendation with only a vague understanding of the company's business model? Or have you plunked down your money for shares of an under-the-radar business because an email in your inbox breathlessly proclaimed it a "can't miss opportunity . . . bound to double from \$0.04 to \$0.08 because of CAN'T-MISS catalysts?" How very foolish of you. Or what about the time you snapped up shares of the International Dashed Hopes Load Fund just because your broker said it was the top performer in its category last year? Terribly, terribly foolish.

And the financial establishment thanks you.

Fortunately, you don't need to be the one who provides the funds for other people's dreams. It's possible—now more than ever—to make informed, intelligent decisions that will help you make the most of your financial future.

The Wall Street Wise would have you believe that "A Fool and his money are soon parted"—we get that a lot. But in a world where more than eight out of every ten mutual fund managers lose to the market averages, year in and year out, how Wise should you aspire to be? In what other realms could such a paradox exist: that the paid professional can do no better than—in fact, cannot even do as well as—dumb luck?

And yet, in few other arenas are the trappings of the profession so enmeshed with the job itself—massive desks, expensive suits, gold cufflinks, precision watches. You be the judge of whether those accoutrements are designed to impress, intimidate, or overcompensate for their underperformance.

And that got us to thinking, working out of a far-from-glamorous 12-by-8-foot backyard shed all those years ago, that we should just go ahead and call ourselves Fools, since our attitude and approach to life were so radically different from what was being passed off as Wisdom all around us.

So we launched the very earliest iteration of The Motley Fool, taking the name from (an admittedly nondescript quotation from) Shakespeare's *As You Like It:* "A fool, a fool! I met a fool i' the forest, a motley fool."

We'd always loved Shakespeare's Fools: they amused as they instructed and were the only members of society who could tell the truth to the king or queen without having their heads lopped off. *The Motley Fool* began as a monthly newsletter distributed to a very . . . let's call it "exclusive" membership base. The printed newsletter soon transformed into a daily feature in the early days of America Online, when users paid by the minute they spent in our community. From those humble beginnings, the Fool has become one of the premier financial destinations online, with millions of investors reading our free analysis and advice, conversing in our community, participating in our stock-picking game, and performing their research in pursuit of winning stocks. The Fool now offers a suite of premium services catered to different investing styles, mutual funds that follow our Foolish tenets, and even a wealth-management business for those who love our style and advice but want to leave the heavy lifting to someone else. And The Motley Fool continues to seek new avenues to achieve its mission: to help the world invest . . . better.

Our goal was and is very simple: beat the market and show others how to do it—whether that's a teenager deciding how to invest the proceeds from her summer lawn-mowing business or a savvy, seasoned investor who wants to profit from advanced options trades. In our decades pursuing this goal, we've enabled millions of people to invest their own money—without the help of Armani suits—and set a course to the financial future they seek.

Our approach is best characterized by our general disinterest in, and mild disdain for, conventional wisdom. For example, the Wise will encourage you to invest your money in loaded mutual funds. (This "double dip" enables them to charge you for that advice *and then* charge you on an annual basis for the funds' management fees.) We, on the other hand, are telling you to buy stocks. They might tell you, "All right, take on that risk of stocks, but only buy the very safest ones." Or, alternatively, some brokers will try to sell you a collection of rinky-dink shares of penny stocks, dubious entities with an even more dubious likelihood of ever paying off. And many brokers, once you've entrusted them with your savings, will quietly rotate you into and out of investment vehicles, maximizing their transaction fees . . . but not your profits.

We want you to buy shares of great companies, sprinkle some more volatile growth stocks in with an array of blue chips, and skip the penny stocks altogether. Then hold those stocks for the long haul—think decades, not days. We espouse this approach for one simple reason: it works. Going back through history, you'll see that the stock market is pretty close to a sure thing, *if* you have the proper timeline (no day trading!) and temperament (no panicking!). From 1871 through 2012, holding periods of a single day were essentially a coin flip—52 percent of those days earned positive returns. But investors with longer horizons fared much, much better. Eighty-eight percent of ten-year holding periods were positive, and (this is not a typo) 100 percent of twenty-year and thirty-year holding periods made money. In pretty much any comparison between stocks and other asset classes, stocks win. According to a Credit Suisse study of the twenty-eight markets it tracks, stocks outperformed bonds, which outperformed cash in twenty-seven of them . . . by a wide margin. (China's the only exception, and that's because the country literally burned capitalistic symbols to the ground under Mao Zedong.) In short, stocks beat all other asset classes around the globe.

In addition to our contrary—though commonsense—approach of buying and holding stocks for the long haul, we're also encouraging you to consider a range of options trades, including *shorting* stocks, an attempt to profit off the decline of a stock rather than its rise. It *is* possible to use options "Foolishly," allowing you to generate extra income or giving you the option to own a stock you like at an even better price. (Fear not, we'll discuss these concepts later in the book, in terms that are neither exceedingly complicated nor scary.) To us, if you're an advanced investor for whom the stock market is more than a passing fancy, we believe you should at least consider the potential advantages of maximizing your returns in a way that matches your timeline and your temperament.

And the list of our outrageous beliefs goes on. It is capped by the very idea that you should manage your own money yourself—that you are the individual most personally invested in your financial success and, therefore, are the one best suited to make your money decisions. To many segments of the financial-services industry today, this idea remains about as logical as a financial-services company calling itself the Fool.

In what follows, then, we hope to help you, and the world, invest better, giving you the confidence and the knowledge you need to succeed as an individual investor. But first, we should introduce ourselves.

WHO WE ARE AND HOW WE GOT HERE

We're David and Tom Gardner, brothers and the founders of The Motley Fool. When we were young, we learned the core concept of investing . . . thanks to chocolate pudding. On trips to the supermarket, our dad would tell us, "See that pudding? We own the company that makes it! Every time someone buys that pudding, it's good for our company." Our childhood family vacations often included visits with the chief financial officers of companies based in the cities we visited. We didn't always understand our dad's conversations, and they cost us a few afternoons that would otherwise have been spent in a hotel swimming pool, but those visits set us on a path to understanding that businesses are only as good as the people who work there.

Years later, we began investing on our own, taking charge of the stock portfolios that our parents had started for us when we were born. For many casual investors, it takes a lifetime to overcome all the most common obstacles to investing in stocks—not knowing how to get started; believing they don't have the time, money, and ability to do it themselves; a willingness to settle for the seemingly safe—yet often underperforming—comfort of mutual funds. Thanks to the foresight of our parents, we were fortunate enough to skip past that preamble of doubt.

Our very first purchase was shares in a trucker called Leaseway

Transportation (long since acquired by a larger company). Using a few elementary measures, we had culled the stock from the pages of *Value Line*, then a seven-inch-thick investment research monstrosity, a format that with the advent of online tools is about as common and timely today as ticker tape. We can't recall the exact rationale for the purchase, but one hot summer, we watched with awe as shares climbed from $26 to $42, where we took our profit. In retrospect, the process of discovering and researching that potential investment left something to be desired—hardly our most inspired work—but it left us with a lesson that endures: If you're willing to take a risk, and you're open to continuous investigation and exploration into the world around you, you can enjoy tremendous financial success in the stock market without paying the Wall Street Wise for the privilege.

We've learned a lot since then, and today we welcome millions of readers to Fool.com each month. Hundreds of thousands of individual investors have come to trust our advice enough to become members of our premium services. In this book, we're going to take much of the guidance we provide daily on our site and in our services and break it down to its primary components. Rather than pointing you to a couple of "hot stocks," we want to give you the tools and tips to build, light, and grow that fire on your own.

We want to help you help yourself make money. This was our intention back in 1993, when we launched *The Motley Fool* as an investment newsletter. Ye Olde Printed Foole, as we fondly referred to it, contained our stock picks, one monthly investment article, and a patchwork quilt of content in keeping with our motley interests. We mailed out unsolicited copies to a few thousand unsuspecting people—we borrowed some friends' and relatives' wedding invitation lists—and wound up our first month with exactly thirty-eight subscribers. After publishing twelve monthly issues, we got a sinking sense that not everyone shared our passion for investing.

But as fate would have it, the burgeoning internet was beginning to connect people in a way previously unimaginable. By sharing our ideas and answering people's financial questions, we could begin a conversation about stocks with people around the world. In 1994, we partnered with a small but fast-growing service called America Online (AOL to friends), providing us greater visibility and reach.

With our dial-up connections and our desire to awaken the world to the benefits of investing in individual equities, we started typing. We offered our investment opinions and advice in response to requests from complete strangers, doing our best to provide them with as much information about their own holdings as they could handle. In so doing, we discovered some wonderful things (like how many people were willing to volunteer their own investment research for the benefit of many) and some bad things (don't get us started on the penny-stock scam artists, who still peddle their false and fraudulent get-rich-quick schemes to starry-eyed investors today). Within a few months, our little gabfest had grown into the most popular financial discussion on AOL, so we shuttered our monthly newsletter and took our show online. We were more interactive and timelier, and we didn't have to run to the neighborhood Kinko's and lick dozens of stamps each month.

Before long, and with the help of a feature in the *New Yorker*, word started to get around, and soon we were AOL's most frequented service in Personal Finance. People were buoyed by the idea that they could do it on their own. And it didn't hurt that our Fool Portfolio, a real-money portfolio invested exclusively in stocks, rose 11 percent in our first few months online, while the Standard & Poor's 500 (or the S&P 500, the index used most frequently to track money managers) stood flat. We closed our first year up 59 percent, almost 40 percentage points ahead of the market. Not so surprisingly, a lot of people were signing into our area to find out what we were up to.

It turned out our strategy for finding and buying shares in great companies, with the help of our growing community, was working. The greater the success of our investments, the more Fools came to the forum. And that itself led to better performance. As the shampoo bottle says, "Lather, rinse, repeat."

In the ensuing couple of decades, our business has changed in ways large and small as we continually strive to educate, amuse, and enrich individual investors like you. We have offices around the world, tackling the specific challenges and opportunities that are present in different countries. From our home office in Alexandria, Virginia, we publish a slew of investing articles each day on our award-winning website, with our talented stable of writers and analysts sharing the news and their views on individual companies, the market as a whole, and advice for making the most of your money. Our groundbreaking CAPS stock-rating service provides insights into what more than fifty thousand Motley Fool community members (as well as more than one hundred professional Wall Street firms) think about the stocks that investors own or are investigating. (Those players who've earned the best track records carry the most weight in a stock's CAPS rating.) We now feature hundreds of vibrant discussion boards, where newbies, individual investors, and industry experts together can weigh in on the prospects of a particular company, where users offer their best advice on living below your means, and where retirees share their successful stories of leaving the workplace long before they hit the official retirement age (to name just a few of the most popular boards). We've written a shelf full of bestselling books, we produce several binge-worthy podcasts, we boast a weekly radio show that airs on dozens of stations around the country each week, we're a mainstay on voice-activated devices like Amazon Echo and Google Assistant, and if you flip your television to the financial news channels, you're bound to see one of our analysts sharing his or her insights. And if you're the type who would prefer someone to do it all for you, well, we've also built a wealth-management business to do just that.

Coming full circle to the early days of the Fool, we also offer a stable of newsletter services for investors who are interested in paying an annual subscription membership for access to a team of analysts who put their heads together to come up with their best stock ideas. Some of them focus on a particular style of investing (dividends, growth, etc.); some of them feature real-money portfolios that members can follow along with at home; some dive into more advanced investing styles, like options (a strategy that we'll explore later in this book). But these aren't your father's newsletters. They offer far more than those early pages of printed text ever could—in fact, we prefer not to even call them "newsletters" anymore, and in a nod to technology, we no longer print and mail them to our members (though they're easy to print at home, for those who prefer). In all of them, we're shooting to better meet the needs of the hundreds of thousands of members who have decided to put their trust in us, and we're constantly refining our strategies for finding stocks that beat the market.

And it's worked out pretty well for the folks who have chosen over the years to follow our advice. We don't want to brag, so we'll just borrow a quote from a 2013 report from the venerable Mark Hulbert, who has tracked the advice of financial newsletters since 1980: "Consider this: The three top spots in the Hulbert Financial Digest's five-year rankings of more than 200 investment-advisory services all buy and hold quality companies. Remarkably, all three are subscription newsletters published by the same advisory firm, The Motley Fool in Alexandria, Va."

2

FOOLISHNESS

Foolery, sir, does walk about the orb
like the sun; it shines everywhere.

—Shakespeare

Some readers will no doubt wish at this point to put the introductions aside and encourage us to get to the point: "When do we get rich?" they might ask. This isn't that sort of book. If you're interested in fast cash, a quick search on Amazon reveals 569,564 results for "get rich." Books with titles like *How to Make $1,000,000 Automatically in the Stock Market* no doubt contain some magical formula that will enable you to become light-cigars-with-$100-bills rich. The book cover might even proclaim, "No thinking required!"

That's not our style. As Mr. Hulbert alluded to, we take the long view. In a world of day traders and sound bites and attention spans that are constantly eroded by our clickbait culture, where the click is somehow more valuable than fulfilling the promise it implies, we measure our success in years and decades. This book, then, is written for those who understand that there's significantly more to investing than just a studio host shouting, "Buy buy buy!" with sound effects added to make sure our interest never wanes.

This book is for those who understand and appreciate that investing is a lifelong pursuit that (done right) will set us up with the financial futures we want, letting us retire early, travel the world, buy a lake house, provide opportunities for our families, or install a two-story chocolate waterfall in our homes (it's our money, we can use it how we please!).

Moreover, we are writing for those who aren't in a hurry, those who think before they act, those who actually enjoy exercising their brains. To that end, let's now turn our talk to Foolishness. It's what we're actually all about once you get past the funny name and the jester caps, and it's not merely a style of investing.

TRUE WISDOM: GO AGAINST YOUR INSTINCTS

Foolishness is not a luxury; it is a necessity. It attacks conventional wisdom. Foolishness is more critical than ever today because everyone is interconnected and communication is instantaneous. That means more bad thinking circles the globe quicker than ever before.

"For every 10 bytes of value online there seem to be 10,000 bytes of drivel," wrote technology commentator Walt Mossberg back in the early days of the internet, when 10,000 bytes seemed like a lot of information. If we're not careful, true wisdom—those proverbial 10 bytes of truly good ideas and approaches—will get lost in the 10,000.

It may take a Fool to notice this, but despite decades of unprecedented advances in knowledge earned through scientific experimentation, archeological discovery, innovations in technology, and globalization, one thing that has assuredly *not* increased over time is the collective true wisdom, also known as common sense. So while modernization has determined that we'll continue to pile up more and more information, technology has no good mechanism for ensuring that we even maintain our common sense. You barely need to squint to see daily instances of it leaking away.

Good straight wisdom is a precious commodity. Benjamin Franklin was a terrific source of it—we're so enamored that we named a conference room at Fool HQ after him. A glance through *Poor Richard's Almanack*: "Three may keep a secret if two of them are dead." "He that speaks ill of the Mare will buy her." "He that's content hath enough. He that complains has too much."

What makes these aphorisms tokens of true wisdom is the way they contradict our basic instincts. We naturally assume the complainer is the one who is lacking what he needs. By twisting our expectations, he forces us to consider this new possibility. And after further reflection, you've probably identified one or another of your grumbling acquaintances who is suffering from having too much, not too little.

True wisdom leads to that kind of insight by challenging our preconceived notions or expectations. In the end, every great investment method succeeds not because of a magical formula or trend lines on a chart with flashing red "buy" signals. Rather, it succeeds by using some of the very commonsense wisdom we're talking about. Good investment practices can almost be called studies in good character. Just look at some of history's greatest investors. The investment career of Warren Buffett (yup, we have a conference room named for him as well) is not so much about balance-sheet analysis as Buffett's own humility, patience, and diligence. The approach incorporated by Peter Lynch (his room's right across the hall from Buffett's) is not so much about price-to-earnings ratios as it is about perceptiveness, optimism, and self-effacing humor. The greatest investors are often paragons of self-discipline and temperament, exhibiting admirable and useful characteristics such as patience, diligence, perceptiveness, and common sense.

Keep in mind that when dealing in money, the default characteristics are fear and greed. The investor must avoid the *instinctive temptation* toward those base motivations. Fear and greed will ruin your investment returns. It is an underappreciated trait of great investors that in putting up consistently superb investment returns, they are demonstrating their relative imperviousness to many of the less optimistic aspects of human nature—or at least understanding the temptations of themselves and others and using that to their advantage. As it says on the wall in the conference room named for Buffett: "Be fearful when others are greedy. Be greedy when others are fearful."

This, then, is the true wisdom: to resist one's baser instincts.

"Do every day one or two things for no other reason than that you would rather not do them. Thus, when the hour of darkness comes, it will not find you unprepared." So wrote the psychologist William James, another fellow who knew that to succeed, we must vigilantly toil against our own wills.

THE CONVENTIONAL WISDOM: "GO WITH YOUR INSTINCTS"

Today, examples of true wisdom are few and far between, culled from the pages of history or found in the rare modern exception. Conventional wisdom has filled the void. This counterfeit, useless, and damaging form of wisdom masquerading as the real thing has roused Fools throughout the ages in a call to arms. The be-all and end-all of Foolishness is its attack on conventional wisdom.

Fortunately for us, conventional wisdom is everywhere, especially in the financial world. That means we have plenty of opportunities to flex our Foolish muscles—to identify accepted thinking that is keeping us from achieving our true potential and knock it down. Television and the internet are filled with "experts" who loudly and confidently tell us where the market is headed over the coming weeks and months. The only reasonable answer to that question is, "I don't know," but that doesn't make for very interesting viewing. Online videos that don't have a "hot take" don't get clicks. It doesn't matter if they prove to be right.

Forecasts are enticing to us because they provide crystal-clear answers to our pressing problems. But they're mostly an exercise in taking recent history and extrapolating it into the future in a straight line. Life, as you know, is rarely made up of straight lines. So, most forecasts are merely a shot in the dark. But they've become so regular and frequent that we take them in stride today; some people almost believe them. The "best" market forecasters tout the one or two calls they got right to build their credentials, but ignore the thirty other predictions that didn't pan out. It's not their fault—predicting the short-term direction of the market is not possible. But based on the frequency of talking heads making prediction after prediction—market forecasts, market timing, and more—we're guessing that the average American doesn't realize that. If we were to hold these "experts" accountable by revisiting their past predictions, we would quickly see the whole enterprise as nonsense and see the conventional wisdom for what it is. (In fact, we track many of the best-known "experts" in our CAPS stock-picking game. Let's just say that not many of them are anywhere near the leaderboards.)

It's true that investment dollars are flowing increasingly toward low-cost, passive, and automated solutions, upending the old way to an extent. But a large segment of the population still believes the conventional pabulum that our mass media features, because they believe conventional wisdom is wise. That one perception is the bedrock of an entire industry: You can't do it yourself. You need experts to help you. You need the Wise.

We can learn a great deal from the Wise, though. In fact, the careful investor can learn so much through a brief analysis of common human error that we can't resist putting it right here. We'll close our chapter on Foolishness by examining the two shiniest pots of gold that many in the financial services industry try to convince us we'll find at the end of the rainbow if we just follow the conventional wisdom. Both can be poison for your brokerage account, and they are opposite but equally detrimental investment mistakes. We're talking about the two idols Wealth and Security.

WEALTH

Let's tackle Wealth first. Author Kurt Vonnegut reportedly said to fellow novelist Joseph Heller while attending a billionaire's party, "Joe, how does it make you feel to know that our host only yesterday may have made more money than your novel, *Catch-22*, has earned in its entire history?" Heller replied, "I've got something he can never have . . . The knowledge that I've got enough."

Literary luminaries aside, we've just about never met anyone who thought he or she had enough, whether we're talking about billionaires or mendicants. In the investment game, this leads people to take stupid gambles.

More often than not, the people most eager and fervent in their pursuit of Wealth are younger. (Security, as we'll see, is quite the opposite.)

Unsophisticated first-time investors often almost instinctively swing for the fences. They've heard the stories about that IBM stock their grandfather once bought and unloaded a few decades later for forty-five times his money. They figure the fastest way to make ten times their initial investment is to buy a stock at $5 that might go to $50, rather than one bought at $50 that would have to hit $500. In fact, perhaps one of the few negative side effects of Peter Lynch's excellent book *One Up on Wall Street* is that he induced a generation of readers to shoot for his fabled "ten-bagger" (a stock that makes an investor ten times her original money). Many people shooting for ten-baggers wind up buying pathetic penny stocks sold to them by people who don't have their best interest at heart. In fact, an online industry has sprouted up in which an ignored stock is suddenly all the rage, thanks to stock pumpers who do a masterful job at insinuating massive profits from a small initial sum . . . then, once the share price soars on the hype and enthusiasm of gullible or greedy speculators, those pumpers sell their shares at a huge profit, leaving the unwitting investors with nothing but remorse. Lynch is the last person who'd ever advocate such shortsighted speculation.

The tales of woe are endless. One of our very earliest discussion boards at Fool.com was titled My Dumbest Investment, and it remains one of our most popular. Sadly, hardly a week goes by without someone new sharing a brief story of the worst investment they've ever made and what they've learned from it.

Take the dentist from Illinois, who wrote of the year 1986, when he was a young, happy-go-lucky investor getting ready to invest in a company called Microsoft. But just then, he got a call at work from an investment banker claiming to have just bought an expensive car with the money made off an investment in (whispered) *platinum*. The poor and self-admittedly naive dentist was convinced by this fellow to put his money into platinum "on margin," meaning that he effectively borrowed extra money beyond what he had in order to heighten his stack of chips on the table. "A few days later my first margin call came in as the bottom dropped out," he wrote. "I had to put several thousand dollars on my credit card to cover my losses." The lesson learned from his Dumbest Investment was an excellent moral so early in his investing life.

Or take the screenwriter from Los Angeles who noticed in an issue of *Smart Money* magazine that a recent recommendation in its pages had dropped from $2 to just 25¢ per share in value. Excited, he didn't even bother to check out what the company did. "Now, imagine this," he went on. "I thought if I had bought it at $2, I would now be down, what, 87 percent or so? But what a deal it was now! A mere quarter! If they thought it was a good buy at two, it must be outta this world at 25¢! When a few months later I received the notice of the company's bankruptcy from my broker, I ruefully rubbed my chin, downed a Manhattan, and considered searching for a tall building." With the characteristic good wit that pervades the Dumbest Investment discussion, the writer concluded, "But I have a family. And, fortunately, I didn't throw away our nest egg."

The stories go on and on, as they will forever. There was the high school student doing a summer framing job for an oil tycoon. The tycoon was praising a little-known Canadian mining company. Unfortunately, the kid didn't know anything about the business except that this "tycoon" had made a lot of money on it, so he bought shares at $2.25 . . . just before it dropped to $1.25. He then doubled his holding, assuming it was an even greater value at the reduced price. Then it dropped to $0.25. Having lost 90 percent, he told us he was just hanging on to the thing, since it would "cost more to sell than just to keep."

Then there's the photographer who, "completely ignorant" about managing money, got to talking with his father's broker at his father's funeral (really). Soon after, he'd opened a margin account so his broker could trade currencies for him: Swiss francs, yen, German marks, Eurodollars. "Five months later, the 'new' broker handling my account (never *did* find out where the original broker went, all my calls were never answered) called to tell me I should close out what remained of the account, or write a *new* check to continue trading. I closed: 88 percent loss."

Finally is the story from a longtime Fool that dates back to the early 1990s when, nervous and new to investing, he visited a broker to discuss the stock he had just purchased, his first-ever investment. "I walked into this broker's office and sat at his nice big oak desk, and behind him were all these computer screens streaming stock quotes and looking very impressive," he wrote. "This gave me a comfortable feeling that this guy knew his stuff."

Unfortunately, the broker talked him out of that stock and into another, one that had recently had its initial public offering. The Fool watched forlornly as the new stock cratered and the one he had been convinced to sell increased in value from $1.75 to well above $12 per share. "Words out of my mouth at the time were, 'First time and last time I will ever invest,' but here I am still going."

The point of these stories is not that brokers and financial planners are evil. Not at all. Some are very good. Some are good and just plain wrong sometimes. Every investment entails a measure of risk. The point we're making is that in every case, the person sharing this sad story was taking on stupid risk—either because of having done no research, or having been baited by a sales pitch, or both. Why? To achieve get-rich-quick returns, in the chase for Wealth.

Hopefully, the lessons are self-explanatory: Don't invest in anything you don't understand. Manage your own money if you have the time and instinct. Don't fall in love with any given investment. Make sure you understand the incentives of the people giving you advice. Fight the urge to concentrate on short-term gains.

The overarching point is that those very get-rich-quick returns will always remain attractive to our human nature. We will be tempted by the conventional wisdom to shoot for the big bucks by "going with our instincts," sometimes on our own initiative, sometimes at the urging of others (who might not have the best motives). Our natural human instinct is toward Greed. To become a good investor, one *must* resist this very instinct. If you are able to focus on the next five years while the average investor is consumed with the next five months, you will have a powerful edge in your investing. After all, markets reward patience more than any other skill. Fortunately, you now have some Fools on your side who are aiming to help you build that advantage.

SECURITY

On the flip side of the coin from Wealth is another obstacle to your long-term financial health: Security. On the face of it, this one seems far less threatening or objectionable than the impulsive chase for Wealth, better known as Greed. How can we seriously advocate that a desire for safety be placed in the same conversation as something so nefarious that it made the ranks of the Seven Deadly Sins?

Easy. We're now talking about the two biggest threats to your (or your family's) long-term investment survival. Chasing Wealth, you may run headlong into a guillotine. But chasing Security is no less deadly a pursuit. In our first-ever issue of Ye Olde Printed Foole, we shared this contrarian line to which we still very much subscribe: "The least-mentioned, biggest risk of all is not taking enough risk."

Portions of the investment community today are infatuated with "risk avoidance" (or "risk aversion"). The primary aim of investing, these Wise tell us, is Safety—holding on to your precious dollars. Whatever happens, you *don't* want to lose what you've already earned through the sweat of your labors.

Now, a perfect Fool might point out that you are *constantly* losing what you've earned, since even low inflation is continuously eroding the value of cash. In fact, a dollar invested in Treasury bills (the *Safest* investment of all) in 1926 increased in real value to $21 by 2014, according to a study by Ibbotson Associates. That same dollar, had it been invested in large company stocks (the S&P 500 and its predecessors) would have assumed a real value of $5,317! Now, of course, with Treasury bills you were ostensibly up every year, and indeed some years you would be elated simply to avoid going down 20 percent in stocks. But here you are at the end of your investment lifetime tearing out whatever's left of your hair over the Grand Mistake you've made in the seemingly noble pursuit of Safety.

The possibility that someone might actually make good money sometimes does not seem to enter the thinking of some Wall Street Wise— particularly the more respectable element, at least. And to be sure, many business schools today teach the Efficient Markets Theory, which, when you boil it down, says that no one can consistently outperform the market over time. (Note: Please keep your eyes closed and pay no attention to those who are outperforming the market.)

The cynic may step in and suggest that many investment "pros" never *will* consistently or impressively beat the market, because of various handicaps that include the requirement to diversify large portfolios, timidity, a lack of imagination, the inability to short the market, and graduate study at business school. Given this, why *not* make Safety our goal? Like the wastebasket by your desk, it's an easy target. And it seems to keep the customers happy . . . those who don't know what they're doing, anyway.

Speaking of which, we've heard money managers tell us, "You know, if the market goes up 25 percent one year, and I go up 15 percent for my clients, no complaints. If the market goes up 5 percent one year and I go *down* 5 percent, I get all sorts of calls." This is a perfect illustration of our point. In both situations, very simple math tells us the money manager has underperformed the market averages by 10 percentage points . . . which, to Fools, is the most relevant year-to-year consideration. But in one situation, the manager's performance is tolerated, perhaps even complimented, while in the other he's berated. So, if *you* were an investment professional in this environment, wouldn't you make Safety your goal?

That's not to say prudence is necessarily bad, but we would advocate that it shouldn't be your primary objective as an investor. Now, since we advise investing in the stock market for long-term investors, we do need to put forth two key elements about playing it safe Foolishly. First, make sure you've paid off your high-interest debt before you get started, and be sure to have an emergency fund that will keep you above water in case of, well, emergency. Next, invest money that you can afford to wait on. The stock market is risky. We like that very much; it helps us make money, because you almost *never* get something for nothing. But in a given period, your stocks could get stomped. In the dark days of the Great Depression, thousands of people lost most of what they had by investing in the market. More recently, the Great Recession of the late 2000s saw the United States shed more than 7.5 million jobs, and American households lost more than $15 trillion of net worth as a result of the market's plunge.

So if you get melted down on Meltdown Day, we want you still to have something left to slap back down on the table. Invest money that you plan on keeping in the market for at least five years. (We recommend a lifetime.) Stocks can and will go down. Sometimes a lot. And sometimes the market will take years to recover and reach new highs. But the long-term prognosis is tremendous. Remember the data we shared earlier: Holding periods of ten years resulted in positive returns 88 percent of the time. For twenty- and thirty-year holding periods, that number jumps to 100 percent.

Second, we aren't buying tickers; we're investing in good businesses. We aim to buy stock in companies that dominate their industry, companies that have a sustainable advantage over their competition, companies featuring honest and efficient management whose interests are aligned with us outside shareholders, and a bunch of other yardsticks that we'll explore later in the book.

And that's about it. Beyond those two points, we advise you to fight the urge to steer your ship to the shores of Security and toward the financial advisor who reflexively strikes the low-risk Safety gong. With low risk comes low returns. The whole point of buying this book is to educate yourself profitably. We expect that even at this early point, you've already graduated beyond much of the rest of the world; much of the rest of the world is going with its instincts—its twin pursuits of Wealth and Safety—and blaming someone else when it fails.

Before we close the curtain on our chapter devoted to Foolishness, we need to include a word about people who require income and high degrees of safety. These are typically older people. Just as chasing Wealth attracts the young in huge numbers, chasing Security can be a fervent hobby among the advanced. We hear every day from our site visitors and our members, "Hey, the Fool investment approach may work for younger people who can take some risk. But I'm seventy-six years old. What about somebody in my situation?"

Well, first we certainly advocate that you get to know your own situation very well and act accordingly. If you don't feel competent to analyze your own situation, hire a financial planner to help (though we have faith in you!). If your money is tied up in an annuity, and you expect to need its every interest payment over the five additional years you expect to live, you should let that money stay put. On the other hand, if your situation requires some income but allows you to contemplate risk in search of greater investment rewards, we think you're selling yourself short to be just sitting in interest-bearing securities. These securities—whether bonds or mutual funds or preferred stock or what have you—*all* underperform the market historically. So if you're looking out beyond five years—but with income needs—you're probably going to do much better by staying invested Foolishly (in good stocks) and annually selling off a portion of your nest egg to meet your income requirements . . . better than any other single investment approach.

Just to make that clear: If you have a $50,000 annuity paying you a flat annual interest of $3,000 (a 6 percent interest rate), consider that you could instead have that money invested in the stock market (historic average return is about 10 percent) earning on average (therefore) $5,000 a year. Assuming an average year, you can sell $3,000 to provide you your income and still wind up with $2,000 to spare, available for reinvestment to produce an account value of $52,000 to begin the next year. To be sure, some years your stocks will lose money, and you'll have to take that $3,000 straight out of capital. But except under the worst market periods in history, which occur very rarely (and from which we have *always* eventually recovered), you'll end up well ahead, even despite the occasional horrible two- or three-year run. Because some years will be wonderful.

This is our reasoning that has us talking down Security and suggesting that people consider keeping their money in the market for their own good, even—perhaps especially—when keeping their money in the market runs against their native instincts. As has been pointed out by many, the market is the best game going, because it pays good stakes and the odds are stacked in your favor. Fear sometimes causes people to lose sight of equity investing's superiority, always (it seems) at the wrong time . . . when the market has just hit bottom. Don't let human nature sway you. Consciously taking on smart risk remains the best way to succeed in investing . . . and in life, too.

◆   ◆   ◆

In summarizing our chapter on Foolishness, we hope we have demonstrated that conventional wisdom—what we call capital-*W* Wisdom—provides society with stale half-truths that encourage us to follow our instincts. Foolishness, a force for reformation and enlightenment (and a heck of a lot of fun, too), attacks Wisdom by providing its adherents contrary truths that enable us to resist our own base instincts. We've addressed the complementary woes of Wealth and Safety, one which tempts us to take too much risk, the other to take too little. We've explained who we are and told you what we believe. Now let us show you the nuts and bolts of how you can play along.

3

HOW TO BE AN INVESTOR TODAY

When we published the first version of *The Motley Fool Investment Guide*, many households didn't have a computer, Wall Street reported share prices in fractions, and "The Macarena" was the top song of the year. Thanks largely to advances in technology, life has never been better for the individual investor. Sure, you can still use a phone to call a broker to make a trade, just like you can play that wedding-dance staple whenever the mood strikes, but there's really no need. Back then, many investors lacked an internet connection at home and had to scour newspapers and other print publications for company and stock price information. Sending off for hard-copy reports from companies' investor relations departments or the Securities and Exchange Commission (the SEC) could take weeks. And before 2000, retail investors couldn't even be sure they had the same information as Wall Street insiders.

We're proud to say we had a hand in bringing about greater ease and transparency for individual investors, leveling the playing field for the little guy. In 2000, we journeyed to Capitol Hill and urged the SEC to support Regulation Fair Disclosure (Reg FD), requiring public companies to disclose material information to all investors fully and fairly or risk losing the commission's mandate to protect investors. The SEC received a record number of comments on the matter, 65 percent of which came from Fools (more than 3,800 in all). Chairman Arthur Levitt later visited Fool HQ, thanked us for our support, and said that we were "as close to being an effective investor advocate as any organization in America." The *Economist* was kind enough to write in 2007 that the Fool stood out "as an ethical oasis in an area that is fast becoming a home to charlatans."

Back in the early days, once you were able to figure out whether you wanted to buy a stock, you pretty much had to go through a broker to make trades, which took time (either to go to your broker's office or call him on the phone) and money (anywhere from $40 to $100 for a single trade). With the advent of online discount brokers in the 1990s, trade commissions were whittled down to roughly $10 per transaction, some even lower. Investing also became a whole lot simpler in 2001, when the SEC mandated a move to decimals. It might seem incomprehensible to newer investors who are used to seeing shares trade in dollars and cents, but Wall Street used to be a matter of fractions—in sixteenths, to be exact. More powerful computers made it possible for trades to go through in seconds.

Today many investors have cut out the well-dressed broker and his mahogany desk and now take advantage of low-cost online brokerages and the vast amount of information available online. Screening tools can help you zoom in on companies that meet your criteria. In moments, you can pull up a company's latest earnings report and all the key filings. And there's a plethora of apps, software, online calculators, news, and analysis that will help you make investing decisions that match up with your timeline and temperament.

Signing up for an online brokerage literally takes minutes. You don't need any fancy certificate to make stock purchases. With low-cost commissions and the ability to buy partial shares of stocks, you can even start your career as a full-fledged stock picker with just a couple hundred dollars. You're ready to roll!

But, before you do, are we sure that buying shares of individual equities is right for you? Or are there alternatives better suited to your needs? We're glad you asked.

PART II

MUTUAL FUNDS: LOVE 'EM OR LEAVE 'EM?

4

MAYBE YOU SHOULD JUST
BUY MUTUAL FUNDS

Think for a moment about Starbucks. For many Americans, there's at least one Starbucks within a short trip of their home. Fool HQ is within a quick walk of four of them. As a headline from the *Onion* satirized, "New Starbucks Opens in Rest Room of Existing Starbucks." With roughly ten thousand shops, the word *ubiquitous* comes to mind.

It might surprise you to learn, then, that even with recent declines in numbers, America boasts roughly the same number of mutual funds. According to Statista, there are nearly ten thousand mutual funds—one for every Starbucks in the United States!—managing assets worth more than $15 trillion. Back in 1980, just 5.7 percent of US households owned mutual funds, according to the Investment Company Institute. That number climbed to 28.7 percent of households by 1995, and to 45.7 percent by 2000, and has inched up since then.

That incredible growth has unquestionably been helped by the shift from traditional defined-benefit plans to defined-contribution plans as the main source of retirement savings, along with the advent of IRAs and Roth IRAs. As fewer Americans could rely on their employers to handle their retirement savings for them, more and more turned to the fund industry.

And it's not hard to understand the appeal. Unlike the latest round of penny-ante pyramid schemes, mutual funds seem safe, understandable, trackable, and well marketed. Mutual funds definitely can and do fail, but the larger fund families—Fidelity, Vanguard, and others—aren't going anywhere. And funds can be held accountable. You can monitor them against the market's average performance and see whether your fund measures up. You'd be foolish not to recognize the comfort in lumping your money together with that of thousands of other investors, passing it to select managers whose performance can be measured, earning instant diversification for your portfolio, and going on with your daily life.

Contentedness and confidence in the long-term profitability of your savings—those are two cornerstones to investing Foolishly. Mutual funds, which sprung up in an industry that had previously been doing a poor job of providing reassurance, filled the void. There are three overriding reasons that the mutual fund has blossomed into a multitrillion-dollar industry today. Let's spend the rest of this chapter digging in, and see whether mutual funds might be the best spot for your money.

MUTUAL FUNDS: A PRIMER

To say the mutual fund business has exploded in recent decades is among the bigger understatements of the century. There are now so many permutations and combinations of different types of funds on the market that it's hard for a regular Joe or Jane Investor to know exactly what to buy and what to avoid.

There have been dramatic shifts into passive products (we'll get to these in a moment), and perceptions have changed in the past couple of decades, but actively managed funds are still what many investors typically imagine when you say "mutual funds." These are portfolios run by sharp Wall Street types who invest your money in stocks and other investments that they think have the best chance of achieving superior returns. The portfolio management team will monitor your investments and buy and sell securities as market conditions change.

In other words, the goal here is to beat the market through careful security selection and analysis of macroeconomic trends. Each fund will have its own specific investment process and will vary with respect to expenses. So, if you want to tap into the brainpower of some of the top investing pros in the business, actively managed funds are a good way to go.

While mutual funds can be one of the best tools for creating long-term wealth, the key to success lies in finding the most well-managed, top-notch funds around. Unfortunately, there are a lot of stinkers out there, and oftentimes, they can look good on the surface. It's true that most funds do not beat the market, and many charge excessive fees for such middling performance. In fact, from 2006 to 2016, between 71 percent and 93 percent of active US stock mutual funds (depending on the type) have either closed or underperformed the index they're attempting to top, according to Morningstar. Bad funds can suck the life out of any portfolio, so it's important to do your homework before bringing a new fund on board. Here are some points to consider when putting mutual funds under the microscope.

How long has the fund's manager been around?

Manager tenure is one of the most important attributes to look for in a high-quality fund. Studies have shown that those funds with longer-tenured managers at the helm consistently perform better than those with newer managers. This makes sense—after all, the more experience someone has managing money in a particular style with a particular asset base, the better he or she should be at it. If a fund changes managers, that means that its previous performance track record is useless going forward, because it may have little bearing on how the fund will perform under the new manager.

Stick to funds with managers who have been around long enough to have seen several types of market environments, both positive and negative. Take a pass on newly minted funds. You don't want to trust your money to untested investment ideas, and this is exactly what most new mutual funds are. New funds open every day, and with little in the way of an asset base, expenses are often high. Investors should demand to see how a fund has performed before they buy in, and the only way to do that is to pick one that has a long track record of investing.

Does the fund have a consistent investment process?

Many funds change their stripes at the drop of a hat to try to latch on to the hottest-performing investment style. While some may think this shows a willingness to adapt to conditions, in reality it shows a lack of conviction in the investment process. A fund should demonstrate a consistent history of investing money in the same manner in both positive and negative market environments before you consider committing money to it.

You might also want to consider sticking to well-diversified, broad market funds rather than narrowly focused specialty funds. Many investors get sucked into obtuse sector- or country-specific funds—the Stock Cars Stock Index! the Herzfeld Caribbean Basin Fund!—because of the high returns these volatile areas can sometimes generate. However, most investors don't need funds that focus only on narrow market segments. They're typically more expensive and are much riskier than those that cover the broader market. Higher returns come with higher risk—meaning that these funds can fall just as far and as fast as they can rise—and many folks fail to remember this until after a downturn.

How much do you have to pay for the fund?

Expenses are, by many estimations, the most important consideration when choosing a fund. Study after study show that fees matter most. Legendary Vanguard founder Jack Bogle wrote in 2003 of what he called the Cost Matters Hypothesis, "a conclusion that is both trivially obvious and remarkably sweeping: The mathematical expectation of the speculator is a loss equal to the amount of transaction costs incurred." In short, money spent on advisory fees, brokerage commissions, transaction costs, and the like is money that you're *not investing*. Fees can be a huge drag on mutual funds, eating into investor returns. Be sure you know exactly how much you're paying for your manager's expertise. The average mutual fund sports an expense ratio of around 1 percent, according to Morningstar—there aren't many compelling reasons anyone should be paying more than that. Actively managed funds charge significantly more than passively managed index funds, so if you're paying for a manager to make active portfolio decisions, he or she had better add more value than the index fund is. Academic studies have proved that funds with lower fees are more likely to outperform more expensive ones, so stick with the low-cost options.

And whatever you do, make sure you don't pay a "load" fee to own a fund. A load is a sales charge or commission that you pay that goes to a broker to compensate the broker for his or her expertise in recommending the fund to you. These charges typically range from 3.25 percent to 5.75 percent of your initial investment—that's a huge chunk of your money, taken right off the top! No-load funds are free of this onerous charge, so that's where you should do your fund fishing.

How has the fund performed in both positive and negative market environments?

In addition to knowing that a fund stays consistent in its investing style, you should also know whether your fund can succeed in all kinds of market conditions. Especially with actively managed equity funds, it's critical that we know what to expect during bear market periods. If the fund dramatically underperformed its peers during down years like 2000 to 2002 or 2008, you know you might not be protected when another downturn hits in the future. (And spoiler alert: there *will* be another downturn in the future!) A solid fund and an effective manager can prevail through up and down markets, so we always check out how the fund has measured up. Also, don't rely solely on how the fund has performed over the past three, five, or even ten years—look at multiple bear- and bull-market periods to see how it has fared in each case.

Are the fund and fund shop shareholder-friendly?

It can be a bit more difficult to judge how shareholder-friendly a fund shop is, but there are some sterling examples, such as Vanguard. Vanguard's shareholders actually own the company, the expenses are some of the lowest in the business, and Vanguard has had shareholder-friendly policies in place for decades, such as fair value pricing and no sales charges to buy its funds.

There are other factors you can check, too. For instance, does the fund's manager invest his or her own money along with that of shareholders? If a manager is unwilling to put his money where his mouth is—we call this "eating his own cooking"—you might want to think twice about investing with him. Furthermore, is the communication to shareholders clear and consistent? Does the firm have a history of closing funds when they become too large? Or do they stay open just to garner more assets? If a fund's asset load starts to hamper a manager's ability to move into and out of stock positions quickly, for example, and the manager doesn't close it, investors will see the effects as the fund moves into more large- and mega-cap stocks, and they may suffer lagging returns. All of these factors should help shed light on how high a priority shareholder satisfaction is for the fund shop.

Of course, equally as important as how you choose funds is how you *don't* choose funds. There are some common mistakes that mutual fund investors are especially prone to making. If you ultimately choose to take the mutual fund route, we strongly encourage you to take extra caution to avoid these traps.

Don't chase performance.

Most investors make the mistake of investing in whichever fund or asset class has done the best in the past year or so. They hop into and out of funds based on whatever the current market is doing, and they don't think of the long term. This is a huge mistake, because most investors are lousy market timers. Too many people do their portfolios a huge disservice, essentially buying high and selling low—precisely the opposite of what you should be doing.

Investment styles come in and out of favor. In fact, a stretch of great performance raises valuations and makes a "correction" (the price will go down) more likely. Trying to catch the hottest-performing style *du jour* is a losing game. Rather, think broadly in terms of asset allocation and try to keep your eyes fixed on the long run, rather than giving in to the temptation of short-term returns.

Avoid trends.

Similarly, stay away from shiny new products that you likely don't need. Just because someone is offering it and marketing it brilliantly doesn't mean you have to own it. Don't buy gimmicky funds if they don't have a legitimate place in your portfolio. Do you really need a fund dedicated just to Chinese semiconductor stocks? Probably not. Think broadly and simply when it comes to investments, and as mentioned earlier, think twice about sinking money into more specialized funds and products.

Of course, once you pick your mutual funds, you're not out of the woods. Now you've got to settle the all-important question of asset allocation, or how you combine all the various asset classes such as domestic stocks, small-cap stocks, international stocks, and bonds. If this is just another headache for you, there is help available from a special category of balanced funds designed for folks who want more of a "set it and forget it" approach to asset allocation.

RETIREMENT SAVINGS ON AUTOPILOT

Called "life cycle" or "target date" funds, these entities are a mix of passively and actively managed stock funds and bond funds—and conveniently include a target retirement date in their name. You simply invest your retirement savings in the fund closest to the date you want to call it a day, and the fund does the rest, providing a suitable asset allocation and gradually ratcheting down the percentage of stocks as the retirement date nears. Today, there are more than one hundred such funds, with retirement dates in five-year intervals extending far into the future—Vanguard recently released a 2065 Fund for retirement-minded investors who are currently age eighteen to twenty-two.

Investing in a target-date fund is essentially like flying on autopilot. As you travel toward retirement, adjustments to your asset allocation gradually reduce your exposure to stocks and increase your fixed-income investments. In fact, and to underscore the flight comparison, this gradual adjustment is often called "the glide path."

It's important to note that there are some fundamental differences in glide paths among the various fund companies. For example, let's compare the three biggest target-date fund companies: Fidelity, T. Rowe Price, and Vanguard. While all three allocate approximately 90 percent of their assets to stocks in their 2045 funds, Fidelity has the shallowest glide path, thereby reducing the stock allocation at the slowest rate. Vanguard's steeper path indicates a more conservative asset allocation as retirement nears, while T. Rowe Price's path is the most conservative.

You'll also find quite a bit of variation when it comes to asset allocation, even in funds with the same target retirement date. Fidelity has a higher commitment to foreign stocks (about 28 percent of its equity holdings as of this writing), but then cuts this asset class at retirement to roughly 13 percent. For the first fifteen years, T. Rowe allocates about 25 percent of its equity portfolio to international holdings, and then steadily reduces the stake to just 5 percent. Vanguard's foreign allocation currently ranges from 30 percent for the most aggressive target-date funds to 9 percent for the most conservative. While those last couple of paragraphs might have caused your eyes to glaze over, they're simply an example to indicate the differences you should be aware of, if you're investigating this approach.

A target-date fund is usually a collection of mutual funds wrapped into a "fund of funds." For example, Fidelity offers a dozen Freedom funds (that's its catchy name for target-date funds) constructed as varying mixes drawn from around two dozen underlying Fidelity funds. The T. Rowe Price target-date funds follow a similar model, but with seventeen or eighteen underlying funds, including an S&P 500 index fund. Consistent with its reputation, Vanguard builds its target funds from its index funds: two stock indexes and two bond indexes, with a third bond index added in for the nearer-term portfolios. T. Rowe Price and Fidelity use their actively managed funds, with index funds sprinkled into the mix.

If you're a self-confident individualist who enjoys picking your own investments and cares deeply about such things as REITs and bond ratings, then target funds won't hold much appeal. However, if you're looking for a mainstream, hands-off approach to asset allocation and rebalancing *and* want to avoid paying a financial advisor to do it for you, then a target-date fund might be just the ticket. Whether bundled within a larger target-date fund or on their own, actively managed mutual funds are a way for Main Street investors to amass wealth and diversify their portfolios, all while getting a helping hand from some industry top guns. But there are both pros and cons to owning funds, so keep reading.

WHY BUY FUNDS? AVOID THE HIGH-VOLATILITY HEARTACHE

Consider this scenario: a broker calls you during dinner for the fifth time this month, pushing Huge Fruit Inc. (Ticker: HUGE), a little-known California outfit involved in "agribusiness biotechnology." HUGE is trading around $3.25, and the nagging broker is certain that the company's Lemon-Larger engineering system will soon be a smash success: "Got any idea how many gallons of lemonade can be squeezed out of a fifteen-pound citrus?" You don't, but you figure it's an awful lot. So you pull the trigger and tell the broker to buy the stock on your behalf.

Those shares of Huge Fruit Inc. bounce around between $5 and $2 over the course of several months. When it trends up, your investment pops to $5,000, and you can't stop yourself from bragging. When it hits new lows, you can't stop yourself from feeling the pain in multiple internal organs. Stock volatility, relative to its ebb and flow, can transform modesty into pomposity and digestion into heartburn.

Mutual funds are often the tranquilizing alternative. By virtue of their diversification, they are typically less volatile than the average equities portfolio of an individual investor. It's calming to know that you sit alongside thousands of other investors owning minute positions in hundreds of companies, sharing the risk. If the weather gets worse, we'll all pop open umbrellas together! And you could only profitably duplicate that diversity using stocks if you had a couple of hundred million dollars in the coffers. (And if you do, you can probably put this book down now.)

Diversification has been called the only true "free lunch" in the investing game, and for good reason. For pretty much every investment out there, if you want to earn a higher return, you've got to take on a higher level of risk. But by owning dozens, or even hundreds, of different stocks, you instantly diversify away the risk of any one particular company's misfortunes sinking your portfolio. That's a great risk-reducing move that won't actually cost you anything! And since, by definition, most mutual funds own scores of stocks, they are an instant diversification tool.

Of course, the flip side of having a diversified portfolio is that you'll be partially insulated from any outsized outperformance, as well. If Huge Fruit tripled in price, and it made up 50 percent of your portfolio because you bought so many shares, your portfolio would see a 100 percent gain, assuming your other stocks were flat. But if you owned Huge Fruit in Mutual Fund XYZ, it might only be 5 percent of that fund's holdings, and the gain to your portfolio would be substantially less. And when you're invested in hundreds of companies, if some of them do very well, their impact is diluted by the many less-stellar performances.

It's also true that as actively managed mutual funds grow in size over time, many encounter asset bloat. When fund assets get too big, managers may have difficulty finding places to put that money to work, and the fund could end up being overdiversified, rather than a carefully curated actively managed portfolio. So the largest mutual funds, by virtue of their reach and dimension, essentially *are* the market. And returns are more likely to end up simply shadowing a market index (which, not for nothing, has expenses that are a fraction of what active funds charge).

Which leads logically to the next question: what exactly is a market index? Glad you asked. The Dow Jones Industrial Average and the Standard & Poor's 500 Index (also known as the S&P 500) are the two primary indexes against which investors compare their investment returns. The Dow is a compilation of thirty huge American companies: Coca-Cola, Disney,

McDonald's, Wal-Mart, American Express, ExxonMobil, to name a few. The S&P 500 tracks (surprise!) five hundred industrial, transportation, financial, and utility stocks (for example, semiconductor, trucking, insurance, or heating companies), weighting the companies to account for their relative size. AT&T, Apple, Ford, Intel, FedEx, Pepsi, and Nike are among the more familiar names in the S&P 500; some of them are also Dow stocks.

Over the years, each index has compounded average annualized growth in the neighborhood of 10 percent per year. And with the help of compounded returns (the concept that the money you make makes you money), that can lead to outsized returns. Think about it this way: If you invest $10,000 and earn $1,000 in year one, you'll have a total investment of $11,000. If you earn 10 percent again, that means a gain of $1,100 in year two. In time, that will snowball (in a good way).

Thanks to the magic of compounded returns, a $1,000 investment back in 1925 would be worth a few million bucks today. In short, it turns out you didn't have to be a railroad baron to prepare for the future of your great-grandchildren. The power of long-term investing, coupled with compounded returns, can make even the simplest of investors look brilliant through the rearview mirror of history.

In that spirit, the Foolish approach to investing rests firmly on the belief that your portfolio should never keep you up at night. Were the market to collapse, dipping 30 percent in six months and pulling your holdings underground, you could rightly think of it as a bummer, but you shouldn't lose a minute of sleep over it. To illustrate our point, let's consider our relatively recent market meltdown. From December 2007 through February of 2009, the S&P 500 lost roughly 50 percent of its value in the lead-up to the Financial Crisis. How did you react?

Now, ask yourself what would happen to your life if, over the next year, *your* savings got cut in half. If your portfolio was $800, it got chopped to $400. If you had $25,000, it got slashed to $12,500. $3.6 million was suddenly $1.8 million. Could you bear the pain and hold tight, even as panic swells and your investment dollars dwindle? If the answer is no, if there's a chance you would cash out and cut your losses, that's probably money you shouldn't be holding in the stock market. Because if you sell at the market's darkest hour in decades, you're going to lose a small fortune—in that recent case, half your money. But if you're a composed investor, you'll be able to hold on tight through those dreary days when it seems like the financial world is crashing down around us. Because when you look at the market's growth from the trough in early 2009 through the end of 2015, you find that the S&P 500 has grown 16.2 percent annually. Even taking the market drop of 2007 through 2009 into account, the S&P 500 was up 6.5 percent annually from December 2007 to the end of 2015. We'll concede that's not as impressive as the long-term market average, but it's not peanuts. While it may endure regular drops and plunges, dips and nerve-jangling free falls over the decades, the long-term graph of the market is a steady march upward.

By buying into a time-tested mutual fund (as long as you don't sell in a panic), you essentially guarantee that you'll be able to participate in America's robust corporate growth in the decades ahead—the growth in companies like Apple, Microsoft, Johnson & Johnson, and Amazon. And you'll be able to sleep late and peacefully on Sunday morning. Broad-market mutual funds are more likely to deliver long-term portfolio stability, lower volatility, limited risk, and unscathed stomach lining.

And that's the second reason mutual funds are so popular.

WHY BUY MUTUAL FUNDS? SO LITTLE TIME . . .

Did you happen to hear the big news? There's a big story about Huge Fruit showing up on all the financial news sites. Take a read:

> RIVERSIDE, CALIF.—Huge Fruit Inc. (Ticker: HUGE) announced that the Food and Drug Administration (FDA), at a meeting yesterday afternoon to consider the LemonLarger® application, recommended rejection of the company's EnGene technology™ used in the genetic engineering of enlarged fruits and vegetables. After further review of additional materials provided by the company, the FDA cited widespread spinal dissolution in laboratory rats exposed to Huge Fruit's altered lemons. In heavy, late-afternoon activity, Huge Fruit Inc. is trading at $0.68, down $2.14, or roughly 76 percent, on the day.

One thing you probably didn't realize when you threw some "play money" into Huge Fruit Inc. is that unfamiliar ventures pushed on you by a broker over the telephone demand *more* research time on your part, *not less*. Imagining a glass of lemonade in every hand at Yankee Stadium, all pressed from a single immense lemon, is entertaining; unfortunately, it doesn't count as research.

You wonder: "How could I have dodged this lemon? Risk comes with the territory, no? What could I have done?" Those are fair questions. While the swift and sharp decline in the value of HUGE shares might not have seemed inevitable initially, more research might have made it so. Did Huge Fruit Inc. have other genetic engineering plans brewing in its labs? Were alternative streams of revenue being developed? Did the company have a load of cash on the balance sheet and negligible long-term debt?

Given the market's reaction to the announcement—the 76 percent loss of value in a single afternoon—the answer to all the above questions was probably "Nope." That's a real shame, too. Those are issues that your broker should've addressed in detail over the phone. It would've taken you or your broker less than an hour of work to uncover.

If you don't have the time outside of your work and family life to scrutinize dozens of stocks, mutual funds have to look pretty enticing. You've freed up time, eluded the bogeyman, and absolved yourself of the responsibility to research the stock market. A sigh of great relief is in order here.

On a train trip to New York, we overheard a retired father confess to his middle-aged son, "I don't know how my funds are doing, but I know they're up, and the money's safe. Somebody told me one of them is up fourteen percent, but does that mean for the last year, or since January first, or for the year to come? I don't know. But the money's safe."

Never underestimate the beauty of delegating the management of your assets. The right mutual funds bring security, profitability, and independence, and it lets you get back to your own business, or your walking tour across Montana, or your child's Little League games. After all, there's nothing wrong with moderate annual portfolio growth on top of moderate annual salary growth. It beats the heck out of Huge Fruit.

And while you may actually have the time and desire to keep up with a few dozen stocks in your portfolio, the sad fact is that you're in direct competition with some smart Wall Street people who have a lot more staff, resources, and connections at their disposal than you do. And even if you have a pretty good knowledge base about some stocks or certain corners of the market, odds are there are other areas where your know-how falls short. By investing in mutual funds, you might be investing in market sectors or other asset classes that you would otherwise probably end up having to guess about.

Of the options we've discussed so far, the best alternative to sitting through brokerage cold calls during dinner and spending weekends digging into financial statements, and suffering $3 stocks that turn nest eggs into eggshells . . . so far, the best alternative is the mutual fund. A majority of mutual funds have clear historical returns, at least somewhat estimable risk, and future returns that can be tracked every day against the performance of a relevant market benchmark. Going forward, counting in decades, you can bet that by buying a few well-chosen equity funds, you're going to outperform virtually every other non-stock investment vehicle. Your $1,000 today most likely will become a few million in the savings account of your great-grandchild.

But if you're still going to invest through a friendly full-service broker, be certain that you're at least getting the same treatment as mutual funds afford. Are you receiving:

- clearly reported historical returns?
- fairly estimable risk levels?
- future returns that can be tracked against a market index?
- a portfolio that is guaranteed to do no worse than mirror the market's average annual returns?

If your load of savings isn't at least mimicking the S&P 500's performance (after the deduction of all costs), you've blundered as an investor. And on that note, we move forward into chapter 5 and what must seem like unlikely advice, given our above treatment of mutual funds.

5

MAYBE YOU SHOULD AVOID MUTUAL FUNDS

WHY AVOID FUNDS? MARKET UNDERPERFORMANCE

It's one of the most damning statistics in the world of finance: Standard & Poor's reports that between 82 percent and 88 percent of all domestic stock mutual funds have underperformed the market's average return over the decade ending in 2014. S&P's annual scorecard of active versus passive investment performance reveals that in the past decade, 82 percent of large-cap managers and 88 percent of mid-cap and small-cap managers underperformed their market benchmark. Keep in mind that the statistics make the industry look even better than it deserves because of "survivorship bias," meaning that they don't reflect those funds that folded because of their perpetual paucity of profits.

Consider, too, that the results don't count the short- and long-term capital gains taxes that mutual funds foist off on their customers every year as they churn their portfolios. (That's not small potatoes, since Morningstar reports that the average domestic stock mutual fund has an annual turnover rate of 90 percent.) Nor do those results count any sales "loads" that funds often charge for the privilege of managed mediocrity. Imagine that: all those oft-quoted professionals in wingtip shoes, with hundreds of millions or billions of dollars to invest, losing to the market average year after year after year. It's like finding out that 80 percent of America's English professors would underperform their students on the Graduate Record Exams (GREs).

Think about the effect that a mutual fund's underperformance has on your returns. Say you put $10,000 in a fund that falls 1.2 percentage points short of the S&P's 11.2 percent return every year. Tack on another "point" for fees and another for taxes. That gives you an annual return of 8 percent. Over thirty years, your mutual fund will be worth just over $100,000. If you'd had an index fund (with its 0.2 percent fees and the current Vanguard turnover of 6 percent), its value would exceed $220,000. Stretch it out another ten years, and your mutual fund would have finally gotten to $220,000, but the index fund would have moved up to $650,000.

Given this data, you'll understand why it's vital that all investors track their annual results against those of an appropriate index, like the S&P 500, the Dow Jones Industrial Average, or the Nasdaq. Simply stack the total dollar growth of your portfolio versus the gains in the indices. That is, if you were to begin investing today, you would track the percentage gains or losses off the current level of the index of your choice versus your own bottom-line profits. It's imperative that you fit your own investment performance into this overall context. Guess what? If you haven't been tracking your investments, don't be surprised to find now that your broker-managed portfolio, or your collection of mutual funds, has done poorly relative to the indices. To be clear, there assuredly are winners out there. Some funds avoid hidden fees and penalties and boast management teams whose interests are aligned with shareholders'. If you're committed to going the mutual fund route, we recommend plenty of diligence and research in finding one that works for you. (As a side note, an affiliate of The Motley Fool, Motley Fool Asset Management, LLC, MFAM for short, manages mutual funds. Industry regulations forbid us from going into detail about them here, but we thought it might confuse readers if we didn't mention their existence. If you'd like more information about MFAM or its investing philosophy, head to foolfunds.com.)

WHY DO MOST FUNDS UNDERPERFORM?

Some of the challenges money managers face are similar to those confronting individual investors, namely a lack of time and a willingness to accept humdrum, average returns.

Further consider that this accelerated growth in mutual funds over the last few years has driven many of them up into the billion-dollar-asset stratosphere. Managing billions of dollars requires greater diversity of holdings. After all, 5 percent of $10 billion is $500 million, enough to buy a basket of small-capitalization companies outright!

But as we—and Jack Bogle—mentioned, the biggest contributor to lagging fund performance is fund expenses. This is the number one, bold-print, don't-forget, critical thing to know about mutual funds: They don't underperform because they're run by people who don't know what they're doing, but rather because the relative drag caused by their fees makes it all hugely challenging to beat the benchmark. The higher the costs of running a mutual fund, the higher the bar is set for the management team. Every penny that goes to pay for stock research, management fees, and trading costs is one more penny that has to be earned back before the fund even turns a profit. And history has shown that fund expenses are one of the key predictors of future returns.

According to Morningstar data, funds with lower expense ratios outperformed their more expensive counterparts over time. And not only that, but the lower-cost funds also tended to actually stay in business longer than funds with higher price tags. This relationship holds true across asset classes, as well when looking at recent three-, four-, and five-year time periods. In other words, the cheapest US stock funds beat the most expensive US stock funds; the lowest-cost foreign stock funds outperformed the most expensive foreign stock funds; and the most inexpensive bond funds did better than the highest-cost bond funds. Keeping costs low means more money in your pocket, both in terms of the fees they're not taking and the performance you might expect.

Of course, fund managers deserve to be paid, and even paid well, for doing their jobs. A Fool finds nothing improper with paying someone millions of dollars to manage a burgeoning conglomerate that outperforms its industry. Honest success needs to be rewarded. Does anyone think Michael Jordan was overpaid, given what he did for Nike, Gatorade, the Chicago Bulls, and the city of Chicago? There's nothing wrong with paying for performance. But some fund shops do a better job than others of containing costs and keeping management compensation within reason. And when expenses creep up, performance tends to creep down.

The final and most entertaining reason that 80 percent of all mutual funds perform sorrily stems from an unusual matter peculiar to the mutual fund industry called "window dressing." Window dressing is the quarter-end ritual during which mutual fund managers belatedly window-shop for the best and brightest stocks of the quarter. Why? To make their portfolio look impressive. In the late 1990s tech boom, when a stock like Cisco Systems (Nasdaq: CSCO) had risen 45 percent for the quarter, you can be sure that mutual funds were lining up to get a few shares of CSCO on their account statement. Why? To let their shareholders know that they were in on one of the hottest stocks of the quarter. That they took a position after the great run-up and perhaps made nothing on the transaction, or lost money, isn't what matters. What does? Appearance. In other words, in this industry it can be as effective to look like you made money as it is actually to have done the deed. Not surprisingly, a 2014 study by a team of Harvard researchers, which analyzed 2,623 equity funds from 1998 to 2008, found window-dressing was beneficial for the funds themselves (in terms of greater inflow of money), but not for the investors in those funds.

With thousands and thousands of funds to research, with brokers selling them on commission, and with many funds sticking their customers with hidden costs, individual investors are really back where they started with Huge Fruit Inc. Namely, weary. They now have to research not simply the investment, but also the myriad costs associated with it *and* the salesman who's cramming it down their collective throat.

WHY AVOID FUNDS? INGREDIENTS, PLEASE!

If Fools are to accept the credo "Don't ever invest in something you don't fully understand," then they should cross 90 percent of all mutual funds off their candidate list. Most mutual fund prospectuses feature a wonderfully rich language—Prospectish—that is indecipherable, uninformative, and legalistic. And the idea that you can ever get a serious grip on a fund through the fundamental analysis of its individual holdings is bunk. You'd be analyzing stocks right through till the next appearance of Halley's Comet.

Sad to say, sometimes even the most scholarly fund investors among us, those who willingly forego summer barbecues to huddle over investment tomes, get backhanded by fund managers who take extra risk on the sly, deviating from their proposed course. What? You didn't know that your mutual fund was dabbling in derivatives? You weren't aware that management was experimenting with some option trading this quarter? You didn't hear that Joe, the new intern at Strategic Diversified Wisdom Fund, decided to try his luck at some "currency swapping"?

Therein lies a primary reason to avoid mutual funds. In most cases, you can't see the *business* in which you're investing. And when you can't see what's going on with your money, it doesn't matter how wise or Foolish you are: You can't evaluate a fund's holdings or its strategy. You can only pay your money and take your chances.

And what tool for valuing mutual funds fairly has replaced the fundamental analyses that turned enormous profits in stocks for the great investors of the past? Performance chasing. The most popular and least meaningful technique used to value mutual funds today is an eyeballing of their one-, three-, and five-year records. Compare it to a baseball game, a Baltimore Orioles–Cleveland Indians game. Disregard whether the game is being played at Camden Yards or Cleveland's Progressive Field, who's pitching, whether any players are injured; in fact, disregard altogether who's on the teams. Now click to your favorite sports website and find out how many games each team has won over the past five years. Whichever team has won more, price studies suggest, should win the game. It's ludicrous.

Oh, but before putting money down on that analysis, *do* check to see if the O's pitching staff is into inverse-floating derivatives.

RUNNING HISTORICAL NUMBERS

Let's look at some of the numbers together to paint a prettier picture of what happens to our dollars when we hold them in the light of compounded returns. We'll work off a base of $10,000, showing pretax profits:

YEAR/VEHICLE	GROWTH RATE	$10,000 BECOMES . . .
I. 20-Year Period		
Huge Fruit Inc.	-95.6%	$0
Crapola Fund	-25%	$32
Treasury Bills	4%	$21,911
Bonds	6%	$32,071
Average Mutual Fund	8%	$46,609
The S&P 50	11%	$80,623
II. 40-Year Period		
Crapola Fund	-25%	$0
Treasury Bills	4%	$48,010
Bonds	6%	$102,857
Average Mutual Fund	8%	$217,245
The S&P 50	11%	$650,008
III. 60-Year Period		
Treasury Bills	4%	$105,196
Bonds	6%	$329,877
Average Mutual Fund	8%	$1,012,571
The S&P 500	11%	$5,240,572

That's the sort of chart that should be stamped on the inside of every investment text published. It ought to be drilled into the minds of business school students and memorized alongside state capitals in grade school:

$10,000 in Treasury bills for sixty years is worth half as much as $10,000 in mutual funds for forty years.

But most astonishing of all is the sixty-year performance of the S&P 500 versus your average mutual fund. The former easily clears $5 million, while the latter struggles to reach $1 million. Pretty damning evidence for an industry that spends billions of dollars each year selling itself to individual investors.

Fools don't while away many hours wondering whether Wall Street is right when it tells us that we ought to have our money broadly diversified in mutual funds, bonds, and T-bills. Fools already know that all of these have underperformed the S&P 500 year after year after year. Seventy-five years of history is sufficiently convincing proof for bonds, gold, and T-bills, and the last twenty years have convinced us that mutual funds often are an investment opportunity that isn't one. So many actively managed funds charge all sorts of fees and fall short of average. In the next chapter, we'll prove that being average is really quite simple.

6

PASSIVELY MANAGED INVESTMENTS

Imagine a single mutual fund whose eminently trackable performance virtually matches market-average growth year after year, whose holdings are clearly outlined for you in advance, and which demands virtually no research. Imagine no more. Your dream is real and available in a variety of passively managed investments.

The index fund—and its descendent, the exchange-traded fund (ETF)—doesn't hogtie you into a lot of investments you hadn't prepared to make, while sticking you with a variety of hidden costs down the line. They simply attempt to replicate the performance of a relevant benchmark by purchasing all the stocks that are included in that very benchmark.

The biggest and best-known is Vanguard's 500 Index Fund. This *many-trillion*-dollar fund simply duplicates the holdings of the S&P 500 by buying all five hundred stocks in corresponding lots. (The S&P 500 does not weigh each stock equally, but by the size of the company. If Huge Fruit were worth

$1 billion, and the total worth of the 500 stocks was $10 trillion, then Huge Fruit would make up .01 percent of the index.) It is thus able to match (and compound) the index's growth year after year.

Index funds such as Vanguard's pace the most profitable vehicle for investing: the US stock market. And now that index funds and ETFs are available that track nearly every corner of the global stock and bond market, you can easily purchase a passively managed fund that invests in domestic growth stocks, small-cap value stocks, emerging markets stocks, real estate stocks, or global corporate bonds. The world is now your oyster!

When you consider that mutual funds have consistently underperformed the stock market, broad-market index trackers (like those that mirror the S&P 500) really start looking attractive. They demand no research and outperform most active funds on the market. For this and the reasons outlined below, you may want to consider making passively managed mutual funds a staple in your portfolio.

As an added bonus, passively managed funds go a long way toward wiping out the broker and mutual fund world's shoddier practices. With no hard selling, no hidden fees, and no confusing monthly statements, the index funds and ETFs have largely been fashioned after the finest of business models: the buyer comes first.

HASSLE-FREE PERFORMANCE

One of our core Foolish beliefs is that investing ought to be a profitable and time-saving venture, meaning that every step of the way, investors should be evaluating how much of their time they're spending and for how much long-term profit.

When you look out over Wall Street, crowded in now by thousands of mutual funds, don't passive investments look inviting? You literally need to do no research to participate in America's corporate growth at a moderate pace. And since we already know that the clear majority of actively managed funds don't beat the market, why not just make things easy on yourself, buy an index fund or two, and call it a day? Why beat 'em when you can join 'em?

And perhaps the biggest draw of passively managed funds is that because you're not paying some Wall Street type to do all kinds of crazy research, fund expenses are a heck of a lot lower. In fact, according to Investment Company Institute data, the average index equity fund has an expense ratio of just 0.11 percent, while the average index bond fund clocks in at 0.10 percent. When you consider that some actively managed funds can cost many times more than a similar passively managed fund, it's pretty easy to be left wondering whether active funds' higher price tags are even worth it.

With passively managed funds, you get one-stop diversified market exposure, lower fees, zero research commitment, a full knowledge of what investments the fund is making (typically market-weighted long positions in a number of well-known stocks), and—not to be underrated—time to spend on other things. All things considered, how Foolish can you get?

LESS ACTION, MORE TRACTION

So let's say you've decided to invest a portion of your portfolio in passive investments. That's one big decision down, but now you have another to go: do you choose a traditional index fund, or an exchanged-traded fund (ETF)?

We're glad you asked, because we've got all the information you need right here to help you make your choice. First, we'll start with this handy chart that highlights the key features of both options.

FEATURE	EXCHANGE-TRADED FUNDS (ETFS)	INDEX FUNDS
Ticker symbols	Two to four letters.	Always five letters, ending with an *X*.
Pricing and trade execution	Trade just like stocks on exchanges (thus, the "exchange-traded" in their name). Their prices change throughout the trading day, and orders are executed very quickly while the market is open.	Are priced just once a day, after the market closes. At that point, any orders placed during the day will be executed.

FEATURE	EXCHANGE-TRADED FUNDS (ETFS)	INDEX FUNDS
Trading costs	Brokerages generally charge a commission to buy or sell, though some offer commission-free trades of select ETFs.	Many index funds can be bought on a "no-load" (i.e., no-commission) basis, especially if bought directly from the fund company. Discount brokerages often charge a "transaction fee" to buy funds from particular fund families.
Investment minimums	No minimum investment as long as you can afford the price of a share and trading commission.	Most mutual funds require a minimum investment, generally ranging from $1,000 to $3,000 (though it can be lower if you sign up for an ongoing "automatic investment" program).
Can be shorted, bought on margin, or used with options strategies	Yes.	No.
Can be bought and sold through special orders, such as limit orders, stop-loss orders, and good-til-canceled orders	Yes.	No.
Available in 401(k)s and 529 college savings plans	Generally not, unless the 401(k) offers a side brokerage account. iShares offers a 529 with ETFs.	Most plans offer at least an S&P 500 index fund.

There are a couple of other differences between ETFs and index funds you may have heard: the former are cheaper and more tax-efficient than the latter. To test those assumptions, let's take a ringside seat in some head-to-head comparisons between popular index funds and ETFs that track the same index.

The table below displays the results of these bouts, in most cases lining up a Vanguard index fund with its ETF cousin.

NAME	TICKER	FUND CATEGORY	EXPENSE RATIO	ANNUALIZED 5-YEAR RETURN	10-YEAR TAX-COST RATIO
Vanguard 500 Index Fund	VFINX	Large Blend	0.16	14.39	0.43
SPDR S&P 500 ETF	SPY	Large Blend	0.09	14.42	0.59
Vanguard Value Index Fund	VIVAX	Large Value	0.22	14.31	0.54
Vanguard Value ETF	VTV	Large Value	0.08	14.47	0.75
Vanguard Growth Index Fund	VIGRX	Large Growth	0.22	14.25	0.25
Vanguard Growth ETF	VUG	Large Growth	0.08	14.42	0.29
Vanguard Small-Cap Index Fund	NAESX	Small Blend	0.20	14.15	0.37
Vanguard Small-Cap ETF	VB	Small Blend	0.08	14.33	0.50
Vanguard Emerging Markets Stock Index Fund	VEIEX	Emerging Markets	0.33	1.60	0.68
Vanguard FTSE Emerging Markets ETF	VWO	Emerging Markets	0.15	1.78	0.83
Vanguard REIT Index Fund	VGSIX	Real Estate	0.26	14.20	1.20
Vanguard REIT ETF	VNQ	Real Estate	0.12	14.35	1.25

NAME	TICKER	FUND CATEGORY	EXPENSE RATIO	ANNUALIZED 5-YEAR RETURN	10-YEAR TAX-COST RATIO
Vanguard Total Bond Market Index Fund	VBMFX	Intermediate-Term Bond	0.16	2.95	1.27
Vanguard Total Bond Market ETF	BND	Intermediate-Term Bond	0.06	3.01	N/A
iShares Core U.S. Aggregate Bond ETF	AGG	Intermediate-Term Bond	0.05	3.01	1.24

Source: Morningstar.

As you can see, the ETF versions are indeed the lower-cost choices, which have led to correspondingly better performance. We should note, however, that in the case of Vanguard index funds, share classes with lower expense ratios (so-called Admiral shares) are available to investors with higher balances.

Looking at tax-efficiency, the argument that ETFs are superior doesn't seem to hold up. In the far-right column, you'll see the ten-year tax-cost ratio. According to Morningstar, that number "measures how much a fund's annualized return is reduced by the taxes investors pay on distributions." Those distributions come in the form of dividends or capital gains that get passed on to shareholders when the fund sells holdings at a profit. The higher the tax-cost ratio, the more an investor paid in taxes if the investment wasn't in an IRA or 401(k). The differences between the ETFs and index funds displayed in the table above aren't huge, but they do demonstrate that—despite popular belief—ETFs aren't always the most tax-efficient choice.

Perhaps more enlightening is comparing the tax-cost ratio of the different asset classes. The Vanguard Growth options took the smallest tax bites, since large-cap funds tend to have lower turnover (i.e., less buying and selling within the funds), and growth stocks are less likely to pay dividends. On the other hand, the REIT and bond options are less tax-efficient because of the relatively high amount of income they produce; also, turnover in the bond funds is very high since it's actually more complicated—and requires more transactions—to try to copy a bond index.

The tax-cost ratio of any fund—active or passive—can help when determining which investments should be placed in your IRAs and 401(k)s and which can be kept out of those accounts without a significant tax consequence. You can get the tax-cost ratio, as well as tax-adjusted return, by looking up the fund on Morningstar.com and clicking on the "Tax" tab in the gray bar. Note that these are calculated based on higher-income tax rates; the lower your tax bracket, the less Morningstar's tax calculations would apply to your situation.

If you look at costs, which ultimately influence performance, ETFs are the winners. Other features further tilt the choice in their favor, such as knowing exactly the price you're going to pay when you buy (or get when you sell).

Transaction costs might also play a role, depending on the size and frequency of your trades. You might have heard that if you make multiple investments over time, and have to pay a commission if you do so via ETFs, then a no-load index fund might be the better choice. However, keep in mind that a discount brokerage commission is a onetime cost—usually $10 or less—whereas a higher expense ratio is a cost you'll pay every year that will grow as your fund (ideally) grows. So consider transaction costs only if you're paying commissions to buy and sell ETFs in amounts of just a few hundred dollars.

Finally, you might not have a choice. If you're restricting your fund investing to your employer-sponsored retirement account, then you'll have to love the index funds you're with, even if they have higher expense ratios than ETFs or even other index funds available elsewhere.

THE SWITCHEROO!

Thus far we've done our level best to convince you to invest in stocks . . . and then not to; to convince you to invest in actively managed mutual funds . . .

and then not to; and most recently, to persuade you to buy an index fund or ETF and now . . . not to. Surely, you've caught on to our tricks by now.

We end this chapter by rescinding everything that, up to this point, might be confused with a buy recommendation. Don't buy just any stock because the market does well (e.g., Huge Fruit). Don't buy mutual funds because you've lost money in stocks. Don't buy an index fund because your actively managed funds have been underperforming the market. Don't buy any of these. Why? Because there are more profitable approaches to investing.

What we have built together, thus far, is the bottom step of the Foolish investing ladder. We ask: is there any reason to garner less than market-average returns, which have rewarded at the rate of about 10 percent per year for six decades running?

Resoundingly, no!

Step onto that bottom rung and start climbing. Two decades from now, you ought to be staring at something close to 11 percent growth compounded on your savings, at the very least. For those with $20,000 to invest, that would grow your portfolio into $161,000 over the next twenty years . . . and more if you were Foolish enough to continue socking away savings there, weekly, monthly, quarterly, and annually for your future.

Should you be happy with 11 percent growth per year without carrying out a lick of research? Compared to what's being foisted upon many individual investors by the investment management business, most definitely yes, you should be pleased. Investors should not settle for market underperformance over any protracted period. And there's nothing at all wrong with 11 percent annual growth, eh?

But what if you actually come to *like* the stock market? What if you think business is interesting? What if you have a streak of competitiveness in you that drives you to outperform? Then no, dear Fool, you shouldn't be satisfied. Throw away all thoughts of index funds and market-average growth, and continue instead of a path of passion and profits—buying shares in tremendous companies with the possibility of far greater returns.

PART III

BUILDING A FOOLISH
INVESTMENT PORTFOLIO

7

STEPPING AWAY FROM INDEX FUNDS

We keep moving forward, opening new doors, and doing new things, because we're curious and curiosity keeps leading us down new paths.

—Walt Disney

So now once again, we've opted to pull apart, analyze, and ultimately de-
nounce the very things we just celebrated. That's how we roll.

In chapter 3, we applauded mutual funds for providing a dependable
way to turn a profit on your savings. Funds give their shareholders diversity,
long-term profitability, and comfort. They're the response to those full-
service brokerage firms that haven't yet proved to lowly Fools that they
comprehend the notion of "service."

Service (n): an act giving assistance and advantage to another.

That means putting your customers' well-being, their short- and long-
term prosperity, before your own. That's a pretty good business plan—as
you'll see, it's one we look for in our own search for great investment choices.
Sadly, the industry doesn't always have service pegged as its priority, though.

That said, don't confuse our criticism of poor service in the world of
brokering for a blanket promotion of the mutual fund construct. Why not?

Because while some do take a Foolish approach to investment success, the majority of mutual funds underperform the market's average return each year. We reiterate that because of frenetic trading, high fees, and a short-term focus, more than 80 percent of all mutual funds with a ten-year track record have failed to be just average. That was true when we published our guide more than twenty years ago, and it remains true today! So the next time you find yourself in the company of five fund managers, ask them if their annual returns have matched those of the S&P 500 over the past five years. Four of them, at least, will hang their heads and sulk. Foolish reader, think how unnecessary the majority of them are, given that we, any of us, can essentially duplicate the S&P 500's returns without doing a lick of research. Investing in an index fund takes no time, little research, no Pepcid, and—assuming you can control your own urges to trade away your success—puts you out front of 80 percent of the competition. To be clear, not all index funds are created equal. Some index funds actually charge loads and additional fees—one especially awful index fund charges a 5.5 percent front-end load and an expense ratio of 0.62 percent, while a similar Vanguard fund has an expense ratio of 0.15 percent and no loads, marketing fees, or other hidden costs. Lighting twenty-dollar bills on fire is arguably a better use of your money. But as long as you don't shut down your brain and blindly accept loads and fees on an index fund, you'll be a step ahead of the average if you select this avenue.

But now we'll push the ante up once more by suggesting that you look beyond index funds and all those other publicly traded exchange-traded funds (ETFs). While no one ought to accept anything less than average returns, if you're able and willing to take risk beyond the index fund, there's a wide, wide world out there. Based on the fact that you're sixty-plus pages into this book, you're almost certainly here to learn how, so give us an opportunity to demonstrate that with some dedication to your task and a long-term, business-focused approach, you can outperform Wall Street's well-heeled stewards.

ETF HYPE: THE EFFICIENT MARKETS THEORY

The Efficient Markets Theory (EMT) backs the traditional, academic approach to the stock market and is the philosophical underpinning of the index fund and ETF industry it spawned. EMT suggests that the stock market is an "efficient" thing, wherein all present prices best reflect the underlying, fair-market value of stocks. Stocks, EMT theorists tell us, are always priced fairly; the only thing that bumps them up or knocks them down are unforeseeable events—mergers, new partnerships, announcements of new products or services, and so on. The future. Because these price stimulants are "unforeseeable," we are told, all future movements on the stock market are therefore random and unpredictable.

The fundamentals of this theory are actually mostly sound. The market's prices at any given moment *do* reflect our collective "best guess" at a company's stock price—a "best guess" arrived at by millions of buyers and sellers who are shaking hands over billions of dollars from opposite sides of the table. This is truer and truer the more liquid (commonly held, highly traded) a company's stock is. On the other hand, like most of their species, these buyers and sellers are rather a shortsighted lot—especially since so much active trading today is done by people (or computers!) whose collective attention span matches that of a guppy. You can expect that the market's prices typically aren't looking as far ahead as the Foolish long-term investor. To our even greater advantage, common sense remains of uncommon value when looking at market prices. Is anyone seriously contending that Farmville creator Zynga or coupon magnate Groupon were ever worth their prices, even at their initial public offerings?

You see, the real problem with the efficient markets theory is not with what it says, but rather what some take it to mean. Some conclude, wrongly, that investing is just guesswork. With guesswork, we admit it would be nearly impossible for anyone to consistently beat the market.

It's unfortunately not surprising that this conclusion has found a home in America's finer universities and business schools, where increasingly the notion of excellence has given way to a soft, sleepy relativism. The collective wisdom of prices is greater than the individual wisdom, they tell us.

And that being the case, there's no reason to study individual stocks and the businesses behind them, nor to prepare, nor to aim high and aspire to outperform. Right? Hey, all stocks at the prices they are today are really just the same! Becoming a part-owner of this company over that one is not worth considering.

But the stock market is not a controlled laboratory experiment, nor does it submit to easy explanations of how much value is in it at any given moment or how accurately that value is being reflected. The stock market is messy and emotional and remains always a little bit wrong in its present estimation, in a charming and sometimes surprising way. Were the market truly efficient—a clean machine—every perfectly valued, publicly traded security would inch forward 0.025 percent per day en route to annual returns of 9.5 percent . . . *every* market day of *every* market year of *every* market decade. It doesn't happen, and it's the inevitable inefficiencies that have Fools rummaging around looking for long-run market outperformers.

Many have gone before and go with us. The market has been beaten consistently and significantly by the high-profile likes of Philip Fisher, Peter Lynch, and Warren Buffett, to say nothing of tens of thousands of Foolish Everymen (and Everywomen) who've logged their time on our website and in our investment services. And this plays out because the stock market isn't propelled by synergistic forces driving toward greater efficiency, but rather by divergent ones generating ever-greater complexity. Pricing in a barter market like the stock exchange isn't the upshot of one mind, one approach, or one analysis, but the consequence of many different attitudes, time horizons, valuation models, degrees of expertise, and varieties of expectation. It's also, critically, the consequence of human emotions, in all their extremes.

Remember the Netflix debacle in the summer of 2011? After growing out the streaming-video library sufficiently to stand on its own, the company announced a huge price increase, and followed up a few months later saying that it'd split the DVD-by-mail business off into a new brand, dubbed Qwikster of all things, and force Netflix users to split their allegiance (and credit card info, and movie preferences) between two websites. The stock sold off to a low around $63 a share. The questions swirled: Would Netflix kill its subscriber growth in one fell swoop? Was Netflix CEO Reed

Hastings really so out of touch with his customers? Would Apple and Amazon use the turmoil to steal subscribers and kill off this upstart once and for all? And for the love of all that is holy, who the heck thought naming the DVD business "Qwikster" was anything other than completely ridiculous? Netflix: a brand name forever scarred?

Now consider the myriad reasons that the hundreds of thousands of institutional and individual investors tracking Netflix bought and sold this fantastic stock during the upheaval. Some felt the company was in serious trouble; others thought the market had overreacted to the news and that the stock was underpriced; some routinely picked up more Netflix shares in their workplace retirement plans; others cashed out, needing capital to buy a home, an iPhone, a Ferrari. Fools recognize that there are an untold number of reasons that stocks are bought and sold at given points in time and at given prices. It's a blooming, chaotic, complex market with few pockets of efficiency—quite a bit like life. And Netflix's stock provided a great example of that untidiness of open barter markets; within a few months of the Qwikster "disaster," management shifted its strategy, dumped the silly name, and reaffirmed its commitment to customers. By the following February, the stock of one of the most innovative entertainment companies in the world was trading at $127 a share—a clean double. A 100 percent return . . . not bad for a few months' time. But of course, Fools being Fools, we don't end the story there. That clean double in a few months would have satisfied most, but those sticking to the long-term Foolish philosophy saw that double *double again* in the ensuing years, and again, and again. In fact, Netflix rose 14 times in value over the next five years! So much for efficient markets!

In this and countless other instances, the markets' supposed efficiency, that idea that future moves are unpredictable, and that every investor in the nation simply ought to buy an index fund and accept market-average returns is all just too simplistic. Vanguard has been one of the great successes for investors over the past thirty years, attracting literally trillions of dollars of investment to the index fund and ETF cause. The index fund provides a wonderful toehold for most of the world's investors. But, by definition, it will never ever beat the stock market. And those who suggest this isn't possible do the world a disservice.

BEATING THE MARKET AVERAGE

There's an extraordinarily important and rudimentary lesson that the vast majority of private investors have yet to learn: if you can't beat 'em, join 'em. If you've had trouble historically with your investments, Vanguard and others are there for you. In fact, according to Morningstar, over the three years ended August 31, 2016, investors added nearly $1.3 trillion to passive mutual funds and ETFs while pulling out more than a quarter trillion from active funds. For this reason, we consider Jack Bogle a genuine modern-day hero of the individual investor. And yes, Fool HQ has a conference room named in his honor, complete with an autographed picture of the man himself standing beside the Bogle nameplate at the door of the conference room. (It's very meta.)

These things said, if you *can* beat 'em, Fool, go ahead and beat 'em! The book would end here if we thought we couldn't direct you to better-than-average returns in the remaining pages. Now that you know the power of compounded returns (remember, the concept that the money you make makes you money), you'll recognize that every extra percentage point we can slap together onto your annualized average return will translate to thousands more dollars down the line. The process can even be relatively painless—even downright agreeable—assuming that you'll enjoy doing some of your own research, and don't mind taking on additional risk and responsibility for your own decision making.

8

OUT OF FUNDS INTO STOCKS

The best servants of the people, like the best valets, must whisper unpleasant truths in the master's ear. It is the court fool, not the foolish courtier, whom the king can least afford to lose.

—Walter Lippmann

The remainder of our investment guide is going to concentrate wholly on finding stocks and building investment portfolios that outperform market average. You'll be surprised at just how simple it is for the individual investor to top mutual fund managers, of which the majority lumber from one investment opportunity to another, follow the herd, underperform the norm, and in many cases, end up so because they have tens of millions of dollars to invest. It may seem counterintuitive, but it's true: *you* have the advantage.

But beating Wall Street is going to take some motivation and mobilization. You're going to have to move out of mutual funds and put your savings into stocks. Stocks have decisively outpaced bonds and cash, making them the most profitable investment over the past five decades, and the previous two centuries as well. Here, from Jeremy Siegel's great book *Stocks for the*

Long Run, are the total real returns (i.e., adjusted for inflation) for $1 invested in popular investment instruments between 1802 and 2012:

Interest-free bank account	$0.05
Gold	$4.52
Short-Term US Government Bonds	$281
Long-Term US Government Bonds	$1,778
US Stocks	$704,997

You don't need an advanced degree in finance to figure out which path wins that contest.

Briefly, we'll detail some of the initial challenges you'll encounter, and some of the initial steps you'll have to take to begin managing a market-beating portfolio, Foolishly.

1. MAKING THE SWITCH TO STOCKS

First, we need to hammer home again that our aim is to top the 10 percent annual growth that the S&P 500 has compounded over the past eighty-seven years. Beating the S&P 500 over the long term should be the goal of every institutional investor in stocks on the planet; sadly, for most of them, that's nothing more than a pipe dream. Ask any number of fund managers whether they could garner better returns with a $50,000 portfolio or a $5 billion portfolio; they're fibbing if they don't name the former.

It's no easy road for fund managers. Why is it tough on them? Not only will they be critiqued weekly with that multi-hundred-million-dollar portfolio—the chief reason that funds underperform the market—they'll also find it difficult to invest in one of the most rewarding segments: small companies on the US market. Try investing $500 million into a company worth $1 billion, and see what happens. It's like being given a million dollars and told to invest it all in the orange stand at the local farmer's market.

The smaller investor can, however, make money on underpriced oranges, or underpriced automobiles, or underpriced land . . . or best of all, underpriced listed stocks. If you're an individual investor with so much money that every time you invest in a small company, you drive the price out of your range (like those oranges above), hand this book over to one of the members of your household staff. You don't need to walk around being Foolish, and you don't need us! For everyone else, however, read on. The niches of inefficient pricing on the stock market are so various, so broad, and so exploitable for the individual investor that it's maddening to see so many substandard returns year after year. Too many investors accept mediocre performance because they think the market is indecipherable. Hooey!

To start, it's a good idea to practice without money on the line. There are plenty of ways to set up "mock portfolios" that track different kinds of investments for a few months before setting out on your real investment voyage. The Fool offers the free CAPS tool (caps.fool.com) to help you become a smarter investor—just do some research into what the community thinks, give a thumbs-up or thumbs-down rating to a stock (will it outperform or underperform the S&P 500?), and see how you measure up. If one of your picks plummets and you find yourself curled on the floor of your bathroom, sobbing over the hit to your CAPS player rating . . . well, you've learned a valuable lesson that perhaps investing real money in individual equities isn't for you. But with no money down and no risk, you could gain plenty of rich experience with the art of stock picking, the vagaries of the market, and the beauty of compounding gains! If your straw portfolio turns south, you can celebrate your patience as an investor! It's the rarest, most essential investing skill you can have.

2. YOUR SAVINGS AND YOUR BROKER

The first thing you have to do is get your capital over to an online discount broker. (If this is an early stumbling block, you can find more on the topic in Appendix A: "Stocks 101: A Primer for Those Who'll Admit They Need It.") Discount brokerage firms are businesses that simply take your investment orders, usually online, and carry them out. You tell them to buy shares (or even partial shares) of a public company, and they do so promptly. You typically won't get a lot of investment advice from discount brokers, but you also won't *pay* for that advice (which, as we've discussed, doesn't always have your investment success as its top priority).

Now, what sort of money should you put away in the stock market, and how? First of all—Motley Fool investing maxim alert!—only invest money that you can keep invested for at least five years. And if you can leave it there longer that's even better. Just look at Warren Buffett: his patience is prodigious! It's the single strongest card that individual investors can play: patience. Stay in front of the eight ball; pick your buy and sell strategies without anxiety; and invest only what you can leave untouched for at least five years.

Once you're ready to tuck away the money, it's time to decide which discount broker to use. Most offer similar services with the amount they charge for each trade, called a commission, in the $5 to $10 range. There are some deep discount brokerages that offer even lower commissions and sometimes even a certain number of free trades. But be careful to read the fine print, including how they make money, so you're completely informed.

Most discount brokers offer the standard services of providing monthly statements; issuing year-end tax statements; offering trade execution online and by phone; offering access to some stock research; offering free IRA accounts; and a variety of other twenty-four-hour information services. Deep discounters often do many of those same things, give or take. Spend some time learning which services are offered by each broker, then determine what you'll need to make prudent investment decisions. If you plan to make infrequent, straightforward purchases of highly liquid publicly traded domestic companies, you can probably skip the bells and whistles. If you've got visions of turning that spare bedroom into a high-powered super-investing nerve center, you'll need to pay up a bit.

We're not going to run through the gamut of all discount brokers here, but we invite you to visit our Discount Brokerage Center at Fool.com, where we provide you an easy one-stop shop for making your decision. The critical tip to making the best decision is to know what you value most. Is your primary need really low commissions, personal service, a good online interface, or something else entirely? Also, be sure to read through the fine print, recognizing that often what looks cheap can have hidden expenses. And that's money that'd be taken away from your actual investments.

3. TRACKING YOUR PORTFOLIO

You can track the details of your account and determine whether you're outperforming the S&P 500 by setting up a portfolio at Fool.com and in CAPS, but you can also buy some personal finance accounting software or set up your own tracking system using Excel to maintain a precise account of your investments. You simply have to know how your investments are performing relative to the stock market; otherwise, "What do you really know?" Stick close to this sort of reasoning from the mathematical physicist and engineer William Thomson:

> When you can measure what you are speaking about, and express it in numbers, you know something about it; but when you cannot measure it, when you cannot express it in numbers, your knowledge is of a meager and unsatisfactory kind: It may be the beginning of knowledge, but you have scarcely, in your thoughts, advanced to the stage of Science.

When you properly account for your portfolio's growth and compare it to market-average growth, you take a giant step toward mastering the art of investing. There are plenty of accounting programs, available both on the shelves of stores and for easy download. Quicken has dominated the financial applications market, and it makes it pretty easy for you to professionally account for your savings without undue hassle. You can also do this with a spreadsheet, of course. Heck, you can do it all on paper if you like, though we don't recommend it! Nowadays, many online discount brokers offer detailed tracking tools, including reports that will help you when tax time comes. Take a few minutes to see what reports and tools your broker offers.

Now, it's true that accurate accounting—telling it like it is—can be painful at times. But remember, with an index fund, there's no reason to do worse than average. Click your heels together three times fast and repeat:

"There's no reason to do worse than average. There's no reason to do worse than average. There's no reason . . ."

Don't forget: when accounting, you should factor in all of your research costs as well; if you choose to join any of our Motley Fool premium services, for example, be sure to deduct the membership cost from your portfolio returns. If you can't beat the index fund after all costs are deducted, you've blundered.

So, account, account, account!

4. WHAT CONSEQUENCES?

We need to address risk because, alas, not every stock is a winner, not every investment thesis pans out, and not every stock will make you money. Some will crater. Some will rebound, but others won't. High-growth stocks—small and large companies alike—can fluctuate by 30 percent to 50 percent or more in a single quarter—occasionally in any month, week, even day. Our 1997 investment in Amazon skyrocketed more than 3,000 percent by December 1999, but then fell more than 90 percent by September 2001. And we won't lie: losing a big chunk of the present value of your investment can be daunting, especially when it's so extreme. But if you've picked high-quality, highly profitable companies in burgeoning industries, the volatility shouldn't faze you as long as your company is still fundamentally sound. Amazon currently sits north of $800 per share, an astonishing return of more than 25,000 percent from our cost basis of $3.18 per share back in 1997.

Your best stocks, if you choose right and remain patient, will often exhibit volatility—but ultimately, volatility to the upside. The best way to minimize and ultimately absorb the risk associated with individual stock investing is to carry out research that is thorough, creative, and logical enough that you're well prepared for a variety of scenarios. After all, some stocks fall 25 percent, then fall another 25 percent, then fall through the floor. So how do we avoid these, as we build our Foolish portfolio?

Part of the answer comes down to a minimum time commitment: the time it takes you to track each of your investments quarterly. More mistakes are made, and more money is lost, by investors who become blind or complacent and simply fail to keep up with the public companies they're invested in. All companies are required by the Securities and Exchange Commission (SEC) to state their financial performance four times a year. The majority of companies run on a December fiscal year, meaning that their quarters end on March 31, June 30, September 30, and December 31. It takes the accountants a few weeks to compile all the information, so you'll find companies typically reporting their quarterly numbers at the end of January, April, July, and October (you might hear folks refer to these parades of pronouncements as earnings season). At the very least, read these reports! Familiarize yourself with what you own. Later in the book, we'll detail what you'll need to concentrate on in those reports; for now, we just emphasize that you should at least expect to review the sales, earnings, and cash-flow numbers every three months.

Another investment mistake to avoid is the opposite: the temptation to overanalyze your investments. Many people hyperactively trade their own accounts, paying huge amounts in commissions, annual taxes, and (worst of all) their own limited time on this planet. Because many traders do not get to know what they're trading much beyond its ticker symbol, the danger of investing in crummy prospects is high. Don't make this mistake. Remember that more activity in investing usually does *not* result in more profits. Some investors check their accounts every day, several times a day, claiming that price movements tell them more about their investments than the strength and long-term viability of the companies behind them. Over the course of a single day, one of their stocks rises $1, then drops $0.50, then lifts again $0.25, then a further $0.20, then it gives away $1 before the close. So that hourly analysis is supposed to tell us all something about the value and future direction of these investments? We don't buy it. We've come across no scientific studies showing that short-term price fluctuations are predictive. And even if we did, unless you're doing this for a living, we don't think anyone should let investing take over his or her life. Investment approaches that compel their adherents to track price fluctuations daily or hourly are bad investment ideas, for both their own bottom line and their quality of life.

Monitor but don't obsess. Turn a particular eye to your companies around the time of their quarterly earnings reports . . . but don't let that blindly dictate your course of action. If your company comes in with $100 million in sales for the quarter, and Wall Street was expecting $115 million, look out below. More often than not, your investment will take a hit, and oh, how you'll be tempted to sell. At those times, a Fool digs through the story to see whether the sales letdown was a short-term anomaly or might signal structural problems symptomatic of some more permanent disorder.

And material changes to the business aren't the only factor that can have a sizable effect on stock price. All too often, abrupt shifts in share prices after earnings announcements are completely out of proportion with the actual importance of the results. A single penny of earnings per share can send short-term traders into a frenzy, with a miss leading to analyst downgrades and questions about a company's future, while a one-penny beat brings upgrades and irrational exuberance. In context, it's natural to ask a simple question: why can a single penny per share of earnings in a single quarter of a single year lead to moves of several dollars in the share price? It's true that current earnings can affect the growth path for a company's earnings down the road, so it's reasonable for an objective assessment of a company's value based on future earnings to move by several times the amount of the earnings miss or beat. But moves of several *hundred* times a penny-per-share disparity between expected earnings and actual results reveals far more about short-term traders' obsession with quarterly results than the underlying strength of a business.

And the short-term traders' obsession has a real effect in the boardroom, despite its inherent ridiculousness. As Roger Martin argued in his book about the "real market" versus the "expectations market," we wouldn't reward coach Bill Belichick for how well the Patriots perform against the point spread. So it's silly that executives are rewarded more for beating analyst earnings targets than for creating real and lasting value in their business.

Particularly with that in mind, taking the long view, being patient and careful, has won—and always will win—on Wall Street.

5. MOVING FORWARD: THE ATTITUDE

It is so much in the financial services industry's best interest to race you through the above procedures at their proposed price that Fools may be forgiven occasional bouts of nausea, amusement bordering on mania, or severe *disillusus Wisdomatum*. There's a basic business principle to keep in mind at all times: let no one rush you.

No one.

Far too many individual investors find themselves trading weekly, daily, hourly, juggling a mishmash of investment vehicles, falling behind in their accounting, and leaving out of their lives much of what is inspiring, rejuvenating, fulfilling, and nonfinancial. These are not stock-market *investors* but rather bettors, players, *speculators*. Our model, however, is designed for actual investors aiming to prepare for their future, the future of their family, the generations beyond.

Investing Foolishly has you looking decades forward and decades back. And yet it can enable you to spend no more than a couple of hours a month on your investments. There is no hurry to investing, and more often than not, there are losses to be had from impatience. *Take your time* locating the best discount broker and practicing investing in mock online portfolios, which will make it very clear how your money is doing relative to the entire stock market. As Buffett has quipped, there are no "called strikes" in investing—you're not penalized for moving slowly and carefully. If you miss a bump in a stock price while you're conducting your research, no big deal. If you ultimately find a great stock, that 5 percent jump will barely register as a blip in the long march upward over a decade or two of that company's dominance. Remember this, above all: *Patience*, Fool. Patience above all.

9

THE MIND-SET OF THE SUCCESSFUL INVESTOR

The investor's chief problem—and even his worst enemy—is likely to be himself.

—Benjamin Graham

Learning to be patient is one of the most important lessons for investors, but one of the most difficult to internalize. When the market is tanking and your portfolio is leaking more money with each hit of the refresh key, the inclination is to do *something*. Just when you should be most patient, your emotions and your brain make you the least.

There are many other ways in which our own minds play tricks on us and try to derail our investing success. We could write an entire book on the field of behavioral finance, but for now, let's just spend a part of this chapter hitting upon some of the most important biases that Foolish investors should be conscious of.

As we've warned over the years, *you are your own worst enemy*. Those are the six most important words in investing. Shady financial advisors, incompetent CEOs, and overpriced mutual funds don't harm your returns a fraction of the amount that your own behavior does. That's because successful investing has far more to do with how you act than with what you know. Traits like good temperament, patience, levelheadedness, and the ability to overcome biases are more integral to doing well in the market than anything you might learn in a classroom. Investing is ultimately a battle with your own behavior. No matter how much technical knowledge you accumulate, the odds are that you'll have an unhappy investing experience unless you understand the behavioral biases we're born with that, sadly, cause most investors to buy high, sell low, and earn subpar returns. With the optimistic idea that awareness leads to improved action, here are a handful of cognitive biases that cause people to do dumb things with their money.

LOSS AVERSION

If you receive a compliment, you'll likely feel good about it for a moment, and then it'll drift out of your mind. But if someone criticizes you, there's a chance you'll be able to recall the details years from now. That's common with money, too. People hate losing money more than they like making it, which makes sense. "Organisms that treat threats as more urgent than opportunities have a better chance to survive and reproduce," writes Nobel Prize–winning psychologist Daniel Kahneman. But that outsized fear of loss causes us to overreact and become too defensive when the market tumbles, almost always to our detriment. Most underperformance is due to buying high and selling low, and loss aversion is at the core of that mistake.

ILLUSIONS OF SUPERIORITY

Most people think they're above average. The bummer is that it's often the other way around: investors who have the highest assessment of their skills actually achieve some of the worst performance. Researchers in Germany asked a group of investors how they thought they performed, then checked their brokerage statements. On average, those investors overestimated their returns by 11.6 percent each year, and investors who self-reported the highest returns in fact had some of the lowest. Confidence increases much faster than skill.

AVERSION TO CHANGING YOUR MIND

We have a natural aversion to changing our minds, because that would imply that our original judgment was wrong. A lot of this is due to something called "sunk-costs fallacy": not wanting to admit that effort you've already committed to an idea can't be recovered. The most successful investors have mastered this bias. They can change their minds with ease and feel no sense of shame.

FREQUENCY ILLUSION

Once you notice an event, it seems to keep happening over and over. But it's often not the case; you're no longer oblivious to it, so you become more attuned. The market crash in the late 2000s was such a traumatic event that investors and the media spent the next several years infatuated with the "volatile market." In fact, the four years following that crash had below-average market volatility. Investors were simply paying more attention to normal market swings than usual.

ANCHORING ILLUSION

The market doesn't know nor does it care what you paid for a stock or what you think a "fair" price is. Anchoring to the price you paid is one of the most damaging biases investors fall for. Being able to admit when you were wrong is key to avoiding this bias. Similarly, if you're holding out to buy a stock as soon as it drops below, say, $40 per share, you could be missing on a huge long-term opportunity. After all, it won't make much difference whether you bought at $40 or $42 if the stock goes to $200, but if it never drops into the range you'd anchored to, you'll be kicking yourself.

OVERESTIMATING SELF-CONTROL

All investors we know say they'll be greedy when others are fearful; few assume that they'll be the fearful ones. But by definition, someone has to be. Nobody says, "If stocks fall twenty percent, I'm going to panic and sell." They're far more likely to aver that a 20 percent decline would be a buying opportunity. That's smart, but the reason there will be a 20 percent crash is that more investors choose panic selling over opportunistic buying. Investors overestimate their self-control—and they eventually realize that they are the "others."

COGNITIVE DISSONANCE

Cognitive dissonance is the uncomfortable feeling of holding two contradictory ideas in your head at the same time. "Doughnuts are bad for me. I'm going to eat a doughnut." That's cognitive dissonance, and we're willing to jump through mental hoops to reduce it. The easiest way to reduce it is to find ways to justify behavior we know is wrong. "I had a stressful day and I deserve a doughnut." Now you can eat guilt-free. Investors do this all the time, too. You criticize Wall Street for being a casino while checking your portfolio twice a day. You buy a stock only because you think it's cheap, and after realizing you were wrong, decide to hold it because you like the company's CEO. Never underestimate your mind's power to convince you to do something you know you shouldn't.

NORMALCY BIAS

It's not uncommon to assume that because something has never happened before, it won't (or can't) happen in the future. Everything that has ever happened in history was "unprecedented" at one time. The Great Depression. The crash of 1987. Enron. Wall Street bailouts. None of these events had ever happened . . . until they did. When Warren Buffett announced that he was looking for candidates to replace him at Berkshire Hathaway, he said he needed "someone genetically programmed to recognize and avoid serious risks, including those never before encountered." Someone who understands normalcy bias, in other words.

LUDIC REASONING

Coined by Nassim Taleb in *The Black Swan*, this is the belief that the real world can be predicted with mathematical models and forecasts. It leads people astray because models are purposely simplified, while the real world is incomprehensibly complex. As author Dan Gardner says, "No one can foresee the consequences of trivia and accident, and for that reason alone, the future will be forever filled with surprises." Accepting that some things can't be predicted or known will help you become a better investor.

BANDWAGON EFFECT

This is the fallacy of believing something is true only because other people think it is. Whether it's politicians or stocks, people like being associated with things that are winning, so winners build momentum not because they deserve it, but because they're winning. This is the foundation of all asset bubbles.

CLUSTERING ILLUSION

Many investors convince themselves that they've found a pattern by taking a small sample out of a much larger one. For example, we know stocks' daily movements over time are random and unpredictable, but you could take a four-day period where a stock went up, up, down, down, and think you've found a trend. Day traders are attracted to clustering like bugs to bright lights. Related is the gambler's fallacy, the belief that future events will be shaped by past events, even when the two have no correlation. A gambler will assume a coin is "due" to come up heads after flipping a string of tails, but the outcome of the next flip is completely independent of the last one—the odds are still 50/50 regardless of prior flips. Investors fall for a version of gambler's fallacy when assuming things like economic data, quarterly earnings, and politics will dictate the direction of the market, when in reality, these things often move independently of one another. Randomness is hard to accept.

BELIEF BIAS

We tend to accept or reject an argument based on how well it fits our predefined beliefs, rather than the objective facts of the situation. When presented with information that goes against our point of view, we not only reject challenges, but also double down on our original view only because the topic becomes more emotional. Voters become more ardent supporters of their candidate when the candidate is attacked by the opposing party. In investing, shareholders of companies facing criticism can become fanatical, die-hard supporters for reasons totally unrelated to the companies' performance. Companies under attack from short sellers have some of the most irrationally supportive shareholders out there. Further, we tend to stick our head under a pillow when confronted with information that makes us uncomfortable. We check our brokerage accounts less frequently when the market is down, ignore dire warnings when we're bullish on a company, and ignore polls when our preferred politician is trailing. Our ability to ignore things we don't want to believe are true is much stronger than our desire to know the truth.

BIAS BIAS

Finally, the most important and powerful bias of them all, "bias bias" is the belief that you are less biased than you really are. If you read this chapter without realizing we're talking about you, you're suffering from bias bias. As Kahneman once said, "I never felt I was studying the stupidity of mankind in the third person. I always felt I was studying my own mistakes." Once you realize that you are as biased as everyone else, you've taken an enormous step forward as an investor.

IS THAT ALL?

Although we've run through enough biases and fallacies to keep your head spinning into next quarter, there are literally thousands more that we haven't discussed. Hopefully, by running through this dozen or so, we'll put you on watch against some of the most detrimental. More important, though, is the underlying theme: you are your own worst enemy in investing. Most of us attempt to become smarter investors by learning more about balance sheets, income statements, valuation models, and other textbook finance techniques. That's all useful, but it's all for naught until you understand how your brain works against you to misinterpret, abuse, and ignore that knowledge.

The world's best investors know finance inside and out. But the skills that set them apart are control over their emotions, the ability to think clearly under stress, the ability to avoid temptation, and the understanding of so many of the behavioral concepts we often ignore. Everyone is prone to cognitive errors—some more than others, but no one is exempt. Coming to terms with the idea that you are your own worst enemy is the single most important thing you can do to become a better investor.

PART IV

COMPANIES AND QUALITY

10

WHY BUY BLUE CHIPS?

As we've discussed, you can find good ideas for investments within your own industry, interests, insight, and investigation. Maybe you work for a robotics company that is doing what you think is groundbreaking work. That might make for a solid investment. You shop at Home Depot every week to get the next perfect tool that's going to prompt you to finish that basement you've been working on for the past five years. Everyone else seems to love Home Depot, too, so that's an intriguing possibility. Every afternoon for lunch you down a tin of Saltee Sardinez from Joe's Fishery, Inc. If America ever catches on to that snack treat, you could have a real winner!

It's useful to classify these investments to get a sense of the level of risk each entails. Any company of any size can rise or fall precipitously in a given year or month or week or day, but you can be pretty sure that Home Depot won't go bankrupt anytime soon. Joe's Fishery is small and relatively new, so it could go belly-up, but its products seem to be catching on. Your robotics company, on the other hand, has a much more uncertain future, since its technology isn't even in place yet. It may never make a dime.

Let's look at the first type first, the Home Depots of the world. These are the large-cap companies, the established leaders, the so-called blue chips of the investment world.

First, a quick word to make sure we're all on the same page with our definitions. Market capitalization is one of the best measures of a company's size. Also known as market cap, it's the total market value of a company's outstanding shares of stock—just multiply a company's shares outstanding by the share price.

Once you've solved that math problem, you can then sort potential investments into a few buckets. We typically divide up the market capitalizations of companies into four categories: large cap, mid cap, small cap, and micro cap. Everyone has his or her own definition of these categories, but the numbers below present a dependable enough guide:

Large cap	Over $4 billion
Mid cap	$1 billion to $4 billion
Small cap	$300 million to $1 billion
Micro cap	Below $300 million

WHY INVEST IN LARGE-CAP COMPANIES?

The Dow Jones Industrial Average (DJIA) and the S&P 500 are loaded with some of the largest corporations on the planet, presenting investors with a veritable smorgasbord of relatively stable and secure behemoths. For the detail-focused, the Dow is a price-weighted index comprising the shares of thirty large public US companies. As of November 2016, those companies had an average market cap of $182.6 billion, with the largest being $609 billion and the smallest weighing in at $33 billion. The S&P 500 is widely regarded as the standard for measuring large-cap US stock market performance, and its companies boast an average market cap of about $40 billion.

Why would you invest in one of these gargantuans? To outperform.

There's no reason to invest in *anything* unless you believe that by doing so you can outdo the uneventful 10 percent in compounded growth you'll get via an index fund. It's risky to ride speculative stocks, bonds, futures, commodities, gold coins; to trade options; to hop in on any cool-sounding, indecipherable Big New Thing. The unfortunate thing is that so many greenhorn investors make unstudied dice rolls each year. If you jump in with a risky approach and limited understanding, it's not investing, of course, it's gambling . . . and an excellent long-term approach to losing money.

Investing in large-cap companies offers considerably less intermediate- and long-term risk. Does anybody think we won't see Coca-Cola, McDonald's, IBM, AT&T, General Electric, and the like in the year 2030? Investors in this group of stocks are a bit like children in a playpen—there aren't a lot of sharp objects, and it ought to be a lot of fun.

The second great reason to invest in large-cap companies is that you end up working from a small sample of potential investments. Perhaps the greatest mistake individual investors make is trying to follow too many stocks. Our major US exchanges—the New York Stock Exchange and the Nasdaq—list about six thousand stocks. It's tempting to fire up your favorite financial website on the weekend, peek in on thousands of stock quotes, and muse, "I will conquer you all!" But it ain't gonna happen. Investors who try to manage too much research typically run unprofitable or underperforming portfolios. It may help you sleep better at night to start by staying on top of only a few stable stocks, selected from five hundred of the strongest, most profitable, and most immense companies in the world.

That's not to say that they are completely safe. Many companies have risen to earn membership in the S&P 500 or Dow 30, only to fall back down the heap. The S&P 500 has dropped the likes of Sears and Avon, for example. Enron, too. You need to watch even the blue chips.

11

WHY SMALL-CAP STOCKS?

Small-capitalization stocks (small caps) make an attractive foil to the world's blue chips. It's not hard to figure out why. For years, small-cap investors have clung to studies that showed that over long periods, small stocks outperformed large ones. This is true, but you have to be careful when looking at these studies, because the data and the conclusion changes depending on what time frame you are measuring and which groups of stocks or indexes you are looking at. For example, a study by Ibbotson and Associates, the esteemed Chicago research firm that tracks the performance of stocks and mutual funds, shows that from 1926 to 2010, small-cap stocks posted average annual returns of 12.1 percent, versus a large-cap return of 9.9 percent over the corresponding period. That may look like only about 2 percentage points, but when you compound that return, the difference (as you now know) is huge. How huge? A $1,000 investment earning 12.1 percent annually is worth $14.7 million eighty-four years later; a $1,000 investment bringing in 9.9 percent over that time ends up worth just $2.8 million. Your grandkids will definitely recognize that meaningful difference!

Now remember, we said that it depends on the study you look at and the time frame you measure. Another study by Pension Partners, LLC, looked at the data from 1979 to 2015—a much shorter period. During this stretch, small caps generated an annualized return of 10.3 percent, while large caps earned an 11.7 percent annualized return. So, depending on the study you look at, small caps either outperform or they don't. But either way, we think they make a great addition to a well-diversified portfolio.

Now, we know that many people resist investing in small caps because of the inherent risk associated with them. You can make a lot of money in these stocks, and you can lose a lot, too. That's because little stocks often react to dramatic news like gnats in the wind (whether the wind is blowing for or against them). Small-cap stocks are not the right choices for people who can't afford short-term risks. Do not risk investing in small-cap stocks if you can't afford to see that money disappear! While that's true of investing in companies of all sizes, smaller companies can become non-companies much quicker than blue-chip behemoths can.

But is that reason enough to avoid some of the biggest opportunities on the market? Of course not. Those who steer clear of small caps are unable to understand and appreciate the value of strong small-cap representation in their portfolios. Consciously taking on smart risk remains the best way to succeed in investing. We embrace risk because the opposite is timidity, which most of the world is good at. Always remember, dear reader, that throughout human history, fortune favors the bold.

Handled properly, small-cap investing can be tremendous fun and exceptionally lucrative. But small-cap stocks should not be your first—and definitely not your only—type of stock. We always recommend balance in your investing (not to mention your life, but that's another book).

WHY YOU SHOULDN'T BUY SMALL CAPS

In Foolish style, let's first spend some time examining why you *shouldn't* buy small caps.

For one thing, you definitely shouldn't buy small caps if you don't know what you're doing. You'd be surprised how many newcomers plunge right into the market just because they happened to get a "hot tip" when they had a little money on hand, without having a glimmer of a clue. While we wouldn't ever make Wall Street's argument that investing is only for "experts," a certain level of curiosity and competence is critical to avoid what amounts to simply lighting your money on fire. Fortunately, you now have your Foolish instruction manual for investing, and you've figured out that no matter how "hot" a tip is, there's homework to do before you make the buy. (Guess what: there's also work to do *after* you buy a small-cap stock.)

You should stay out of small-cap stocks if you don't have the time or are unwilling to follow them. Small-cap investors must pay attention to their investments on a more regular basis than equity investors of other stripes. A gale-force wind might rattle the shutters of a behemoth like Apple, but it could blow a smaller company way off course.

Another reason to avoid small caps is if you instinctively shy away from risk. While we celebrate taking risk—the *right* risk—we don't look down on those who eschew it. Everyone is different, and the good news is that a motley variety of market-beating stock-picking approaches exists. If you're not risk-tolerant by nature, don't try to be something you aren't. If you're the type to lose sleep if you lose money, if a higher level of risk causes you to break out in hives, you'll want to avoid small caps.

We've already mentioned yet another reason not to buy these things: If you need the money elsewhere. If you're putting your lunch money (or its equivalent) down on the market, you're hoping to hit the Lotto jackpot. Again, the most frequent mistake new investors make is to invest as if they were playing the lottery: buy enough long shots, and one of them has to hit! Neither the lottery nor a shoot-the-moon investing strategy is a path to wealth.

All right, that's enough on why you shouldn't buy small caps. If you've worked your way through the above and decided that you're still interested, then carry on.

WHY EVERYONE SHOULD HOLD SOME
SMALL CAPS: GETTING IN FIRST

Having learned what "small cap" means, and in which situations these stocks should be avoided, let us delve more deeply into the advantages of small-stock investing and why everyone should probably own a few of these shares.

The primary reason for buying small-cap stocks is that mutual funds and institutions often cannot buy them . . . yet. Or even if they can, mutual funds and institutions cannot build up any meaningful holding. "Meaningful" here is defined as "in a sufficient quantity to make any noticeable difference to the fund's overall performance."

At last count, the average US mutual fund had about $1.8 billion in holdings. So let's set up our own fund for discussion's sake. We'll call it Jack Fund, and it's going to be absolutely average; it has $1.8 billion in holdings and wants to make lots of money. If Jack Fund's manager (Jack) wanted to hold ten stocks, he would divide that money into ten parts, or $180 million each. Now, the total value (as measured by market capitalization) of many excellent small caps is between $300 million and $1 billion. Furthermore, the management team often owns 15 percent to 40 percent of the company, meaning that a large portion of shares are simply not available on the open market. Thus, you can see that any serious attempt by Jack Fund to establish a meaningful stake in these companies would often involve owning a huge chunk of these companies or, in some cases, undertaking virtual buyouts of the targeted companies! At the very least, if mutual funds were to attempt to buy 20 percent to 30 percent of a stock they loved, they'd push up the price so quickly that the latter half of their buying would be at prices far beyond the attractive initial entry point. Not a formula for good investment returns . . . especially when it comes time to *sell* a big stake. The price could be driven down just as far and as fast as it was driven up.

So, what would *you* do if you were Jack managing the Jack Fund and wanted to invest in small caps? You'd end up having to spread out your holdings into, say, fifty separate stocks, to avoid the dangers of buying "too much" of a company. Do you have fifty good investment ideas? Perhaps, over time, you could pull together a roster of small-cap companies you expect are on their way to larger caps. But for the average investor, that's an impossible task. Add in the necessity of keeping up with the companies' performance over time, and this is starting to look like more than a full-time job. In addition, every additional investment makes it that much more likely that an investment portfolio will do no more than duplicate the market's performance.

To reiterate: the first reason that you want to buy these stocks is that many mutual funds cannot . . . yet. But the small investor *can* buy these stocks, getting in early on some of the great emerging growth stories of American business. Microsoft, Intel, and Wal-Mart all began simply as initial public offerings on the Nasdaq. Mutual funds couldn't really buy them back then, when they were small caps. Over time, as these companies became mid-cap and then large-cap companies, mutual funds and institutions moved in, in a multibillion-dollar way. The ideal for the individual investor in this situation is to have been the person able to *sell* the shares to the institutions when the big guys finally became convinced that one or another of these stocks was worth owning and that they were big enough to buy into. (Although in the case of these three companies, the best plan of attack would have been never to sell at all—but that's a story for later.)

Now, it must be said that some of the best-performing mutual funds historically are small-cap funds. These include, among others, Fidelity Small Cap Growth, T. Rowe Price New Horizons, and Janus Venture Fund, which have compiled excellent track records over the past decade (past performance being, of course, no guarantee of future returns). But what happens then? More investors hear of these funds and invest *their* money in them, too. The fund's assets swell, forcing managers either to invest that money into new stocks they don't like as much, or put more and more money into their favorite existing ones, at significantly higher prices in most cases. And if a small-cap fund's assets *still* continue to grow via appreciation, it often has to close itself to new investors altogether or risk walking away from investing in small caps anymore!

By investing directly in the stocks yourself, you gain the ability to profit hugely from stocks that mutual funds couldn't buy for their customers in sufficient amounts. You get in before the big guys get in, and once they decide to get in, the big dollars they throw at your stock help push it up for you. The best buy of all is the purchase of a small cap just before the institutions "discover" it. By concentrating a portion of your portfolio in excellent small companies, you give yourself a great shot at beating mutual funds by a wide margin.

MORE REASONS EVERYONE SHOULD HOLD SMALL CAPS

You already have a couple of good reasons for buying and holding small-cap stocks for the long haul: they have historically produced excellent returns, and you can beat the institutions into these stocks and then *use* the institutions to prop them up further. The good news doesn't stop there, though.

Small numbers multiply much more rapidly than big ones. When earnings double, a stock's price could also double. But which company is more likely to double in size in the next two years (all other things remaining equal): a company with $10 million in sales or one with $10 billion in sales? Right, the smaller one. It's a lot easier to triple and double again in size quickly when you're starting from a base below $100 million . . . a lot more difficult anywhere above that.

Earnings grow fastest among small companies. And what often accompanies earnings growth is share price growth. That argument has been made down through the decades, perhaps most convincingly by Peter Lynch in his wonderful book *One Up on Wall Street*. It didn't hurt that Lynch put his money where his mouth was. He made a whole career out of expounding his love of growth stocks and generating superior returns by investing in them.

This concept has found such acceptance since Lynch wrote his book that you'll often find a lot of future growth priced into a stock. Companies that would have remained small caps in earlier markets are now finding themselves bid up into mid- and large-cap ranges, based much more on future rather than present earnings. That has made our job harder, since we have to pay very close attention to business quality and potential instead of spying power in their financial statements. It also depletes the returns and augments the risk that investors in low- or no-earnings companies take, since they are already priced for success. If they don't deliver, the pain share-holders feel will be significant. That hasn't, however, stopped us from look-ing for quality among even younger companies. We believe that it is still possible to score big gains, even in this environment.

Another reason to like small companies is that they are typically closely held by management. That means that the people running the company have a significant financial stake in the success not *just* of the company, but also of the stock itself. In fact, in many cases, the performance of the stock has a greater influence on the wealth of the management team than does their annual salaries.

Imagine, if you will, the founder and owner of a small company. In the earliest days of the business, it's probably not generating enough cash to pay massive salaries to the team, even at the upper levels of the organiza-tion. The money they do bring in often is reinvested back into the company to spur growth and tackle new opportunities . . . and occasionally to move out of a shed and into proper offices. But these intrepid employees aren't working solely out of the goodness of their hearts and a fervent belief in the mission. In many cases, they're granted shares of the company, essentially tying their futures to the success of the business. They're making a bet on themselves.

That's great news for outside investors, because the people making the decisions and running the operations are focused on the long-term success of the company. In fact, it matters far more to them than it does to us, even though we have some money on the line. That founder-owner is probably running the business as if it were the make-or-break opportunity of his fi-nancial life . . . because it probably is. If he's like the typical small-company management, most of his wealth is tied up in his company's stock. Thus incentivized, the goals of the team are aligned with the goals of outside investors like us. And that can be a very good place to be for early investors in a company, as it (hopefully) begins its long and steady march from a small cap up the capitalization ladder.

12

HOW DO YOU FIND THE
BEST STOCKS?

If you don't study any companies, you have the same success buying stocks
as you do in a poker game if you bet without looking at your cards.

—Peter Lynch

By now, you've hopefully come to understand that whether you're pursuing small caps or blue chips or something in between, investing can be fun and rewarding, opening up a world of opportunities for you as a result of the life-changing wealth you've accumulated through shrewd decisions and savvy insights. Or it can be as productive as shoving $20 bills into a blender set to mince.

The difference is largely in the specific investments you make. With so many companies publicly traded in the United States and around the globe, how do you determine which stocks to buy? There are as many answers to that question as there are stocks in the market. Some people rely on fancy-looking charts and graphs that show the very lowest a stock can go . . . right until it goes lower. Others follow the advice of TV talking heads . . . who, it must be remembered, are focused more on ratings than returns. As you've hopefully gleaned by now, at The Motley Fool we embrace a long-term, buy-and-hold strategy that focuses on finding great businesses and investing in them for years or even decades.

Broadly speaking, we recommend "business-focused investing"—that is, seeking out great and amazing growth-opportunity businesses, rather than relying on a mechanical formula. We ask ourselves where the company, not the stock, will be in the next three to five years and beyond. We look at criteria such as competitive advantage, market opportunity, strength of leadership, and other characteristics that are tough to plug into a financial calculator. Don't get us wrong—there's value in uncovering and understanding a company's financials . . . and we promise we'll get to that in a few chapters, when we take a closer look at the criteria we use to help us find small-cap stocks. But as we've evolved and refined our investing philosophies over the years, we've now reached a point in which we approach the market with a "business owner" mentality rather than a "stock buyer" one.

And with that sweeping overview in place, let's dig deeper into some of the thinking that now—more than twenty years in the making—sits at the core of our investment philosophies.

PART V

TOM'S TAKE:
AN EVERLASTING
APPROACH TO
INVESTING

13

FIVE TENETS TO EVERLASTING INVESTING

We opened our book with a cannon shot across the bow of the USS *Wise*—the mainstream financial media, Wall Street firms, and anyone who provides poor investing or financial advice without transparency or accountability, who doesn't put your needs first over their own.

Our weapon: a team of analysts and a community of investors hanging out at Fool.com.

Our ammunition: More than 80 percent of active mutual funds and a fair share of expensive hedge funds underperform the market for long stretches of time. And way too many unscrupulous brokers or financial planners care more about the fees they charge you than the results they deliver (or don't, as is often the case). The Wise are slowly changing, thank goodness, as more individuals choose more Foolish investing solutions. Yet we still have a long way to go.

One of the great—though tragic—ironies for individual investors is that the advice peddled from mahogany desks on Wall Street or by traditional financial media (both pillars of the Wise class) is the exact reverse of what individual investors really should do. Because their goals often are not your goals, their outlook tends to revolve around the fees they charge, their short-term thinking, and their lack of transparency. The Wise are obsessed with what's happening minute-by-minute, hour-by-hour, day-by-day. What's the market doing *today*? What did the Fed decide? How is stock ABC moving after earnings? What will the election win mean for next quarter?

It's all so incredibly short-term, and it's the very antithesis of how we invest at The Motley Fool. The vast majority of wealth is built in the public markets for people who want staying power—who want to build family wealth over decades, not over the next couple of weeks. (Sorry to break it to you, but those kinds of quick gains are impossible). Organizations and businesses are already building long-term wealth, and to achieve the same goal, you'll have to learn to ride with them over long periods. You have to find the right cultures, strategies, and businesses to do so. An organization that has built, for example, a culture of proven innovation will continue to churn out positive results (and corresponding profits) long after it misses analysts' expectations by $0.02 per share in the second quarter.

It might seem like backward thinking to focus on *holding* a stock before we tackle *buying* a stock, but this is one of the most important and under-rated lessons we've discovered in our investing careers. With that crucial idea, we'll begin our dive into Tom's approach to investing.

INVESTING FOR THE LONG TERM

We're kind of math nerds here, so let's start with some reality: mathematically, the worst thing you can do as an investor is to lose any of your big winners. If you buy a stock, there's always the chance you could lose 100 percent of your investment. It's unlikely that, say, ExxonMobil is going to go bankrupt, but there's *a chance*. But while your losses are capped at 100 percent, there is no limit on how much your investment can *increase* in value. As of April 2017, fifteen of our recommendations to members of our *Stock Advisor* service had increased *more than 1,000 percent!*

If you miss a few monster investments—those multibaggers, as Peter Lynch referred to them—it doesn't matter how many times you save a couple percentage points by selling a stock on its way down. You'll never catch up to the gains you missed out on had you stayed committed to the ones that eventually become your great winners. So much of the financial media and the financial services industry is focused on transactions—stay active, trade a lot, move things around. But that's done more to prove that they're doing *something*. Unfortunately for you, that approach only generates commissions for brokers, hits you with unnecessary taxes, and leads to mediocrity and underperformance. It's a terrible way for people to run their investments.

A better, more Foolish approach is to find great businesses and add money regularly to them. That's the way we think about investing. And that's your best path to lasting wealth.

Countless times, we've heard otherwise talented investors lament, "If I had held . . ." And sadly, people often *underestimate* the damage that an itchy trigger finger can cause. The human mind has trouble managing exponential growth numbers. We don't realize that 25 percent a year isn't just 23 percentage points ahead of keeping money in the bank. That growth spirals, turning early investors in, say, Starbucks into millionaires many times over. If they'd focused on the short term, they would have missed that great business story and the riches that came with it for committed investors. They didn't have to put a lot of money in to make a fortune.

There are thousands and thousands of public companies, and many of them will do poorly as investments. But the ones that end up being multibaggers? You don't want to trade your way out of those. That's why a long-term, patient approach is a defining feature in our investing.

Okay, so how do you find those stocks in the first place?

FIVE TENETS OF A GREAT INVESTMENT

Here at the Fool, we're enthusiastic fans of frameworks. Whether we're assessing the strength of a company's "moat" against competition, or figuring out where to go for lunch, we seek roadmaps that organize our ideas into clear and memorable categories or tenets.

Switching to the first-person singular, here is the framework that I've (Tom here) built and refined over the years, and still employ today. (In the ensuing chapters, you'll learn about David's "6 Signs of a Rule Breaker" framework that he built years ago, and which he's put to work in hundreds of recommendations over the last decade-plus.)

These are the five tenets that I use in my Everlasting Portfolio inside our *Motley Fool One* service. For those unfamiliar, these are companies I view as the world's greatest investments for the very long term. I aim to crush the market as I hold these stocks for a minimum of five years. These Everlasting stocks are the only ones I intend to hold in my personal portfolio for the rest of my life.

The tenets are ranked in order of importance to my thinking, starting with culture and finishing with valuation . . . which makes me different than probably 98.4 percent of the investors out there, who start with valuation and, if they consider it at all, give a passing glance at a company's culture or leadership.

We'll start with a brief overview of the tenets, then spend more time in the following chapters explaining exactly what I mean and what I look for within each tenet. And I'll be naming names of the companies and leaders I admire and invest in! (With one addendum: things don't always go according to plan, so it's possible some of the companies or individuals might have hit on rough times by the time you read these pages. That's a danger of publishing and of investing—we don't know what we don't know, but we have to content ourselves with making the best decisions possible based on the information we have.)

1. Culture

What's the ecosystem of that organization? What matters most to the company? Culture isn't whether there's a foosball table and kegerator at the headquarters. It's how businesses treat their employees, their customers, their suppliers, and their stakeholders.

My assessment of a company starts there, because that's the greatest determinant of long-term success for a business. The companies that focus on treating all their key constituents well tend to thrive over decades, and that kind of positive culture is far more important to my focus on being a business-owning investor than quarterly earnings reports and short-term share price fluctuations.

2. Strategy

What is the company's strategy? What advantages does it have? Is that the very best solution that the customer is coming to in the industry, or are there superior alternatives?

Every business faces competition, so it's critical to understand a company's strategy for winning. A big part of this involves understanding pricing power and competitive edge, and how a business is widening its lead in both.

3. Financials

What are the financial underpinnings of the business? It might be a great place to work, and it might have a tremendous strategy in place, but if a company has a massive amount of debt on the balance sheet, that burden could knock it out of consideration. Excessive debt could deny a company the resources to reinvest in its business and grow. Before making an investment, I need to examine that business's financials and understand its capital structure and financial underpinning.

4. Safety (aka the optimistic side of "Risk")

How safe is this business? Things may be going great right now, but what happens if the CEO retires? Is the company using leverage in a low-interest-rate environment? What happens if interest rates rise? Could Amazon put it out of business?

I aim to explore all the ways a business could run into trouble and assess the likelihood of each. What has the company done to mitigate those risks, and how safe do we think that investment is? After all, we're holding these companies for five years and more, so we want to be sure we've given thought to what could go wrong in the meantime.

5. Valuation

While we could list dozens of other categories for assessing public companies, the final one on my short list is the value that the market is placing on the business. What's the valuation today, and how does the market price its growth prospects?

Valuation—whether I think the market is giving a company too much or not enough credit for its underlying business and future—matters a great deal to me. But it's only fifth on my list, because a lot of valuation concerns get cleared up with my unwavering long-term-hold philosophy.

Think about it this way: if you find a way to travel back in time to 1998 and have a chance to buy Starbucks, it's not going to matter to you in 2017 whether you bought it at $7.25 a share or $9.15 (split-adjusted). If you're able to find a truly outstanding company, especially in its earlier stages of growth, it doesn't make sense to concern yourself deeply over the matter of a dollar or two in the purchase price. It just won't matter if you get the other four tenets spot-on.

14

CULTURE

Culture reflects all the connections happening for an organization. Your culture is how you interact with your customers, your shareholders, and the communities in which you function, and how your employees interact with each other. And the culture of an organization is only becoming more important in a world of increased globalization and interconnectedness. It's harder than ever for organizations to hide. Whether a company commits outright fraud or subtler instances of taking advantage of its stakeholders— whether customers or employees—we're more likely than ever to find out about it, and that could have an impact on the stock's performance. So, from our perspective, it's more important than ever that the companies we invest in work diligently to do right by their constituencies.

UNDERSTANDING CULTURE

Great culture doesn't just happen. A tremendous amount of work goes on behind the scenes to make sure an organization is setting up its people for success. That's not just about trying to make people happy; happy, productive, passionate, *and* purpose-driven employees are the ultimate aims.

I look at all the different slices that I can. I look at the *Fortune* Best Companies to Work For list and the Ethisphere Most Ethical Companies list, both of which have been shown to outperform the market. And I look at Glassdoor.com, where past and present employees can anonymously review their employers. Analysts at the Fool have shown correlation between Glassdoor rankings and stock performance: top-rated companies tend to outperform the S&P 500, and the bottom fifty public companies have significantly underperformed the market.

EVALUATING CULTURE: START AT THE TOP

To many, culture feels vague and amorphous. It's difficult to quantify, and that can make some people edgy as they look to assign value in their analysis. But it's where we find our edge as investors.

As Chuck Royce, chairman and portfolio manager of the highly successful Royce Funds, told me in an interview, "I focus on culture, as well, because all the numbers of earnings and financial performance . . . those are very easily sorted, searched, and analyzed . . . and conclusions drawn from that are very consistent with what other investment organizations are doing. So you need to go into the qualitative, vague, gray areas and try to gain advantages there because those advantages are multipliers on returns."

Without numbers, how do you measure? I start with the CEO. It's not true with all my investments, but when I see a founder who is CEO, I pay attention. This is especially true when the founder has stuck with her company through the IPO and well past needing money. If she chose to stick around after raking in millions from an IPO, there's clearly continued passion for the business she created. And that passion spreads to the team that works there.

Let's look at Facebook. I was analyzing the company after its unfavorable IPO, with the stock well off its fifty-two-week highs. *The Social Network* was in theaters, painting Mark Zuckerberg in a highly unflattering light. Yet Glassdoor was exploding with hundreds of glowing reviews that made Facebook (at the time) the highest-rated public company on the platform. And then I read Zuckerberg's vision statement for his company. Facebook isn't about cat videos or political rants or reconnecting with that high school sweetheart. Its vision is nothing less than to connect the world.

I like to see that Mark Zuckerberg is leading Facebook and is the largest individual owner. Ditto Jeff Bezos at Amazon or Warren Buffett at Berkshire. I loved when Herb Kelleher ran Southwest Airlines. And we saw the massive impact of Howard Schultz at Starbucks when he returned to the CEO role in 2008.

On and on, you can find these companies, but that's not a guarantee of success. There are many founders who are ego-driven, incompetent, and fraudulent. But overall, if you find a great company with a great culture and a founder who's the CEO, that should be a very positive sign when fishing in the public markets.

ARE EMPLOYEES STAYING?

The second data point that I love to understand—although it's a tough number to find—is a company's employee retention rate. Ideally, we want a place that is keeping its people, promoting from within, and building a lasting culture that supports employees as key stakeholders.

We want a culture where people are staying, because the cost of retraining new employees is expensive and painful. This is especially true for positions steeped in institutional knowledge. If you're thinking long-term, you want to find that culture that makes everybody feel connected to the purpose.

Whenever I meet any employee at any company I'm thinking about investing in, I want to hear from them: "I am grateful to work here. I'm proud to work here, and I'm thankful for my job." I want to see a two-way connection between the employee and the employer. That's a strong indicator to me that long-term value is going to be created.

GOOGLE: DRIVEN BY DATA

Google is one of the greatest companies in American history, no question. In my conversations with the company's longtime SVP of People Operations, Laszlo Bock, the author of *Work Rules!*, I learned that Google is an extremely data-centric culture. Google measures everything. It surveys employees frequently in an effort to understand deeply what drives each person. With more than fifty thousand employees, that's not easy. But Google makes it work. It uses data and technology to connect with each employee in ways that companies with seventy employees don't.

Data is in Google's DNA. Information runs through the organization. From its mission to organize the world's information to its weekly all-hands meeting, Google is constantly thinking through the uses of information and data. Successfully scaling its culture is an enormous achievement. So I'm learning from Google while I'm also enjoying investing and profiting from it.

CHIPOTLE: DRIVEN BY FOOD WITH INTEGRITY

Another great example is Chipotle Mexican Grill. Founded by Steve Ells, a chef by training, Chipotle created a culture driven by a foodie and run by Monty Moran, a former lawyer who ran his law firm like few others: transparent with fees, committed to a higher purpose, passionate about the work, and big on collaboration.

Ells and Moran's goal was to build a culture unlike other fast-casual restaurants. They aimed to develop talent internally and promote people up the ranks to give them more and more responsibility. They built a training program with a goal to optimize anyone's potential and take an employee further than she imagined she could progress. Someone who started as a crew member warming tortillas could advance to a management position. The result is a retention rate that far exceeds the average restaurant company. Employee passion increases. The passion to serve customers increases. The passion to find solutions to improve throughout so people can get their food faster increases.

I'm looking for cultures where employees are engaged, and where they know that their companies treat them as partners or owners—not just with development opportunities, but also with the chance to make a real difference. I want employees thinking like they do at Chipotle: "If I add value, I have opportunities beyond working at the register. If I see a problem I can solve, if I can solve it here in this one store, we can roll it out across all our other stores."

Could Google or Chipotle ultimately be a loser for me? Sure, because that's the nature of investing. There is uncertainty. Even great investors are wrong four times out of ten. But I'm very optimistic about these companies, and others like them, because I believe in the cultures created and fostered by passionate founder-CEOs. In my view, the real drivers of long-term winners will be leadership, culture, and engaged employees driving a business full of purpose forward. And that's why culture stands alone on the top tier among my five tenets. (For those scoring at home, I'd put strategy and financials in the second tier, and safety and valuation in the third.)

OVERVIEW: WHAT TOM LOOKS FOR

1. An ownership structure that is vested and aligned with the interests of shareholders.
2. A higher purpose that inspires long-term growth.
3. Evidence that when the business wins, customers, employees, and the world also win.
4. High levels of employee engagement and retention.

THE DETAILS: WHAT TOM LOOKS FOR

Ownership and compensation information, including the number of shares owned by insiders and major investors, is available in a company's proxy statement (also known as a Form 14A). You can usually find this online at a company's investor relations website or at SEC.gov. You can keep track of insider buys and sells by looking at the company's Form 4 filings at SEC.gov. And you can read about the executive compensation structure to see that it aligns with your personal beliefs.

A company truly delivering on its purpose will have a passionate and loyal fan base. If you don't personally use its products or services, see what customers have to say. Interested in a product? Read the Amazon reviews. Curious about a restaurant chain? Check out Yelp or Zagat.

Tom's go-to resource for employee data is Glassdoor.com. You're looking for high overall and CEO approval ratings, especially those that have been consistently high or are trending higher. Also, read the employee reviews. You're looking for energized, loyal employees.

Don't forget to visit the company's website. There you can not only learn about the company's products, but also its founding history, leadership, values, and mission. All that information will help you develop a sense of the company's culture.

CULTURE CHECKLIST

- ❏ A company founder who serves on the board or in company leadership.
- ❏ More than 5 percent insider ownership or executives who own meaningful personal stakes.
- ❏ Executive compensation that seems fair relative to the size and performance of the business.
- ❏ An employee-based CEO approval rating of more than 80 percent via Glassdoor.
- ❏ A workplace that more than 60 percent of employees would recommend to a friend via Glassdoor.
- ❏ An employee benefit you wish your employer offered.
- ❏ Evidence that customers love the company's product or service.
- ❏ A clear, transparent purpose that resonates with you.
- ❏ Diversity (race, age, gender) on the board and within management.
- ❏ Ability to hire and retain talented workers.

15

STRATEGY

There are plenty of factors to analyze when evaluating the strategic landscape for a company, but I focus on three key things.

1. Does the business have pricing power?
2. What's the size of its market opportunity?
3. What's the level of loyalty of its customer base?

PRICING POWER

Warren Buffett's top factor for his greatest-performing investments is understanding a company's ability to manage its pricing over time. Looking back on his greatest investments, like Coca-Cola or American Express, his companies were able to raise prices sustainably, with staying power, over long periods, and that created a compounding machine.

Because when those companies raised prices, they often could invest in scale and operations and technology, gaining even more marginal benefit from their pricing strategies. And that's why pricing power is the lead factor for me in a company strategy. For each investment, I ask: "Can this company raise prices? How predictable is it? How sustainable?"

Because of inflation, the dollar you have today is dwindling in value. If a company is losing the value of its dollars, it needs to be able to increase prices faster than inflation (and/or continually lower costs). If inflation averages 3 percent, you want to know, "If I'm paying $3.00 for this cup of coffee at Starbucks, would I be willing to pay $3.09 for it next year? Would I be willing to pay $3.25? Would I be willing to pay $4.00 for it?" How high and how fast are you willing to go?

You don't have a lot of pricing power if you're selling an automobile that somebody buys once every eight years. A company more commonly forms pricing power by creating a habit—a reliance on repeat purchases without blinking twice at a price. With its ubiquity, along with the consistency and quality of the experience, Starbucks has some proven pricing power.

Note that I said "some." If Starbucks doubled the price of a cup of coffee overnight, there would likely be enough outrage to break many people of the Starbucks habit. A dime increase isn't a big deal to consumers, but it is a big story for the financial performance of Starbucks relative to its competition. Across the landscape of Starbucks' operations, a few cents here and there can make a huge difference over time.

So I'm looking for businesses that have the ability to raise prices steadily. As a consumer, ask yourself with all your purchases, "What would I have been willing to pay for that? What would I pay more for?"

Other examples:

- Would you pay more for Netflix? Netflix faces competition from Amazon, HBO, and other challengers, along with many international first-movers. But considering that Netflix is expanding its product offerings and, critically, has the vast consumer data to feed its recommendation engine to enrich *my* viewing experience, that's worth more to me.

- Speaking of Amazon, how about Amazon Prime? I know many people who wouldn't second-guess paying a few bucks more for their Prime membership.
- A Costco membership. The unique Costco shopping experience and the dirt-cheap prices keep the company's membership retention numbers strong. Costco customers are extremely loyal.

That litmus test for identifying pricing power is a very helpful investing tool.

MARKET SIZE

The second factor I look for is the size of the market opportunity. I've invested in businesses that were thriving, but they were running out of room to attract new customers. The ultimate market size just wasn't there. And if the pie is static—or worse, shrinking—then a five- or ten-year investing timeframe doesn't work nearly as well.

Roughly twenty years ago, I invested in a snowboard company. It had a great culture, a founder-CEO, and solid financials . . . but I didn't consider deeply enough the size of the possible market (how many people make regular trips to mountains?) or related markets it might jump into (are hoverboards next?). Even if the company became the hoverboard king, how many customers might there be? Those are the questions I should have been asking. (Looking through the archives, I see that the stock was actually a two-bagger when we sold our position in 1995, but that positive outcome doesn't excuse the incomplete thought process that went into the original purchase. Thankfully, my investing style has evolved over the past twenty years.)

But it's not just about the market size for a company; I need to see that management is smart about grabbing more of it. Let's go back to Starbucks, and the satirical article in the *Onion* that described a new Starbucks opening inside the bathroom of an existing Starbucks. The joke was that Starbucks had saturated its store locations, and had nowhere left to grow. But Howard Schultz and his team went abroad; there are now more than ten thousand Starbucks outside the US and growing. The company started adding drive-thru stores that offer quick service and have smaller footprints with lower costs from real estate to people. Starbucks has been expanding its consumer products division to sell coffee in other retail outlets, such as grocery stores and warehouses. It's moved into licensing. The leadership team sees the global growth opportunity in coffee, tea, and food (and now liquor in some spots). Starbucks knows its customers, and it's moving aggressively to identify market opportunity and then capture it. That's what I look for when I consider market size.

CONSUMER LOYALTY

The successful investor Bernard Baruch was once asked at a party for some stock picks. Rather than share his favorite ticker, Baruch explained his simple methodology for finding winning investments—one I've embraced as well:

Find companies whose product you buy, use, throw away, or however you've used it, you need to repurchase it within thirty days.

Consumers are creatures of habit. Start with your own experiences. Look where you spend your money consistently every thirty days. Often, this will lead you to some fabulous companies for your investment dollars.

Of course, there will be massive disruption, and we'll talk about that in the Safety section. But generally, you want to see where you and other people are going, repeatedly, to spend more and more dollars. Look for that repeat-purchase, recurring-revenue kind of business with deepening relationships with its customers.

Put these three factors together, and you'll find:

A company with pricing power with a large and growing market opportunity, whose customers are enthusiastically going there over and over again, because it is the best place to find what they want or need.

HOW TO ASSESS STRATEGY

Assessing these three factors (pricing power, market opportunity, and customer loyalty) is as much art as science. There are numbers you can pull together from a company (many provide what is called TAM for Total

Addressable Market) or from online research. But there's also your intuitive read, based on both your experiences and those of others you talk to.

Beyond that, a great step is to contact any company you're considering. Companies have never been so available and accessible as they are today. Just visit the company's website to start (as we'll discuss in the following few chapters).

Another source of research is frequently overlooked by the Wise: You-Tube, or other sites that feature a range of user-generated videos. Search any of the leadership names (primarily the CEO and CFO) for online speeches or talks they've given, and you'll often find fabulous insights into the company's strategy, directly from the individuals responsible for setting that strategy.

Finally, check a website like Amazon. By looking at customer ratings and sales ranks, you'll find a treasure trove of valuable clues about pricing power, market size, and customer loyalty.

OVERVIEW: WHAT TOM LOOKS FOR

- Companies with pricing power—the ability to successfully raise prices over time, often reflected by increasing gross margins over three to five years.
- Businesses that serve growing, dynamic markets with years of expansion ahead of them.
- A business model built on repeat purchases or recurring revenue.
- A track record for capital allocation that suggests long-term shareholder success with limited asset write-downs or charges against earnings.
- A company that has created or is transforming a niche business that has lots of growth ahead.

THE DETAILS: WHAT TOM LOOKS FOR

Read the company's annual report. A management team that can articulate how it will handle shareholder capital—clearly outlining its uses and how acquisitions, dividends, or repurchases have contributed to historical successes—has an enormous advantage in the marketplace. You will also learn about the company's products and services, including the markets it serves and the key customers.

Often at a company's website, you can learn about the corporate strategy or new initiatives.

Think about what you buy regularly. If you keep paying for a product or service that you think is expensive, or you would be willing to pay more for the products you use, that company has a strategic advantage. Of course, you might discover a less expensive alternative that others are starting to buy. That disruptor may enjoy an even stronger strategic position.

Are your friends and family excited about any particular businesses? Some neighborhoods beg certain companies to open there, while other businesses draw residents' protests. If your neighborhood is excited about a company coming, that's a strength that could turn into pricing power. As with any single data point, that shouldn't be the sole basis for a decision, but it can be instructive.

STRATEGY CHECKLIST

- ❑ Evidence of pricing power.
- ❑ A stable, ideally expanding, long-term gross margin.
- ❑ Evidence of repeat purchases.
- ❑ A "brand flock"—customers who are not only loyal, but also celebrate the company's brand.
- ❑ An addressable market that's growing.
- ❑ Evidence that acquisitions are successfully integrated.
- ❑ Smart use of debt and equity to enhance shareholder returns.
- ❑ A management team that is clear about its growth strategy and has a successful past.

16

FINANCIALS

I've gone back and done historical research on the best-performing stocks over the past twenty-five years, and my conclusion is that the number one factor was awesome rates of sales growth. In other words, you don't end up with a twenty-bagger because that company was growing its top line at 4.8 percent per year. Don't get me wrong. There is nothing inherently wrong with 4.8 percent annual growth rates. There are wonderful companies that grow at twice the level of GDP—but they usually don't end up delivering multibaggers for their investors.

TOP DOGS GROW THEIR TOP LINES

The companies that end up being the twenty-baggers, the thirty-baggers, the forty-baggers—the ones that change the course of your portfolio and grow your family's wealth from $50,000 into $700,000 (or from $300,000 into $4 million)—have very strong demand and very strong sales growth.

Here's a telling fact I learned while researching Starbucks and Whole Foods: since they went public in the early 1990s, the sales growth for both companies outpaced their stocks. Those stocks have gone up between 15 percent and 25 percent per year for almost a quarter of a century, and those rates of return are astonishing. But their sales have grown even faster! That means demand has grown faster than the value that they've created, and the value they've created has grown so much faster than the average market or coffee shop, or the vast majority of other investments you could have made.

So I like to find sales growth. In my dream scenario, I'm finding high, accelerating sales growth. That's a challenge to find because of the law of large numbers. It's happened with Facebook. When Facebook IPO'd, it was transitioning (slowly, it turns out) from desktop to mobile. It was retraining all its developers to be mobile developers. That slowed its growth rates, which knocked down the stock. Then things flipped. The top line started to accelerate, and the stock followed. It's my largest holding, and one of our best performers.

RETURN ON CAPITAL INVESTMENTS

If you go back to the late 1990s, you had some incredible sales-growth stories that went bankrupt because companies were burning through so much cash. So sales growth alone isn't a great thing. It reminds me of the joke: "Hey, we're losing money, but we'll make it up in volume."

I like to find high rates of return on invested capital and smart allocation decisions. As for a number, I look for returns on equity of at least 10 percent, with manageable debt levels. That means every dollar invested into the business returns at least $0.10 back. Ten percent is about average for US companies, so ideally I'm looking for those businesses that are generating returns on equity of 15 percent, 20 percent, or more. And I like to see that management teams can continue reinvesting that capital at those attractive rates.

CAPITAL ALLOCATION SKILLS

Great capital allocation doesn't just happen. Yet every great-performing stock that has staying power north of five or ten years has a talented financial team and makes intelligent capital allocation decisions.

Here are some of the questions I like to ask (and if you're interested in this topic, I encourage you to read *The Outsiders: Eight Unconventional CEOs and Their Radically Rational Blueprint for Success*, by Will Thorndike).

Is the company using excess cash to pay dividends?

That might indicate that it doesn't have healthy growth prospects, attractive market opportunities, or the best reinvestment opportunities.

Or it could indicate awesome discipline, like we've seen with the Dividend Aristocrats over the years (a group with a tremendous market-beating history).

Is the company buying back its stock?

Is it a routine schedule just to offset dilution from stock options? That would be a negative for me.

Or does it have a plan to jump in headfirst and buy back shares at discounted prices? In this approach, it stockpiles cash, then buys back huge chunks of stock at the right prices.

Is the company making smart acquisitions that build long-term value for shareholders?

Does it issue stock for a large acquisition (the dreaded "merger of equals")? Studies show that two out of three acquisitions fail, so be careful about companies that bite off a lot.

Does the management team have a long history of successful acquisitions, with zero or few write-downs on what it buys?

Do the acquisitions enhance the company's competitive edge, or are they part of an empire-building strategy by a CEO simply interested in running a larger business?

One company that has thrived with acquisitions over the years is Middleby, the commercial and residential oven maker run by Selim Bassoul. Middleby is an acquisition machine, making more than forty smaller "tuck-in" acquisitions over the past fifteen years to enhance the company's leadership position in its core markets. Since taking over Middleby in 2000, Bassoul has increased the stock more than 100 times in value.

How does the company use debt? Excess leverage (aka debt levels) can lead to bankruptcy, fraud, or desperation. There are awesome managers who use debt brilliantly (like Bassoul for the aforementioned acquisitions), and others who got in way over their heads.

For the most part, I like companies like Buffalo Wild Wings, Chipotle, or Arista Networks, which are extreme outliers on the other side. They have grown, they're continuing to grow very rapidly, and they have no or very little debt.

These are extreme cases, because most public market companies, and certainly restaurant companies, use debt to expand. Their individual units aren't profitable enough to open another twenty units, and open another forty after that, and another sixty after that. That costs a lot of money, so they take on leverage. I'm not making a blanket statement that this is a terrible thing. But when you can find the outlier restaurant that is unit-by-unit so profitable that it can pay for expansion out of internal cash flows, that's a strong, positive indicator.

When you read through the numbers that I'm looking at (sales growth, return on investment, capital allocation, debt levels on the balance sheet), none of these sound like the quarterly earnings numbers that you'll see quoted so much by the Wise. I won't knock Wall Street analysts, because I use their work, and many times the analysis is quite good. But if you take the Foolish approach and you're thinking about your investment as a business of which you're a part-owner, you want to think about the long-term inputs of that business. And those inputs are much more tied to market opportunities, capital allocation, and growth rates.

OVERVIEW: WHAT TOM LOOKS FOR

1. Growing companies with exceptional business models that generate bountiful earnings or cash flows.
2. High returns on capital and talented management teams that put money to work in even higher-return ventures.

3. Strong balance sheets with appropriate levels of cash and debt to take advantage of growth opportunities without sacrificing long-term flexibility or being beholden to the capital markets.

4. A high but sustainable profit margin—ideally one that's expanding.

THE DETAILS: WHAT TOM LOOKS FOR

Public companies generally release financial information quarterly. You can find these filings—known as 10-Qs and 10-Ks—on a company's investor relations website or at SEC.gov. Although these filings highlight different aspects or segments of a company's business, they will all contain three key financial statements: an income statement, a balance sheet, and a cash flow statement. You can also find this information at caps.fool.com by pulling up a ticker.

The income statement can be used to calculate growth and profit margins (the percentage of every dollar of sales converted into profit). Look for increasing sales and rising profit margins, which would indicate that profit is increasing even faster than sales.

The balance sheet is where you can examine a company's capital structure, or how—and how well—it's able to fund future operations. There are many ways a company can build a balance sheet based on its needs. Generally, you want to see that the company has ample cash to fund strategic growth and debt restrictions that will not force it to make short-term decisions at the expense of long-term growth.

The cash flow statement lets you determine whether a company is generating cash. To measure that, look at "owner earnings," Warren Buffett's preferred metric (we'll touch more on this in the Valuation chapter). This starts with fully taxed net income, then adds back non-cash charges—such as depreciation and amortization—and sometimes stock compensation, depending on the type of company (tech stocks, for instance). Buffett then subtracts growth capital expenditures to determine the run-rate of cash flow available to shareholders. Tom loves to see this number growing aggressively, and to discover companies set up to grow owner earnings at a healthy pace over the next five years.

FINANCIALS CHECKLIST

- ❑ Sales that were higher this year than last year.
- ❑ A sales growth rate that was higher this year than last year.
- ❑ Profit margin that was higher this year than last year.
- ❑ Healthy returns on equity with manageable levels of debt relative to operating earnings.
- ❑ A healthy balance of cash and long-term debt.
- ❑ Owner earnings growth that can accelerate.

17

SAFETY

Risk is a part of investing in equities. There's no such thing as a risk-free stock. If someone insists there is, hide your wallet, because an *unbelievable offer* is coming next. We must consider the safety of the companies in which we invest, the risk of losing our capital. I look at three key factors.

LEADERSHIP SUCCESSION PLANNING

As you've hopefully figured out over the past couple of chapters, my style of investing involves putting our capital (and our faith) in the hands of corporate leaders. Imagine they're flying an airplane, and you're the passenger. Just as in a plane, you're not controlling things in the public markets (so stop thinking you are). How confident are you that your pilot will get you to your destination safely?

That's why I placed so much emphasis on Howard Schultz when he was at the helm of Starbucks or Mark Zuckerberg and his leadership at Facebook. You can feel confident that pilots like these won't fall asleep at the stick or try a loop-de-loop midflight.

And just like you won't frequently be changing out your pilot midflight, you won't change your CEO or cofounder very frequently, if at all. You'd better like him or her. But when the time comes—and one hopes it doesn't come while cruising at thirty thousand feet—your pilot will call it quits. Who is going to take over? Is it the copilot? Is she ready? Is she the right person to land you safely?

Business is the same way. But with many of our investments, the first transition is from the founder to the next leader. This worked well when Jim Sinegal handed the Costco reins to Craig Jelinek. But will it always?

Howard Schultz left Starbucks, and the results weren't pretty. When he departed, a large part of Starbucks' culture and success went with him. For five years, Starbucks wasn't a good investment, and there were no signs that the lull was temporary . . . until Schultz returned and revitalized the company. When he rejoined the company, he made it his priority to focus on long-term strategy and innovation, leaving the day-to-day operations to others. He surprised us by announcing his retirement as we were putting the finishing touches on this very book, but we are optimistic he'd learned a lesson and put together a solid plan for the company following his departure this time around.

Because we are long-term investors who might hold stock in a company longer than any one person's tenure as CEO, succession planning is an important consideration. Warren Buffett has been talking succession planning for decades, and he has a plan in place that only the company's board knows about (though I would prefer it to be more transparent).

DISRUPTION ON THE HORIZON

The second thing I look for is the threat of disruption. I focus on the company's platform, looking for potential shifts.

Taking a look at one example, for years we bought books at places like Barnes & Noble. We drove to the store, bought our book, and went on with our lives. That was the experience, the platform for our purchase, and it was a huge growth story in the 1990s. Then Amazon showed up and shifted the platform dramatically. Once that platform shifts, start thinking very seriously about the threat to your investment.

Or think about the shift from desktop to mobile. More and more people are spending time with their iPhones and Androids and less with the clunky machine that ties them to one location. What companies will benefit—and which will be harmed—by that platform shift? Who is most suited to the mobile environment? Identify changes that are coming then try to figure out the companies best positioned to capitalize.

TOO BIG TO SUCCEED

There's also a risk of the law of large numbers. The bigger a company gets, the harder it must work to outperform the market. It's harder to steer an aircraft carrier than it is a tugboat. Think Microsoft, Intel, and Cisco in 2000. In a newly technological world, they were the biggest companies with the most cash. They had the best talent. They had the most evidence of their own awesomeness. They seemed certain to win. And they were the darlings of the stock market. Yet over the next ten or fifteen years, this rosy outlook proved not so true. Those companies have proved to be mediocre investments, as other, smaller, more nimble companies moved ahead and created new industries and new ways of doing things.

So I'm wary of the superpowered winner that everyone loves. It's possible, even likely, that Facebook is heading in that direction, and before long, I might decide to stop adding to the stock. It'll get too big to succeed.

One of the beautiful things about our markets is that we're constantly refreshed, and the markets are constantly changing. Creative destruction is always happening in every industry and to every company, in some way. There's always something new that's coming up, and that's where you'll find the great long-term investment opportunities.

POSITIONING YOUR PORTFOLIO

And now, a few words about portfolio management and temperament. History tells us that the stock market falls 10 percent every three or four years, and that there'll be a drop of 20 percent every decade. We can expect a tumble of 30 percent or more once or twice a generation. If you are investing in public equities, your portfolio (assuming that it's not hedged) will fall significantly at some point over the next couple of decades.

You need to determine what you'll do when that happens. Will you be one of those who sells everything in a panic? Will you sit on your hands and stick with your great companies? Or will you have some cash ready to add?

My final safety trait is the structure of your portfolio, and most important, getting in the mental state that your portfolio will drop and figuring out what you'll do when it does. Positioning yourself to always be able to take a positive action in a negative market is critical to your long-term success as an investor. Again, you can follow all my precepts, end up with awesome companies, and have the wrong portfolio structure, and your best efforts can fall apart because the markets are volatile and you haven't prepared mentally for such occasions.

OVERVIEW: WHAT TOM LOOKS FOR

1. Evidence that the company is being proactive about disruptive forces or competitors.
2. A talented management bench (plus a leadership succession plan).
3. A company that still has room to grow.
4. Diversification among customers and/or suppliers.

THE DETAILS: WHAT TOM LOOKS FOR

What's changing in the world around you? Are this company and its vision in line with how things are evolving? Does the business reinvest in itself by devoting adequate resources to research and development? Is there a thriving culture of innovation?

Companies are often mum about potential succession plans. But you can study up on executives' work histories to get a sense of how deep a talent bench exists at a company. In a company's 14-A (or proxy) or on its website, you can find bios of the leadership team, including their ages. Also, search online for videos from the company; you can sometimes learn about the next CEO before he or she takes the seat.

As companies grow larger and generate more cash, it gets harder to invest that capital profitably. Watch how the company is reinvesting its cash flow. If it can do that at higher and higher rates, it still has room to grow.

A company's 10-K includes information about any customer that accounts for 10 percent or more of revenue. Pay attention to concentrated client groups.

10-Ks also comment on potential regulatory risks. Follow the mainstream media's coverage of any proposed regulations, and you'll find more information in industry publications.

SAFETY CHECKLIST

❑ Evidence that the company is anticipating changes in its industry—and making plans to address them.

❑ An array of talented managers who could lead the company if the founder or CEO was no longer involved.

❑ A consistently rising rate of reinvested cash flow.

❑ Enough diversity among customers that the company doesn't depend on just a few of them for the majority of its revenue.

❑ Evidence that the company is aware of regulatory threats and has plans to deal with them.

18

VALUATION

Each of us at The Motley Fool has a different methodology for determining the value of a company, and none of them is wrong. Here are a couple of steps I would recommend for everyone looking to strengthen their approach to valuation.

First, stop looking at earnings and start looking at cash flow. I would look at owner earnings: the cash generated by the business if it didn't need to grow at all. It's a steady-state level of cash flows for owners. The formula is simply after-tax net income, plus depreciation and amortization, minus maintenance capital expenditures (or what the company will need to spend to maintain its equipment). That will give you a pure look at how much cash the business is generating for its owners, which is an entirely different number from the earnings the company releases on a quarterly basis.

Next, run your valuation exercise over the next five years—not the next quarter or even the next year. A lot of valuation work we see from the Wise says things like, "The intrinsic value of this stock is $29 and it sells for $24. So it's undervalued." That's not the way I think, because that's short-term in nature. Taken to the extreme, that means if it goes from $24 to $29, you're going to sell. And that's great. That's more than a 20 percent gain. But 20 percent gains are not going to transform your portfolio and your family's wealth, no matter how many times you get it right.

Instead, figure out whether that $24 stock could become a $100 stock at some point in the next five to ten years. If so, that looks like an awesome investment (for those with the patience to hold those winners).

I don't run short-term valuations. I'm trying to understand five-year sales growth rates, five-year growth rates in cash flow and earnings. I try to understand whether this business has the potential to grow at a rate that will far exceed the way it's being valued today. And if there is one thing I've learned in valuation over my thirty years investing, it's that other, non-Foolish investors consistently undervalue proven long-term growth stories.

Let's go back to Starbucks. If you had invested in Starbucks at any point in the 1990s, you would have paid a multiple of 50, 80, even 100 times current earnings. And most of the Wise, especially in the Wise media, would have laughed at you. But if you have a growth engine that's going to generate north of 20 percent sales growth each year for almost a quarter of a century in the public markets, the market can't get a handle on that, because it just strikes people as absurd.

When I run a valuation, it's over five- to ten-year periods. I consider what I think it could be worth in ten years, and I try to ensure that I'm getting a 15 percent annualized return over that ten-year period if my expectations play out.

Finally, I look for some negative conversation around the company. Because most members of the media tend to focus on the short term, bad news can create opportunities to buy a stock at a discount, for reasons that will be forgotten long before we take our profits. Seeing the bigger picture is a huge advantage for an investor.

Let's take a look (again) at Facebook. When the stock went public at $38 per share and zoomed toward $70, I thought, "I love the business, but not that stock. There's too much positive energy around it."

Fortunately, the bad news we discussed earlier gave people plenty of reasons to doubt the company and its founder. Facebook wasn't profitable, and there wasn't an obvious and immediate way for social media to generate revenue. *The Social Network* painted Mark Zuckerberg as a jerk: he was young, he was inexperienced, he wore hoodies. The stock cratered to $24, and that's when I first recommended *Motley Fool One* members purchase shares (and I bought some myself and kept adding on the way back up).

Those looking beyond the next quarter could see that Zuckerberg was making tough decisions at the expense of short-term profits, even though he owned a ton of stock himself. He didn't bow down to investors or dress up the numbers (or himself). He went through the costly process of retraining all of Facebook's developers from desktop to mobile because desktop usage was collapsing, and he admitted that he had missed spotting that trend for too long. He basically said: "I made a mistake. I didn't see this. I missed this opportunity. Now we're all going to pay for it, but we're going to set it right, because we're thinking ten years forward."

Even in the early days, he was thinking about the long term, while many investors were fixated on petty, picky details that were destined to blow over in short order. As of April 2017, shares were closing in on $150.

When you're running a valuation, try to find out whether there's something people misunderstand about a company—some clouds that are obscuring the long-term vision for those who aren't patient enough to look out several years. That's when you can find amazing long-term bargains.

OVERVIEW: WHAT TOM LOOKS FOR

1. Companies that stack up well in Culture, Financials, Strategy, and Safety.
2. Based on owner earnings growth and the current balance sheet, a stock that should—looking ahead five years—have an annualized growth rate above market expectations.
3. Companies and management teams that have a history of outperforming growth expectations.

THE DETAILS: WHAT TOM LOOKS FOR

Start with Culture, Financials, Strategy, and Safety. If a company passes the grade there, then it's time to move to valuation.

As a long-term investor with a minimum holding period of five years, focus on per-share cash flows and where they will be in five years, once you account for capital expenditures and share dilution. Management teams that can grow cash flows consistently faster than expectations deserve to lead companies with higher market valuations. On five-year earnings expectations, apply an earnings multiple to value the equity portion of the business. Then add in cash and subtract debt to predict the business valuation. Compare that to today's market valuation to calculate the annualized expected stock return.

Don't do this in a vacuum! Develop and strengthen your ability to recognize the contenders versus the pretenders. Then pick the companies that you think give you the best shot at outperforming the market over the next five years.

VALUATION CHECKLIST

❑ Passing grades in Culture, Financials, Strategy, and Safety.

❑ Expected long-term growth rates that fit with historical performance and pass a commonsense sniff test.

❑ Positive owner earnings, adjusted for the normalized tax rate, non-cash charges, and reasonable capital expenditures.

❑ Expected growth rate in owner earnings that's greater than the S&P 500's expected return.

SUMMARY

None of the factors that I'm giving are absolute necessities—not in Culture, not in Strategy, not in Financials, not in Safety, not in Valuations. There are no ultimatums. I've invested in companies whose founders had long departed from the business. I've invested in a company whose financials were in tatters—but its valuation was incredibly low and new leadership had just joined, and I believed they'd be able to correct the problem.

The point is, there are no hard-and-fast rules.

The key is to begin with a framework that works for you—whether you want to build your own or go with somebody else's system that makes sense to you. If you like my system, terrific! Welcome to the club. In the next chapter, you'll learn more about my brother David's Rule Breaker approach. If that's more to your liking, fantastic. Or pick and choose the pieces you like from each. Or build your own from scratch. Whatever avenue you take, I encourage you to prioritize it, test it over time, adapt, and then enjoy.

But keep in mind that no system works if you can't master your emotional temperament. Warren Buffett has said the main reason he turned $10,000 into $7 billion is not that he met with management or understood competitive advantages or knew which products would work and which wouldn't. It's that he's been able to manage his temperament and emotions through ups and downs over decades.

For me, there are two keys that have helped me retain that mind-set. The first is my self-imposed, mandatory five-year minimum holding period. While many of us investing at the Fool carry long-term preferences (the portfolio "turnover" at many of our services is far lower than average), I take it an extra step by *committing* not to sell a stock for at least five years. Ideally, longer.

This means I'm not trying to get out of company ABC after two years when it's down 24 percent. I believe there's more folly in trying to dodge in and out of positions at precise time points than in simply holding and riding. Even if a stock keeps dropping, I'm going to learn from it, and it'll become a smaller and smaller percentage of my portfolio overall as I continue to back my winners.

And that's how we make a portfolio grow: finding great companies with long-term missions and cultures we're aligned with; holding them and adding to our winners through all the short-term noise; and enjoying and learning as our theses play out over the years in the market.

PART VI

DAVID'S TAKE: BREAKING THE INVESTING RULES

19

SHAPING (THEN BREAKING)
THE INVESTING GAME

We'll now turn to David's approach, which we proudly call Rule Breaker investing.

Where most of Wall Street, mutual funds, insurance companies, and individual investors are playing by one set of rules, I (David here) play by another. This approach has led to dozens and dozens (and counting) of multibagger winners at *Motley Fool Stock Advisor* and *Rule Breakers*: companies such as Netflix, Priceline, Disney (through our original recommendation of Marvel), Baidu, Intuitive Surgical, MercadoLibre, and Amazon, which is perhaps The Motley Fool's greatest recommendation of all time.

Investors don't often find returns of 500 percent, 1,000 percent, or even 6,000 percent by following traditional Wall Street rules of "buy low and sell high," "sell in May and go away," or any other approach that can be summed up in a simple rhyme. In Fooldom, we find that those truisms are more like *falseisms*.

As you'll see, Rule Breaker investing is about seeking growth in dynamic companies that are disrupting and shaping industries, businesses, economies, and even our daily lives. Some of these companies you know well and others are entirely unfamiliar. What they all have in common is a desire to break the rules of business to create products and services that truly change the world for the better. They want to shake things up, topple kingdoms, speak truth to power, and otherwise change the way we see the world.

Not only are these the companies that will shape our future, but they also can make for outstanding investments; as it turns out, changing the world can be lucrative. But that calls for a rather stiff upper lip, because backing world-class underappreciated disruptive companies requires the Foolish long-term perspective that we've discussed throughout this book.

Changing the world doesn't happen overnight. And neither do multibaggers.

Settle in, and I'll share with you the investing philosophy that I've refined with a team of Fools over the years, and introduce you to the Rule Breaker investing world.

IN THE BEGINNING OF RULE BREAKERS . . .

There are companies, like Visa, Johnson & Johnson, and Home Depot, that steadily grow earnings over the years by doing pretty much the same thing they've done the year before—just maybe a little better or with a little greater profitability. There's nothing wrong with stellar and stable companies like those. They've been great investments, and you'll see many of them recommended across Motley Fool services.

But they're not exactly what we would call Rule Breaker exemplars . . . at least, not anymore. Home Depot was early in its history when it disrupted hardware stores across the United States. Johnson & Johnson was just starting out in the 1880s when the Johnson brothers invented new surgical dressings.

Every great business begins as a Rule Breaker. It enters the status quo of the commercial world driven by a vision that says, *"That's not good enough."* Rule Breakers by their nature actively break the "rules" of how business is done, how things have always been. They bring great promise to customers: Rule Breakers solve old problems or invent new possibilities. Like Glendower in Shakespeare's *Henry IV*, part I, these companies say, "The earth did shake when I was born." The truest Rule Breakers aren't anyone's hidden gem. One of the acid tests for a Rule Breaker is, if a company disappeared overnight, would anyone notice? Would anyone care? For the biggest Breakers, there would be *great* awareness and shared distress. If a company could drift away with nary a murmur, that's a Faker Breaker.

So not every new business is a Rule Breaker. Not nearly. And just because it's an established business doesn't mean it can't be a Rule Breaker. The number of anniversaries since a company's founding is far less important than a list of commonalities that we've identified as our 6 Signs of a Rule Breaker (about which we'll go into much more depth below):

1. They are the top dogs and first movers in important and emerging industries.
2. They have visionary leadership and smart backing.
3. They have identifiable competitive advantages.
4. They're good brands.
5. Their stocks have *already* done pretty well.
6. Stodgy backward-looking observers will be jumping all over each other to declare these shares "overvalued."

Now, every business ultimately dreams of *making* the rules. It might be more fun to break rules (it is), but over time, it becomes more important and impactful to shape and rule the world around you instead. Most usurpers ultimately want to rule. Hence the title of our 1998 book, *Rule Breakers, Rule Makers*: great businesses begin as Breakers and hope to become Makers. Both types of stocks can be valuable additions to your portfolio.

There is a middle, pupal stage between the Breaker and the Maker: the Tweener. *Tweening* occurs when a Rule Breaker's key product or service becomes almost perfectly duplicated by a competitor in the marketplace. If the company can face down this type of threat, it's in a good position to become a Rule Maker. If things aren't looking good, this is often when we'll exit.

WHY RULE BREAKERS INVESTING?

Maybe you're thinking that this all sounds great. Maybe you've embraced much of what you learned in the previous section, in which Tom laid out his approach. That's great, because as you'll learn, we have far more in common than not when it comes to investing. Tom has said we're 90 percent alike in our investing approach, with a 10 percent difference. And that often shows in the kinds of companies we like to invest in: great businesses, with visionary leaders making bold strategic decisions that lead to ever-higher growth in both sales and profits. Heck, you can find some of the same companies on both of our scorecards in our respective investing services.

For more than a decade, our *Rule Breakers* team has been bringing our members a delightful combination of winning stock picks, helpful postings to our community discussion boards, updated research with each quarter's earnings revelations, and a focus on the future—minds always alive to new innovations and new investments.

Buoyed by a strong market, the service in early 2017 sat right near all-time highs. With roughly three hundred recommendations under our belts, our average stock carried a gain of around 97 percent (that's averaging every return, from No. 1 to No. 300). By contrast, the directly comparable return of the S&P 500 was around 56 percent, which means that at that point, we were outpacing the market by more than 40 percentage points *per pick*.

Now, when you express that as a sum across the history of all our picks (about 300 at the time of this writing), we get to an impressive total of around 12,500 points of alpha (one point of "alpha" equals one percentage point of market outperformance). That data point says something truly remarkable about *Rule Breakers*' strategy, legacy, and the staff and community that have managed this achievement.

Always remember that we perform against the conventional wisdom (incorrect, in our minds) that says, "You can't beat the market"—that you should just mail it in and go with the index fund. All the other kids are doin' it.

But if you're reading this, you're not one of those kids. You're the kind of kid who, when she builds her lemonade stand, is thinking not only about topping her grandmother's fifty-year-old recipe, but also about how to change the franchising model, build a world-class branding campaign, or recruit her Eagle Scout brother to fund her first-mover business. And if you *currently are* a kid like that, call us. We have an internship for you at Fool HQ.

This chapter is designed for you, Fool, to learn about Rule Breakers investing, and to employ a framework (remember, we like those!) to identify companies breaking the rules. And, equally important, to avoid those rule *fakers*. Before we jump into the 6 Signs of a Rule Breaker, let's look back to a section from our earlier book *Million Dollar Portfolio: How to Build and Grow a Panic-Proof Investment Portfolio* to describe what a Rule Breaker is not.

FINDING BREAKERS, AVOIDING FAKERS

Rapid growth can lead to big returns . . . or painful mistakes that will drag down your portfolio. Just *how* do we find the companies that will win the Darwinian struggle for survival in a hostile and competitive business environment?

First, recognize that this isn't just a numbers game. Screening stocks for high rates of revenue or earnings growth may lead you to businesses that experienced brief spurts for transient reasons. Think of generator makers or modular-home builders that saw a spike of sales and earnings growth after Hurricane Katrina or Sandy. They then saw, and investors experienced, the painful reversal, as sales growth normalized without the catalysts of more major natural disasters.

Indeed, investors who don't love spreadsheets and math may feel a special affinity for Rule Breakers. These companies are hard to assess by traditional valuation metrics, like P/E ratios or discounted cash flow calculations. While all companies are ultimately valued on their ability to produce cash from their operations, Rule Breakers tend to operate in such a state of flux that trying to predict their future with any kind of numerical precision is a questionable prospect.

Think of all those analysts who can't successfully pin down what a company will earn in any given quarter, even after the sales are all in . . . yet who still think they can predict how much the same company will sell for five years from now, out to three decimal points. That problem gets much worse when the company in question is rapidly gaining market share, creating new demand, and seeing high-double-digit growth—all subject to a lot of volatility. Then, the analysis involves more variables, moving less predictably, and in larger swings. To paraphrase the statistician John Tukey, you're better off being approximately right than precisely wrong, which is where most numerical analysis will get you with these kinds of companies.

That doesn't mean analysis is unimportant. In fact, it's more important than ever in the world of Rule Breakers, even if it requires less feverish use of your calculator.

Here are six criteria you can use to help identify a Rule Breaker. Not every great growth investment has all these traits, but then again, not every growth company is a Rule Breaker. The companies with these characteristics deserve special attention. They are more likely to sustain extraordinary growth over a long period and defy investors' expectations.

20

6 SIGNS OF A RULE BREAKER

Investing in great companies early in their high-growth stages, then holding them for the long term, will provide the highest possible returns. Period. We call such companies Rule Breakers, and as we've highlighted, they are some of the most innovative, forward-thinking companies operating today.

To find companies like these, you need a new set of tools. You already operate with various theories about human nature. Your experience gives you some horse sense regarding which efforts will succeed or fail and how to juice the odds. These mental constructs help you make decisions, weigh the possibilities, and predict outcomes. But we believe that most of us don't have *enough* such frameworks.

Think of a new investor tasked with plunking down her money for the long term. Can her selection of stocks be nearly as good if she doesn't understand what it means to disrupt a market? *Frameworks give us pattern recognition.* To see more patterns, we need more frameworks. Otherwise, we risk winding up like the proverbial problem solver who, possessing only a hammer, sees only nails.

As a quick refresher, here's our framework for Rule Breakers investing.

THE 6 SIGNS OF A RULE BREAKER

1. "Top Dog" and First Mover
2. Sustainable Advantage
3. Past Price Appreciation
4. Good Management
5. Strong Consumer Appeal
6. Overvalued, According to the Media

WHY BUY GROWTH?

When we talk about growth, we're essentially talking about a company selling more goods and services this year than it did last year—and expecting to sell even more the following year. But you shouldn't just search out hot companies or high growth rates in isolation.

Rule Breaker investing is about identifying companies that are likely to turn a high growth rate, or an anticipated high growth rate, into sustainable cash flow for a very long time to come. With the right principles and a little discipline, you can be a successful growth-stock investor—and the payoff can be huge.

Companies go through various phases of growth, and a Rule Breaker investor needs to be aware of where their companies sit. To help, we can use—you guessed it—*yet another* framework, called the Hype Cycle. Created by Gartner Research, the Hype Cycle can assist Rule Breaking investors in tracking the five phases that often play out with the introduction of new technologies:

1. Technology Trigger

This starts the hype: the introduction and growing awareness of the technology in question, be it the Human Genome Project, 3-D printing, cloud computing, next-gen video-game consoles, or Twitter. The Hype will frequently surround many of our biggest Rule Breakers. Why? We latch on to game-changing technologies well ahead of the curve. We first bought into Netflix not only because it was going to be about delivering DVD movies by mail (how quaint!), but because it was leveraging technology and the internet to deliver a far superior solution than we could get from our local Blockbuster (may it rest in peace).

2. Peak of Inflated Expectations

As awareness of the exciting new technology grows, the public transitions from dreaming to *expecting*. The technology isn't nearly ready to deliver all that we can foresee, and some of what we can foresee will never come to pass. Thus, we hit the peak of the Hype Cycle. In Gartner's framework, the "visibility" of the technology will never again rise this high! However, Fools are not short-term players, so we don't systematically (or cynically) sell into phase 2. Guessing the peak is very tough—if not impossible—and buying in at the exact right moment is even more difficult.

3. Trough of Disillusionment

From boom to bust: as it becomes clear that the technology's immediate impact has been overstated, we turn against it. Cynicism sets in; all that hope, just a year or so ago, now looks ridiculous, maybe embarrassing. But there's a good chance it'll all be up from here, because everyone got *too* disillusioned.

4. Slope of Enlightenment

The actual ways the technology will be adopted manifest themselves. Acceptance ensues.

5. Plateau of Productivity

Finally, we have become smart implementers and practitioners of the technology. While we can look back and see how truly overhyped it once was, we also can see how relevant and visible the technology has become. This long plateau continues until the technology gets disrupted or loses relevance.

In the end, owning great innovators from phase 1 all the way into phase 5 is how Rule Breaker investors pile up the big returns. It's not about guessing the growth periods so much as identifying, buying, and holding many companies through the five Gartner Hype Cycle phases.

WHY IT WORKS

Rapid growth that turns into sustainable growth can lead you to some of the biggest returns you'll ever find as an investor. Yet at the same time, chasing growth by itself is a ticket to mediocre performance . . . or worse. How can you find the companies that will lead to superior returns and avoid the mistakes that will drag down your performance?

Enter our 6 Signs of a Rule Breaker. As we've mentioned, not every great growth investment has all these traits, but the companies that do exhibit all of them deserve special attention. They're most likely to sustain extraordinary growth over a long period of time.

RULE BREAKER PRINCIPLE NO. 1

TOP DOG AND FIRST MOVER IN AN IMPORTANT, EMERGING INDUSTRY

This is the most important of all the six Rule Breaker attributes. And it should be the first place you focus your search as you look to grab hold of your next great investment.

A top dog holds the dominant market share in its industry; often, it's the largest by market capitalization. The first mover is the innovator that first exploits a niche—essentially creating its market. And finally, that niche must be actually worth dominating.

One company that comes to mind is Baidu, the leading internet search provider in China. While Google is the dominant global search provider, Baidu dominates China, home of the world's largest population and still a growth force in global internet traffic.

Or consider Salesforce.com, a tremendous Rule Breaker investment up ten times in value since 2009. Its suite of tools started as a customer relationship solution, but then quickly moved into the cloud, an important and timely evolution that allowed it to become the top dog in the world of cloud-based services. That's a critically important emerging market for all kinds of companies, including Netflix, Amazon, and Google.

Who else has put all of this together? Think of Microsoft in software, Starbucks in coffee, or Whole Foods in natural and organic groceries. Starbucks didn't invent the coffee shop, and Whole Foods wasn't the first natural food store. But these companies were the first to conceive of these businesses on a national and ultimately international scale when others didn't see growth opportunities.

There are emerging industries all around us: robotics, cloud computing, virtual reality, artificial intelligence, and many others. Rule Breakers aren't hidden; they're right there before our eyes, bringing disruptive technology, clever and effective marketing, or a brand-new business model.

RULE BREAKER PRINCIPLE NO. 2

SUSTAINABLE ADVANTAGE GAINED THROUGH BUSINESS MOMENTUM, PATENT PROTECTION, VISIONARY LEADERSHIP, OR INEPT COMPETITORS

Successful businesses attract competition. The critical question is how well a company can fend off that competition.

In some businesses, like the pharmaceutical industry, patents can enforce a lasting competitive advantage. On the other hand, patent protection can be problematic in the software industry, where protected inventions can often be worked around. Luckily, there are other ways of protecting a competitive advantage.

Companies have trade secrets (the formula for Coke isn't patented; it's a well-guarded secret), and they can build expertise that others find hard to duplicate. Some businesses require daunting levels of capital investment to establish, while others invest in their reputations and brand names. Sometimes a company's leaders are just smarter than the competition, and sometimes competitors find they just can't adapt to a changing world. The key is to find what we call a company's *moat*—its bulwark against inevitable competitors—and figure out how many alligators are in it.

Let's look at some examples.

Business Momentum

Amazon was one of the pioneers in online commerce, starting as an online bookseller before expanding its reach into . . . well, pretty much anything you can imagine. Its visionary founder and leader, Jeff Bezos, always intended Amazon to be more than just books, and he quickly moved the company into movies and DVDs, and then nearly anything and everything anyone needs. Amazon built customer relationships and success so quickly that it became a retailing force. There is no "Pepsi" to Amazon's "Coke." Other retailers quaked at the "Amazon effect," which changed the dynamics and playing fields in industry after industry. That real business momentum has carried Amazon to become one of the most amazing success stories in commerce history.

Patent Protection

This trait is the most reliant on government protection, so it's probably our least favorite, but it's still important. Biotech and drug companies come to mind, as do many tech companies. This is especially true for companies that design intellectual property that goes inside our iPhones, laptops, televisions, or connected cars. Chip companies are another example.

Visionary Leadership

Steve Jobs, Mark Zuckerberg, Jeff Bezos, John Mackey at Whole Foods. Not every leader is a visionary; some are more operations driven. And that's important, too. But true Rule Breaker companies (as opposed to Rule Fakers) are led by strategic visionaries who have their hearts and souls (if not their bank accounts, through stock ownership) tied into their company's success.

Inept Competition

Netflix comes to mind as a perfect example. In its early days, Netflix completely disrupted the movie-rental industry with its ubiquitous red mailers. Instead of trudging to the local Blockbuster, viewers could pick the movies they wanted and—*poof!*—they arrived in the mailbox. In response to that disruptive threat to its business, Blockbuster did . . . not much. First, it turned down offers to buy Netflix for a paltry $50 million. Then it waited six years from the time of Netflix's launch before it decided to enter the online DVD rental-by-mail space. Netflix has been an amazing investment, and it couldn't have done it without Blockbuster's bungling.

If you can find a company that can check off each of the four categories, you might have yourself a Rule Breaker.

RULE BREAKER PRINCIPLE NO. 3

STRONG PAST PRICE APPRECIATION

This principle is the most contrary to what investors are taught. You'd be hard-pressed to find an investor who isn't familiar with the phrase "buy low, sell high." It's simple, concise, and on the surface, at least, quite logical. They're probably the most common four words in investing . . . and in our minds, the most dangerous, as well.

First, "buy low" can be interpreted to mean, "buy penny stocks." After all, if a $0.35 stock goes to $0.70, it's doubled! Many individuals see that simple math problem and miss all the far more important variables that make up the more complicated calculation of investing. Many penny stocks trade so cheaply because the businesses behind them aren't worth much more than that.

Second, many people prefer to buy a stock that has been crushed and try to catch it on the rebound once the market warms up to it. They are shopping in the discount rack, rather than on Fifth Avenue. Who doesn't like a bargain, either on purchases or stocks?

We prefer to flip that thinking. While there's nothing wrong with getting something on sale, we don't mind buying high. In fact, we even seek it out, because a high price means the market has recognized a winning company. In fact, there are plenty of times over our decades-long history where we've bought a stock after it has doubled . . . only to watch it go on to double again, and become one of our outstanding performers.

Consider an investor's take on Newton's law of inertia: a stock on the rise tends to remain on the rise, unless an outside force disrupts its path.

The best growth stocks continue rising, because their advantages allow them to sustain remarkable earnings and cash flow growth, and to continuously win new converts among the ranks of both customers and investors. Don't count on momentum to save your bacon in the absence of other strong fundamentals, but a strong company firing on all cylinders can sustain a remarkably extended run.

When we invest in Rule Breakers, we're investing in excellence. And that includes a company's leaders, as our next principle shows.

RULE BREAKER PRINCIPLE NO. 4

GOOD MANAGEMENT AND SMART BACKING

We're not going against conventional wisdom here. Few investors make it a point to invest in only incompetent, unscrupulous, short-term-focused leadership teams. But we are saying, as Tom emphasized earlier, that leadership teams matter. Their culture matters. Their backers matter. They matter a great deal.

If you are a truly a long-term owner of businesses rather than a trader of stocks, the people who run your companies, make strategic decisions, choose the right market, hire well, build cultures, design products, guide the organization, and more, will be more important to the success or failure of your investment than just about any other factor.

Good management trumps almost all other concerns. Think of a company like Target: At its core, it's just another discount retailer with few structural advantages over its rivals. Yet by dint of good management, it's been very successful and returned a lot of value to shareholders. Better a mediocre business with great management than a great business with mediocre management. Over time, those latter guys will screw up a free lunch.

Now imagine adding great management to a great company. Judging the quality of a management team is a bit subjective, but that's because human beings head these companies. Luckily, we're human beings, too, and most of us are equipped with skills to assess the more subjective aspects. Listen to conference calls and investor presentations. Even if you can't talk to management directly, the internet makes it easy to hear how the top brass thinks and how they interact with investors. Are they smart? Visionary? Inspiring? The heads of Rule Breaking companies are often career entrepreneurs with business track records you can study. Even if you can't put a number on it, you can certainly get some idea of whom you're dealing with.

Note that we also put smart backing as part of this principle. That's because Rule Breaker investing often has us looking at young, earlier-stage companies that have money and support from venture capital and private equity firms, or even other corporations. We want to invest behind proven venture investors like Marc Andreesen or Kleiner Perkins to give us more confidence that our companies will succeed. After all, such investors make their living by finding the companies with the best chances of success.

If you can find a company that has smart, visionary leaders backed by successful, long-term venture investors, you have a potential delicious Rule Breaker cocktail on your hands.

RULE BREAKER PRINCIPLE NO. 5

STRONG CONSUMER APPEAL

For most of us, consumer appeal ties closely to a company's brand. Our favorite definition of brand is, "a promise that you make and have to fulfill every single day." This is much harder to do than it is to say, and the companies that can achieve it will win over time.

It's almost impossible to overstate the power of a strong brand. If a business has mass consumer appeal, sustaining extraordinary growth is that much easier. We want to buy products from companies with strong reputations and brands. A brand eventually reinforces itself—that's why a company like Starbucks rarely needs to advertise.

A brand also becomes associated with an *experience*. We're creatures of habit, and when we have to think less, it makes our lives seem easier. The habit that comes from a strong brand—for instance, stopping by your favorite coffeehouse each morning for your cup of joe—immeasurably strengthens a company against its competitors. For us at Fool HQ, the question is usually which of the two nearby Starbucks locations we'll be heading to for coffee (we call them Nearbucks and Farbucks). Consumers don't have to think about the decision on what to buy or when. They know, without exerting brain power, the action to take. That's immensely powerful for a business and its investors. A company with a strong brand saves its consumers time. And time is our dearest commodity.

It also gives a company pricing power over rivals. You expect to pay more for a brand name, right?

Of course, some great companies work in specialty businesses that simply don't have mass consumer appeal. That's okay, but we want to know that the company's product, name, and reputation constitute a brand among *the people who matter*. If you're looking at an esoteric software business, ask yourself this question: could this company price its product 5 percent or 10 percent higher than its competitors, yet still maintain market share because of its reputation and loyal customers?

One real Rule Breaker reason we love brand so much is that it's not easily represented on the financial statements. You can't screen for brand strength. There isn't a balance sheet ratio to use to compare Brand A to Brand B to Brand C. Quant funds can't point their supercomputers to find disrupting, innovative brands. And that's why we love consumer appeal so much—we feel like we have an edge here.

GROSSLY OVERVALUED ACCORDING TO THE FINANCIAL MEDIA (THE WISE)

Finally, perhaps the most iconoclastic principle to Rule Breaker investing, and the one that makes us truly different than the Wall Street Wise and their adherents: grossly overvalued stocks, according to the Wise.

This might sound like an odd factor. Who wants to buy a stock that all those financial commentators say is too expensive and poised for a tumble?

In fact, being derided as overvalued is a trait shared by many Rule Breakers that supposedly smart investors avoid . . . stocks that go on to double, triple, quintuple, and more over the years. The "too expensive" label comes from underestimating how a Rule Breaker can disrupt its industry, displace competitors, and grow over a relatively short period. Fear of paying too much may leave many investors on the sidelines, only to come in later and drive the stock up further as the writing on the wall becomes more apparent.

Here's a thought experiment for you. Imagine you find a company that scores an A or B on each of the first five Rule Breakers criteria. Then you read in *Barron's* or hear on CNBC that the company's stock is so overvalued because its P/E is too high. Or its stock price has run up too much to make it a good value.

We can almost guarantee you that you're looking at a very good investment.

Why? Because it has all the Rule Breaker traits we look for. And when the financial media calls it overvalued, that tells us that other investors are sitting on the sidelines precisely because it is "overvalued."

We've seen this play out many times before. As your company continues to perform and prove skeptics wrong, the company and the stock will converge as doubters become believers and buy the stock. And as more money comes into the stock, it will go up.

In more than twenty years of picking stocks, going way back to the early days of The Motley Fool, many of our best-performing stocks were considered "grossly overvalued" when we recommended them to our readers. Those companies include Amazon, Netflix, Priceline, Baidu, and Google.

That's because first-rate companies and stocks are often priced higher than second-rate or third-rate ones. And those first-rate ones are the Rule Breakers we're hunting for.

SUMMARY

These six criteria aren't guaranteed to weed out every dog or to point you to every winner. But they offer a framework for evaluating fast-growing companies. We think they can focus your attention on the characteristics most likely to be shared by companies that turn growth into extraordinary performance over a long period.

Finally, we want to emphasize that anyone can be a Rule Breaker investor. You just need to appreciate, understand, and pay attention to the 6 Signs we've laid out. Like most Foolish investing, it's not overly complicated.

Peter Lynch, the famed manager of the Fidelity Magellan fund, enjoined investors to be able to convey their reasons for owning a stock in two minutes or less. Think of it as the Lynch KISS ("Keep it simple, stupid") approach. If you couldn't succinctly and easily tell your friends why you own any given stock, Lynch argued, you should probably sell it.

Lynch was championing the practice of thinking simply and deeply, always keeping the big picture in mind. But let's push beyond Lynch. Let's look not for *good* actions and *good* stocks, but for *great* stocks. With that in mind, here's our Rule Breakers challenge:

Great stocks take not two minutes, but *one sentence* to explain. If you can't cogently communicate to your friends in a few words why they should own the stock over the next five years, chances are it's not a great stock. It might be a good one, or a winning one (and no complaints about that), but it won't be a *great* stock.

And we're looking for great stocks here. So aim high. As my Motley Fool motto says: Excelsior! Ever higher!

21

IS RULE BREAKER INVESTING
RIGHT FOR YOU?

Are you ready to go out and discover the ultimate growth companies? If so, that's terrific. I think it's the most financially rewarding and the most exciting way to invest. But I encourage you to keep a few things in mind when you do. Let's start with a story.

Years ago, a friend recommended I read *McElligot's Pool*, by Dr. Seuss. "It's perfect for a Rule Breaker," he told me. I had thought I'd already read and enjoyed all of Seuss's books, but I hadn't heard of that one, so I ordered it and read it. I'm glad I did.

> *"Young man," laughed the farmer,*
> *"You're sort of a fool!*
> *You'll never catch fish*
> *In McElligot's Pool!"*

McElligot's Pool has a simple premise. A boy is sitting on the edge of a small pond, fishing. "I've been here three hours without one single bite," he admits to the farmer who encounters him at the beginning of the story. Challenged by the farmer in the stanza above, but ultimately undaunted, he spends pretty much the rest of the book imagining out loud all the different sorts of fish he could catch.

It isn't much of a story (and as an early Seuss book, it's illustrated in colored pencil, which I don't like nearly as much as his later inky style). But ranked against all other possible (non-Seussian) reads, it's well worth reading! Rereading *McElligot's Pool* provides us four relevant insights.

1. *The farmer ridicules the boy from the start*—a sure sign that the pool might be a great investment. Some of our best Rule Breaker investments will draw ridicule from the "intelligent" proponents of the status quo. Like the farmer laughing at the young Fool who's fishing at the pool, so did observers laugh at Baidu ("overvalued untrustworthy Chinese search engine"), Tesla Motors ("electric cars will never sell"), Facebook ("failed IPO"), and many more. We Foolish investors actually *need* these farmers. They are excellent indicators!

2. *The boy is honest with himself that he might be wrong*—how very Foolish! When confronted by this older ridiculing figure, does the boy do what most of us might—either acquiesce or become defensive and attack back? No. The young Fool simply concedes that the "Wise" might be right. We have to do that as investors. Don't let anyone talk you out of a great investment, but also don't overload on any one stock. You could be wrong. (You won't hear that often from Wall Street brokers.)

3. *Patience!* The young Fool says it best: "Oh, the sea is so full of a number of fish / If a fellow is patient, he might get his wish!"

4. *Imagination that says, "I might catch a . . ."* The best indicator that this young Fool might be a good Rule Breaker investor is that he brings a formidable Seussian imagination to his endeavors. The people most likely to invest in (or hey, invent!) surgical robots,

better lasers, and cures for cancer are the very people whose imagination is broad enough to allow that these things *might* just work.

If you, too, find yourself drawn to the metaphor of a boy fishing on the edge of the pond, then Rule Breaker investing is for you. With that, welcome aboard . . . but please keep in mind:

Every investor, no matter what style or strategy he chooses to pursue, makes mistakes—our illustrious analyst team at our *Rule Breakers* service included. We can make reasonable assumptions and sensible inferences about the future, but we can't predict it with unfailing accuracy.

When it comes to growth stocks, your mistakes are likely to cost you. You're buying companies that are priced with the expectation that tomorrow is going to be a lot better than today. That new technology is going to work, that product is going to reach the market, that demand is going to climb.

If it turns out that tomorrow is only a *little bit* better than today, you'll pay. If tomorrow turns out to be *worse* than today, you'll *really* pay. Rule Breakers tend to be volatile because necessarily rough predictions of the future are constantly being reevaluated. Both good news and bad news get amplified.

For that reason, you've got to have the stomach for some volatility if you're going to invest in Rule Breakers. If the very idea that an investment might lose 30 percent or more of its value in a single day gives you a stomachache, this might not be the approach for you.

Buy Rule Breaker stocks as part of a broader portfolio. If you own equal amounts of ten stocks and one drops 50 percent, your portfolio goes down 5 percent. If you own equal amounts of ten stocks and one goes up 500 percent, your *whole portfolio* increases in value by 50 percent—from just one stock.

Across our *Rule Breakers* service recommendations, our accuracy (picks that are beating the S&P 500) stands in early 2017 just under 50 percent. That means about half of all the stocks we pick don't beat the market. And some, as we've said, go down . . . a lot. We're not happy when a stock takes a nosedive, but we also don't reflect too much on it. We're not rearview-mirror investors. The future is out the front windshield, and that's where we'll find the next double, triple, or more.

But it's critical for investors to know up front that you will experience more volatility with our approach than with more traditional, conservative investing styles. We take a venture capital philosophy of swinging at a lot of great opportunities with the expectation that we'll hit a few home runs to balance out some strikeouts. And so, if your investing stomach can't handle some of the expected volatility with Rule Breakers, then think twice before you begin.

On the other hand . . .

If you apply the *Rule Breakers* approach with diligence and patience, you will find stocks that go up 500 percent and more. You will also pick some that go down 90 percent—we certainly have. The secret to coping with that is knowing that your Rule Breaking investments are part of a broader approach to wealth creation.

THE FOOLISH BOTTOM LINE

Where are the creative disruptions happening today? Some are undoubtedly just bubbling up now, invisible to all but a few eyes. But others have matured enough to become apparent to investors willing to break a few rules. Are those opportunities in solar power? In robotics? In the new world of cloud computing? Virtual reality? Bank on it. Maybe all of the above? The future is uncertain . . . and we embrace it.

Finding these companies will pose a challenge to your sleuthing abilities. *Buying* them will challenge your well-honed impulses as a cautious investor. Just remember this: Rule Breaker investing isn't about taking giant gambles on unproven, blue-sky ideas. It's about recognizing the companies that are already succeeding in creating a new niche—and identifying the ones that are going to keep succeeding tomorrow.

In other words, it's the ultimate in growth investing.

PART VII

DIGGING INTO
THE DIGITS

22

CLIMBING UNDER THE HOOD TO FIND THE BEST SMALL-CAP STOCKS

Now that we've taken the broad view of companies, digging into Tom's and David's big-picture approaches to finding great opportunities, you've likely noticed that we don't spend as much time on the numbers behind the investments as many others in the field (or, at least, we don't talk about it as much). For some investors, particularly those who took the bare minimum number of math courses required for graduation, that's a godsend. But we understand that other investors take comfort in analyzing financials to arm themselves with cold, hard numbers.

In fact, once upon a time, we drew our conclusions based to some extent on complex ratios and backward-looking formulas. One renowned approach had us buying the five worst-performing Dow Jones stocks from the previous year (the "Dogs of the Dow" theory). As you've read in the previous chapters, our investing philosophies have evolved, but we understand that many investors appreciate numeric screens and financial tools to either screen for stocks worth watching, or dig into the digits to confirm or break down what they've discovered from a higher-level view.

Moreover, understanding the formulas behind the scenes—what a P/E ratio is and what it means for your business—will make you a better investor. Even if you don't personally calculate and compare the P/Es among the companies you're considering, it's valuable to know *you could*. If your car's head gasket blows, no one will insist that you replace it on your own. But knowing the part's role in proper engine function, and what the repair bill might mean to your bank account, will help you understand your options.

And to be clear, even though we rely on many of the qualitative factors we've outlined, we still care about the quantitative side as well. In the next chapters, we'll walk you through a process to develop a list of quality stocks to watch, with some insights on the tools you can use to determine whether these are the companies you want to buy and hold for the next decade. We'll explain a technique we created years ago, in which we use eight key metrics to identify potentially winning small-cap growth companies. It provides a starting framework that's easy to use (and, not for nothing, one that's helped us pick plenty of big winners over the past decade or two). We'll also provide an introduction to and a snapshot of the three important financial statements that a company files: the income statement, balance sheet, and cash flow statement.

Is it glamorous, thrilling, and fascinating? Perhaps not. But you can't play a symphony without learning first how to hit each note on the scale. And who knows? You just might like it.

Let's start our exploration into small-cap growth companies by introducing Messngr (Ticker: MESS), a potentially fabulous (and sadly fictional) upstart company bringing some ingenious new ideas to a fairly dull, mature business. Based in, let's say, Reno, Nevada, this company exhibits dynamic growth of the very sort Fools favor, though the situation grows more complicated as we delve deeper.

Suppose your friend Chris (no, not that Chris, the other Chris) recently sent you an email about a new investment idea. Chris caught an online story about Messngr and sent you a link to its website. According to investor information at the site:

Messngr™ manufactures, markets, and distributes written communications included with traditional novelty items. The company's primary business involves tiny scrolls inserted into fortune cookies, except that Messngr has radically redefined the meaning, function, and popularity of these items. In 2007, the company pioneered the use of flavored scrolls with the introduction of its new TastiScroll® technology, a line of paper breath fresheners. In late 2010, the company introduced new concepts for the messages themselves, creating the popular InfoCookie®. InfoCookies, whose predecessors focused entirely on conveying "fortunes" of little redeeming value, now feature stock tips, winning picks for NFL games, revenue-generating suggestions for entrepreneurs, and other information that customers crave. The InfoCookie won the Best of Show prize at the 2011 Consumer ProductFest, and helped Messngr reach 25 on the Forbes 200 Hottest Small Companies list for 2012.

The company forecasts dynamic growth on the wings of its two-tiered expansion strategy: (1) vertical growth, involving further development of message concepts for the InfoCookie (Braille messages, smart phone videos, text messages, custom birth and death announcements, etc.), and (2) horizontal growth, involving the deployment of messages over a wider range of consumer gift items (airline snack packs, virtual reality headsets, piñatas, packaging slips, etc.). Messngr's InfoCookie brand name poses significant barriers to competition. Messngr markets its primary product line under the service marks, "More Than Just a Cookie" and "We're Talking to You."

With interest, you dive into the company's press releases, mentions in the media, and online consumer reviews. You notice that much of Messngr's publicity revolves around stories of people whose lives were radically changed by messages they'd read: investors who made money on stock tips and entrepreneurs turned on to winning product ideas by suggestions contained on the company's edible scrolls. Amazing.

You wonder whether Messngr has run into legal problems from people who acted on some of these moneymaking tips, failed, and blamed the cookie. But in a precedent-setting 2014 case, Judge Calissa Richards ruled the company "not responsible for losses incurred as a result of its products," adding that "these are basically just a novelty item, fortune cookies whose messages adults shouldn't take seriously." While the company itself might disagree with the reasoning, it obviously agreed with the ruling. Legal problems appear to be a nonissue for an investor (and there are no fiduciary requirements for the fortune-cookie-message maker).

Business is booming. Sales have already reached $50 million over the past twelve months, and they're still climbing. A few analysts have trotted out rosy earnings estimates for the next few years (the company is actually making some money). That's not surprising, considering the production cost of these tiny TastiScrolls must be negligible, while the market's enthusiasm for them has enabled the company to charge rates far above its production expenses. Many are now speculating that Messngr might make an attractive acquisition for a bakery-products conglomerate, like Mondelez International, or for a media-tech company expanding its audience, like Comcast.

A few days later, a *New York Times* op-ed piece skewers the company's newest business plan to make a large portion of the "Inspected by . . ." messages in new garments *edible*. The article contends that by conditioning consumers to blithely ingest their "Inspected" slips, the company will induce thousands of people to eat non-Messngr chemically treated paper that is not at all edible. That's because Messngr's TastiScrolls are expected to penetrate only 30 percent of the "Inspected" slip market, meaning that *fully 70 percent* of these slips will remain quite inedible. Reacting to the piece, the stock drops from $15 to $10 in one day, as critics reach a consensus that the *Times* article has put a significant hurting on Messngr's aggressive "horizontal" expansion plans.

Ah, but the competitive business advantages of the product eventually outweigh short-term doubts, and in the coming weeks, the company continues to announce sales deals with domestic and multinational corporations. Corporate partners cannot deny the entertaining enhancement of including InfoCookies and other imaginatively placed messages in their products. The "brand enhancement" of inserted messages enables a diverse group of manufacturers to differentiate their product from competitors by creating incredible—and edible—goodwill with the customer. It's a winning formula, and the company is looking like a huge winner.

Whether you prefer to examine Messngr's financials as a screener, to pare down all the stocks in the universe, or as a back-side check after your analysis of management, market opportunity, and more, here's one route to determine whether the company's financials earn it a place in your portfolio (and what "the financials" even mean). This is our "Foolish Eight." While it doesn't factor into decision making with the prominence it did in our earlier investing days, the screening principles still hold.

Each of the concepts below is simple—in most cases, nonmathematical—so anyone can use it. Remember that these measures are best used for finding growing companies, often from the smaller side of the spectrum. Many of these measures work for other asset classes, but we focus here on small caps because we think they give us the best opportunities for outsized gains. After all, it's hard to double or triple in size for a company as big as Google or Apple, as much as we admire them and their teams.

EIGHT KEY ITEMS

1. The Company's Sales: $500 Million or Less

If we can agree that all stocks *can* be reasonably valued, then it follows that the least followed and least familiar ones have the greatest potential for not yet having been fully evaluated. Among America's small companies, you're most likely to find a hidden gem—one that, as we explained earlier, institutions won't be able to buy yet. That's why we use limits on a *company's sales* to weed out the ones we want to follow. For this exercise, leave behind all the monster corporations for now—ExxonMobil, Coca-Cola, Pfizer, and all the rest—and set your sights on the lesser-knowns.

Companies that have $500 million or less in sales are more likely to double and triple in size over the next few years. By limiting yourself to $500 million in sales, you can quickly eyeball an earnings report online and see whether a company falls within these bounds. Since Messngr racked up sales of only $50 million over the past twelve months, it's certainly small enough for us. We move ahead.

2. Average Daily Dollar Volume: From $1 Million to $25 Million

We've discussed market capitalization, but when it comes to small caps, the company's *daily dollar volume* is also important. Whereas capitalization measures the total amount of value of a company's equity (remember: *share price times number of shares*), our daily dollar volume figure tracks the total amount of money that trades in a given stock on an average day. This figure enables us to measure and follow a stock's "liquidity." To get the figure, just multiply a stock's share price by its *average daily trading volume*, which is included in most online stock charts. If you were to click to Fool.com or Yahoo! Finance and type in MESS in the quote box (if it were, in fact, real), you'd see:

Stock	Avg. Vol.
Messngr	980,000

From these figures, you'll need to deduce the average daily volume in dollars. Online quotes often will list both the day's volume and the average daily volume over a few months. Use the latter. Diving in deeper:

Stock	Avg. Vol.	Closing Price
Messngr	980,000	12.65

From here, calculating the average daily dollar trading volume is simple multiplication: average volume (980,000) times the closing price of $12.65, for an average daily dollar volume of $12,397,000. That means that a typical six-and-a-half-hour trading day sees more than $12 million of Messngr stock change hands. That's within our guidelines.

A daily dollar volume of $12 million might sound like a lot, but it's peanuts compared to most stocks you've heard of. Apple, for example, trades more than $3.5 billion a day. But companies in our range remain relatively "undiscovered" by institutions, providing an advantage to the small, private investor. And by limiting our search to companies that trade more than $1 million a day, we eliminate companies that are too illiquid—and possibly too sketchy—for our needs. Stick to higher-quality companies that trade over $1 million a day and have NYSE or Nasdaq listings.

3. Minimum Share Price of $7

The third Foolish requirement is also mainly to limit the field: simply, a stock's *share price. We want stocks trading above $7.* Anything lower than that drifts into the land of instability. While it's true that low-priced stocks move more than their higher-priced brethren, it's also true that businesses don't see their stocks drift this low without good reason. Stocks with prices below $7 also become much more difficult to trade, and we don't waste our time with illiquid junk.

4. Net Profit Margin: At Least 7 Percent

The fourth Foolish requirement is also designed to limit the field. But whereas a company's sales and dollar volume and share price relate merely to size, a high *net profit margin* relates mostly to quality.

Let's learn what the net profit margin is by examining Messngr's financial statements. If you're right now looking at an income statement for the first time, you'll soon see how little you had to fear all those years:

STATEMENT OF INCOME (NUMBERS IN 000)	MESSNGR
Revenue	**50,000**
Cost of sales	21,000
Gross profit	**29,000**
Operating expenses:	
Selling, general & admin.	12,000
Research & development	6,000
Total operating costs:	18,000

Income from operations	**11,000**
Interest income/(expense)	**50**
Income before taxes	**11,050**
Income taxes	3,650
Net income	**7,400**

All numbers in bold represent sales and profits; nonbold represents subtractions, or costs.

The income statement shows a business's sales on the top line and its profits on the bottom during a specific period. (Note that all numbers above are expressed in thousands, as the "numbers in 000" indicates. Numbers are sometimes listed in millions and even billions, so always check the multiplier.) Between a company's top-line sales and its bottom-line profits are its costs of doing business, appearing on the income statement as deductions from the top line.

In Messngr's case, we see that it did $50 million in revenues for the year last year, almost all of it via TastiScroll. From this figure, we must deduct $21 million for the factory costs of manufacturing these products, also known as "cost of sales." The number we're left with is gross profit, or $29 million. Some financial analysts like to use a measure of profitability called the "gross margin"—gross profit ($29 million) taken as a percentage of (divided by) overall sales: $50 million. Messngr's gross margin (29 divided by 50) is thus 58 percent.

The next deduction is in the operating costs, comprising "selling, general, and administrative" costs (SG&A), and "research & development costs" (R&D). SG&A typically includes advertising and marketing expenses, office expenses, insurance, rent, and other miscellaneous fun stuff, like company-wide putt-putt golf tournaments. Messngr racked up $12 million there. Research and development expenses represent the amount that a company pays to develop new products; in Messngr's case, psychologists are studying human behavior to determine which products will serve as the best vehicles for new messages by the year 2020. The psychologists' conclusions cost $6 million last year in development expenses. Adding SG&A and R&D together, we reach our operating cost of $18 million.

Income from operations isn't too difficult to calculate next: $29 million in gross profits minus $18 million of total operating costs. Hmm. Looks like $11 million. (Even the math-averse could handle that one!)

Many profitable small companies have little debt and not much cash. So the line item that follows, interest income (or it could be expense), is usually small enough that it's approaching insignificant. That's the case with Messngr.

Now it's time for income taxes. Messngr paid the IRS almost exactly one-third of its revenue last year, or about $3.7 million. What's left over is the bottom line: profits, aka "net income," since it's the income remaining after you've netted out everything else.

We're in search of "net profit margin," which is simply *net income* (Messngr's is $7.4 million) taken as a percentage of sales. Thus, Messngr's net profit margin is $7.4 divided by $50, or 14.8 percent. Our Foolish requirement is that our companies should show a minimum net profit margin of 7 percent.

What does 14.8 percent—or our minimum of 7 percent—mean? And why do we bother making this our fourth Foolish requirement? Fools prefer this figure high, because a high net profit margin indicates a company that is either soundly beating its competition or (Fool's choice) has barely any competition at all. In our capitalistic world, a high net profit margin is a mark of excellence. Anybody who can manage to make 14.8 cents off every dollar of sales (as Messngr is doing) must be doing something right. High margins automatically invite copycat competitors who will try to run you out of business by selling the same product for profits of $0.10 or $0.12 off every dollar of sales. That's capitalism—darling of the consumer, bane of the complacent business. Now, a company that maintains a high net profit margin over many years and through economic cycles gives clear numerical proof of its superiority.

A bit more context helps here. The typical net profit margin will vary from industry to industry, but in America, the average business carries a net margin of about 6 percent. Bargain-basement retailers and supermarkets typically sport margins of less than 3 percent, many closer to 1 percent. The reason isn't complicated. Retailers like Amazon and Wal-Mart have built billion-dollar businesses out of offering consumers the lowest price. In a cutthroat competitive world, it stands to reason these guys ain't taking too much to the bank. In fact, Amazon founder Jeff Bezos is famous for telling competitors, "your margin is my opportunity."

You'll typically find the best profitability and highest margins among technology companies. When a successful company carves out its own niche with a revolutionary product, it can get away with charging higher prices (taking in more profits) because no one else is making, say, cold-fusion automobile engines. But high margins aren't necessarily only for high technology. We've found some great small companies in a wide variety of industries, everything from prototype manufacturing (Proto Labs) to microbrewing beer and cider (Boston Beer, makers of Sam Adams).

Messngr, at this point, has met all four of our Foolish criteria, being both small enough and profitable enough. Time to push on.

5. Earnings and Sales Growth: 25 Percent or Greater

Our fifth Foolish requirement calls for a company to demonstrate *sales and earnings growth of at least 25 percent* when compared to the same period the year before. That number makes it clear we're on the hunt for significant growth, but it doesn't narrow our field so drastically that we're left with few options to explore.

Corporate financial statements are prepared and published once a quarter. Especially with small caps, you'll want to check in on your stocks at least this often so that you're on top of your company's developing story. Messngr's sales and earnings are up more than 80 percent in its most recent published annual report. No significant competition yet . . . the innovative company was first to market with its product and carved out a brand name. Messngr easily passes our fifth test.

6. Insider Holdings: 10 Percent or More

As we mentioned, a respectable amount of *insider holdings* is an attractive attribute in a stock. *Fools typically prefer to see at least 10 percent of a small-cap growth company owned by management, if not a good deal more.*

We've covered this, so we'll just add that you shouldn't panic if you hear insiders are selling their shares. Many insiders have most of their wealth tied up in their own company's stock. Just like you, they have loved ones to send to Space Camp, vacations to take, new homes to buy. They, too, have costs that their salaries cannot always cover. Selling their stock is their way of getting rich, and in most cases, they've worked hard to earn it. Insider sales occur about ten times more often than insider buys, and are only in the very rarest situations cause for concern (e.g., multiple insiders sell out all or most of their positions in one pop, at about the same time).

Back at Messngr, 3.5 million of the 10 million shares outstanding sit in the coffers of the company's founder and CEO. Indeed, 35 percent is a high mark. If the founder continues to think positively about holding his shares, it makes us feel good about owning some of our own.

7. Cash Flow from Operations: A Positive Number

Cash flow from operations measures the movement of money through a business. It is reported in the statement of cash flow that usually appears at the end of a company's financial statements. We want this number to be positive. That means that in the course of running its day-to-day operations, the company has managed to *generate* cash rather than consume it (which would be indicated by a negative number). You want your companies to crank out positive cash from operations, making the necessary funds available for internal expansion, acquisitions, dividend payments, or whatever. A company that has negative cash flow must borrow money in order to maintain and grow its business. For a small company, that's a discouraging indication that the company will either have to take on debt (borrow money for the short or long term) or issue more shares of stock (diluting its earnings per share). And that means it doesn't control its own destiny—a killer for a small business.

One other important metric is *free cash flow*, which is simply the cash left over from operations after subtracting required capital expenditures. Free cash flow is essentially the cash available to management to invest in growing the business, paying down debt, buying back shares, or paying a dividend.

Many successful companies will run a negative free cash flow at times because they are making hefty capital expenditures to add to their operations. Buffalo Wild Wings, the popular sports bar and wings concept, had at times made capital investments in excess of its operating cash flows as it added and remodeled restaurants early in its growth years. In other words, free cash flow was negative. And during that time, the stock continued to do very well; investors had faith that the capital investments would pay off down the road, and they did.

You might ask, "Doesn't *every* profitable business generate positive cash flow?" The answer is no. Messngr is unfortunately one such example. Following the strong fiscal 2016 report that we've been examining, the company will turn in a disappointing 2017 (stay tuned for details). So despite its profitability, Messngr goes cash-flow negative, which is perhaps the only thing we don't like about MESS shares right now. Let's preview the situation (the brunt of the analysis of the company's finances for 2016 appears in the following chapter).

In 2016, Messngr reports sales of $97 million in a further explosion of market penetration, based both on brand-name expansion domestically and an unexpected swelling of international sales, as the concept seizes the imagination of the Far East. But in order to grow its sales so quickly and generate publicity, Messngr has extended extremely favorable payment terms to these foreign customers, allowing them to finance their purchases of Messngr products at a low, low, low 0.5 percent annual interest charge, no money down. In other words, Messngr has practically been giving the product away overseas. All of this has substantially bulked up the company's accounts receivable.

Additionally, you discover that Messngr's customers are taking an average of more than four months to pay for their TastiScrolls. Meanwhile, the company has to pay salaries, advertising and marketing costs, the rent, and its sugar suppliers, within *one month* of services rendered. The predicament hurts Messngr's finances, though it simply represents a natural outgrowth of the company's business plan. Messngr now must pay its costs three months before getting paid by its customers. Despite the impressive profitability we discovered in the income statement, Messngr is cash-flow negative; the act of growing its business consumes cash, rather than creating it. Unless the company can turn this situation around by making stricter payment demands of its customers, more business will only mean more short-term cash consumed and an even greater need to either borrow money (the likely course of action) or sell more shares to generate the cash on hand necessary to meet a three-month cash shortfall.

A company with *positive* cash flow, on the other hand, signals a savvy management team and a strong business, the sort of situation we like to buy and hold. (We'll discuss cash flow statements a lot more in the next chapter.)

8. Relative Strength—Strong Price Appreciation

Companies that meet all the previous criteria have proven financial performance and are small enough to show superior gains. The last step in the Foolish Eight is to look at the actual stock price performance. Our original Foolish Eight included some pretty fancy calculations to determine a specific measurement of relative strength performance, but we've moved away from that. Today, we're more concerned with the broader concept that the stock is generally moving upward. In short, we believe that winning businesses with winning stocks will keep winning.

Messngr, at $12.63, just so happens to meet our final Foolish requirement. Although the company's stock still sits a few points off its recent high, it's nevertheless up from a low of $3.50 toward the end of last year, and it's been a stellar market performer.

With seven out of our eight criteria met, we're happy to stick with Messngr for now. Let's head on to the income statement.

23

MAKING SENSE OF INCOME STATEMENTS

Whether you're looking online—you can search for a company's most recent 10-K file on SEC.gov—or in its beautifully designed annual report, a company's financial statements can be a bit confounding and intimidating. Our aim is to help weed out the meaningless stuff, so you can spend all your time examining what counts. Please excuse us as we skip over many of the footnotes and exceptions, and steer clear of deep discussions about amortization, revenue recognition, nonstatutory stock option plans, and warranty reserves.

Below is what a perfect Fool should spend time investigating and pulling out of the standard available financial information.

THE INCOME STATEMENT

We've already seen the income statement, but in somewhat abbreviated form. Let's now look at the actual version as it appears in the company's annual report:

STATEMENT OF INCOME (NUMBERS IN 000)	MESSNGR INC.		
	2016	2015	2014
Revenue	50,000	27,000	8,000
Cost of sales	21,000	12,400	3,400
Gross profit	29,000	14,600	4,600
Operating expenses:			
Selling, general & admin.	12,000	5,250	2,200
Research & development	6,000	3,750	2,000
Total operating costs:	18,000	9,000	4,200
Income from operations	11,000	5,600	400
Interest income	50	50	50
Income before taxes	11,050	5,650	450
Income taxes	3,650	1,875	0
Net income	7,400	3,775	450
Earnings per share	$0.74	$0.38	$0.04
Shares outstanding (000)	10,000	10,000	10,000

All numbers in bold represent sales and profits; nonbold represents subtractions, or costs.

The picture that emerges is of one of the nation's best-looking up-and-comers, the sort that should keep making next year's "200 Hottest Small Companies" lists until it's no longer a small company. Sales and earnings growth is outstanding, profit margins improve with the passage of time, and management is allotting a healthy amount to develop new products. Messngr seems to epitomize what every small-cap growth company fan could possibly seek.

And that's why it's so disturbing, to savvier Messngr shareholders, when the company posts the numbers below, for fiscal 2016:

STATEMENT OF INCOME (NUMBERS IN 000)	MESSNGR INC.	
	2016	2015
Revenue	**97,000**	**50,000**
Cost of sales	46,500	21,000
Gross profit	**50,500**	**29,000**
Operating expenses:		
Selling, general & admin.	27,500	12,000
Research & development	4,500	6,000
Total operating costs:	32,000	18,000
Income from operations	**18,500**	**11,000**
Interest income	**100**	**50**
Income before taxes	**18,600**	**11,050**
Income taxes	6,000	3,650
Net income	**12,600**	**7,400**
Earnings per share	**$1.05**	**$0.74**
Shares outstanding (000)	12,000	10,000

All numbers in bold represent sales and profits; non-bold represents subtractions, or costs.

On the face of it, we still see tremendous growth. Revenues exceeded analysts' expectations, coming in up 94 percent to $97 million, while net income rose some 70 percent. But look deeper, and you may change your mind about this report. Certainly, the market didn't like it, dropping MESS stock from $18 (to which it had risen) to $14 in one day, a drop of 22 percent!

Let's examine this income statement for a few more Foolish indicators that we seek in every statement of operations. (Hooray, another checklist!)

1. Make sure margins rise at best, or hold steady at worst.

A company's profitability directly affects its stock price, mainly through its earnings per share (EPS). If a company's margins (aka level of profitability) decline, that decline shows up in the bottom line, or earnings per share, dramatically affecting the stock's performance.

Messngr's net profit margin in the year 2015 was an impressive 14.8 percent ($7.4 million divided by $50 million). But in 2016, the company followed up with only a 13.0 percent net margin (remember: $12.6 million divided by $97 million). Still very high, but lower than the year before. A bad sign. Stocks often trade off forward expectations, and forward expectations are deeply rooted in trends. Because the trend here is falling, even a Fool couldn't express much surprise in MESS stock's decline the day that these numbers were released (though a 22 percent drop might be a little too harsh).

We prefer margins to remain at the same levels or (even better) rise slightly and consistently over time. This is the sign of good management and a healthy and competitive enterprise. Always make sure you examine the cause of rising or falling margins. Try to understand the reasons behind any significant change in a company's financial statements, just as you would in your own bank account. In Messngr's case, we find the primary problem relates to its cost of sales, which ate right into the company's gross margins. It appears that in the effort to ramp up production of new messages for innovative new inserts—particularly the construction of its scratch-'n'-eat mentholated series—the company couldn't achieve factory efficiency. Perhaps it shouldn't have introduced the new product, or maybe this is just a onetime stumble.

2. Make sure research and development (R&D) expenditures aren't getting shortchanged.

Perhaps the foremost financial trick that companies use to match or exceed their earnings estimates is to reduce research and development (R&D) expenditures. While this makes one number look better, it jeopardizes the company's future by enhancing (or just preserving) its present.

Unfortunately, most companies feel tremendous pressure to meet or exceed Wall Street analysts' quarterly earnings estimates. If a company fails to meet estimates (as Messngr did), it can expect its stock to star in that day's "Market Losers" news articles. And it can sometimes take a long time for institutional confidence—and strong stock price performance—to reappear.

Still, it's key that we carefully watch the amounts our companies are spending on R&D, particularly at high-tech and medical companies, which rely on developing superior technology to maintain their edge. A Goldman Sachs study of the one hundred largest tech, internet, and biotech companies in the Nasdaq shows a strong correlation among R&D spending, sales growth, and stock performance. In effect, companies that invest in their mad scientists deliver better shareholder returns!

Look back at Messngr's financial statement. Horrors! It spent less on research and development in 2016 (just $4.5 million) than it did in 2015 ($6 million). That's a bad sign, and it suggests that management might have underfunded its development efforts in order to prop up its earnings per share. Sure, a company's R&D needs can change, permanently reducing the amount spent. That's quite unlikely for a small, high-growth situation, but possible. Your job is to find out what really happened.

The traditional and best approach involves looking at R&D as a percentage of revenues for that year. Doing so, we see that R&D accounted for 12.0 percent of revenues in 2015, and just 4.6 percent of revenues in 2016. This is a dramatic reduction. The company might have managed to keep earnings per share up over $1.00 for the year, but how well will earnings fare in another year or two? The company has claimed plans to release its Virtual-Reality InfoCookie Experience modules in the first half of 2018—do you still think it's going to make that schedule?

If Messngr is not willing to maintain a consistent annual percentage for R&D costs, it'll only be that much more likely to get swept under the rug when Google comes out with a better Virtual-Reality InfoCookie Experience module. Watch this figure carefully, Fool.

3. Make sure the company is paying full income taxes.

Always look at your company's corporate tax rate: the amount paid in income taxes as a percentage of income before taxes. Refreshing our memory in Messngr's case, we see:

MESSNGR	2016	2015
Income before taxes	18,600	11,050
Income taxes	6,000	3,650

So the company paid 33 percent ($3,650 divided by $11,050) in 2015, and a slightly lower rate (32 percent) in 2016. This is fine—about what one would expect. Don't get hung up here on fine distinctions regarding a percentage point or two. The rules change slightly every year to keep accountants in business. Don't let this bog you down.

We make a point of talking about income taxes because some companies record much lower income tax rates due to "tax-loss carryforwards." Our government gives money-losing enterprises credits against future taxes when (and if) they eventually turn a profit. Messngr lost a bit as a start-up, and paid no income tax at all in its early years as a result.

Don't worry too much about taxes. Just be sure you're not judging its merits based on net income and earnings-per-share figures that swelled artificially high thanks to an artificially low tax rate (in most cases, below 20 percent).

4. Keep an eye on growth in the number of shares.

Companies issue more common shares when they need to create cash; with an investment bank serving as liaison, the public purchases the new shares, filling the corporate coffers. Reasons to issue new stock abound. Some companies are cash-flow negative, as we learned earlier, and therefore need the bucks to fund expansion. Others might issue new shares or convertible warrants to pay off a new acquisition. Whatever the reason, whenever new stock is issued, the market generally devalues the existing stock.

As mentioned, when we start actually valuing stocks, earnings per share is an important figure to watch. To review, earnings per share is simply the profits of the company (net income) divided by the total number of shares of common stock. So when a company issues more shares, the earnings per share will decline, all other things remaining equal. (If you divide the same-sized pie into a greater number slices, each slice is smaller, and therefore worth less than before. The same goes for shares in a company, and the amount of its earnings that each share commands.) Because many stocks trade mainly off a multiple of earnings per share, this is not a good thing.

In 2015, Messngr issued 2 million new shares for no good reason we know of at present. (We may learn more later.) So, despite sales and profits gains of greater than 70 percent, earnings per share rose only 42 percent. We've already discussed what that did to the stock.

Keep an eye on total shares outstanding. If you see significant increases, or hear of a new company share offering, ask yourself *why*. Did your company need the money, or did it just want to cash in off a high share price following a great run in its stock? And if your company did need the money, did it need it for *good* reasons (like launching a new subsidiary or developing of a new product) or *bad* reasons (like fighting to stay in business)? By the way, you have no cause for complaint if total shares outstanding increase in bits and pieces from quarter to quarter. Companies often award extra shares to management and employees as incentivized compensation. But if you see a large unexplained jump in the company's share total, or a consistent pattern over three to five years of significantly more and more and more shares, your guys are diluting the growth of their earnings per share. You can find better investments elsewhere.

THE P/E RATIO: THE MARKET'S PRICE TAG

Now that you've got a handle on the income statement, here's a quick word on one of the most common methods people use to evaluate stocks: the price-to-earnings ratio (the P/E ratio). P/E equals the price of a stock divided by its company's earnings per share over the past twelve months.

Let's take two examples:

YUCKIE YOGURT CORP. (TICKER: YUCK), the retailer of exotically flavored frozen yogurt, has earnings per share of $0.50 and a stock price of $5. *Its P/E ratio is 10.* ($5 divided by $0.50 = 10.)

DOORS, INCORPORATED "C" (TICKER: REMAC), the software conglomerate whose operating software—Doors—has suddenly cracked a competing brand's seemingly unshakable hold on the computing market, has earnings per share of $0.50 and now trades at $30. *Its P/E ratio is 60.* ($30 divided by $0.50 = 60.)

The P/E for a given stock varies based on changes in price (which happen every day) and changes in earnings (which happen once a quarter). Think of it as the price tag that the market has put on the shares. The market is saying, "If you want to buy stock in Doors, you're going to have to pay 60 times the company's earnings." Buying stocks like Doors, Inc., that trade at 35 times earnings or higher (as do many of the best growth stocks) is akin to shopping at Tiffany—you'll pay high prices for desired goods. Purchasers of stocks at ten times earnings or less have opted to shed their discretionary income on the equity equivalent of the bargain bin.

Looking closely at the examples, notice the extreme disparity. Both companies, after all, have trailing twelve-month earnings of $0.50 per share, but YUCK is trading at $5 per share, and there's REMAC at $30. This seems just too good a deal to pass up, so you push all in on Yuckie—after all, for the same amount of earnings, you have only had to pay $5 per share, compared to the Fools who are paying six times that for Doors. Darned clever of you; you've outsmarted the market. Yuckie's share price, you convince your in-laws, should race to $30 sometime soon . . . a cool 500 percent profit.

But before you start pricing yachts, consider the woeful state you'll be in when, a year later, Doors has run to $52 a share, while YUCK's management has closed its seventy-third Yuckie Hut of the year, sinking the stock price to $1.25 per share.

The lesson: Not all P/Es are created equal. Some stocks may be considered underpriced at 50 times earnings, whereas others may be grossly overpriced when their P/E rises to 12. The market's price tag is based on past history, present circumstance, and future projections, all of which vary from company to company. The P/E represents the present circumstance (stock price) divided by past history (trailing twelve-month earnings per share). Finally, analysts' future projections (the company's expected growth rate) have a great effect on how high a stock's P/E gets. Remember that those analysts are giving you their best guess . . . and they're usually guided by the company itself.

THE PEG RATIO: A STEP BEYOND P/E

Many investors make the mistake of viewing the P/E ratio alone, in a vacuum, as if the number 17, or 5, or 43 could serve as an effective valuation tool on its own. You'll occasionally hear such an investor blurt something like, "That stock's got a P/E of 60! It's *outrageously* overvalued!" To our Foolish ear, that's kind of like saying, "The thermometer says the temperature is sixty! Outrageous!" But unless we know what season it is, where we are in the world, and what the average temperatures are, we have no context to understand the comments. They're non-sequiturs.

First Foolish lesson on P/Es: place them in a context that gives them meaning. In a fully and fairly valued situation, a growth stock's price-to-earnings ratio should equal the percentage of the growth rate of its company's earnings per share.

The growth rate is the subjective piece of the pie. The P/E ratio is hard fact, reported everywhere. Thus, you'll have to use your noggin in this scenario to analyze a company's growth. When we talk about growth rate, we're talking primarily about the future earnings per share (EPS) growth rate. Sales growth doesn't help if swelling costs counteract it. We want EPS to outpace everything else on the income statement.

Let's say Doors, Inc., has just reported EPS of $0.60 this year. How much will EPS be next year? The most relevant numbers—earnings estimates—haven't been reported yet. In the case of Doors, a quick check (in the event the company existed) would show that the company is currently earning $0.60 per share, and that analysts expect EPS to grow by 50 percent over the coming year to $0.90.

If you want to look more than one year into the future (and what Fool doesn't want to look as far forward as possible?), simply use analysts' growth estimates for two, three, or five years into the future, if they're available. Yahoo! Finance is a good place to look for these longer-term estimates, under the "Analysts" tab.

All right. We know the P/E now, and we can calculate growth rates. Here comes the fun part: putting the two together.

Again, the axiom says that a stock's P/E should, conveniently enough, equal the company growth rate. Thus, if a company is growing at 20 percent, the P/E should be 20 for a fair, full value. The technical underpinnings of the theory have something to do with anticipated cash flows looking years ahead, but the actual principle itself has melted away over the years.

This is the basis for the PEG ratio. You calculate this by taking a stock's current P/E ratio as a percentage of its growth rate, to bring you to the "Price-to-Earnings-to-Growth Ratio," or "PEG." It's that easy.

Let's apply the PEG ratio to Doors, Inc. We know that the P/E is 60 and that analysts expect the company to grow at a rate of 50 percent next year. Simply divide 60 by 50 to find that the PEG for Doors is 1.2.

Simple, isn't it?

Now what to do with that number? We said that the PEG ratio takes as its basis that the P/E and growth rate would be equal when a stock is fully and fairly valued. That means that a PEG of 1 would indicate full valuation. Anything less than 1 would mean that the expected growth rate has sped ahead of the P/E, which means that the stock is selling for less than its growth rate would normally demand. A PEG more than 1 points out a stock that is more expensive than you would expect, based on its growth rate.

We used to interpret results of the PEG—we went so far as to refer to it as the Fool Ratio—as a clear indicator of absolute over- or undervaluation. We would make buys based on low PEGs and sell or short high PEGs. We've found, however, that Mr. Market often has a good reason for his valuation. If the Street doesn't have confidence in Doors' ability to reach its 50 percent growth targets, it will price it accordingly, leading to a low PEG. If the market starts to believe that Doors will blow the doors off its 50 percent annual growth estimate, it will bid the stock up, giving it a high PEG ratio. That means that, counterintuitively, a high PEG ratio often points out a company in which the market has great faith. And the market is very often right to believe in the best companies.

Also, a "normal" (or mean) level for a company's PEG ratio will, in our experience, change based on the present-day environment for interest rates.

When rates are low or going lower (as they were in the years after the 2008 financial crisis), money piles into the stock market, fleeing from interest-bearing vehicles like CDs and money markets, since the rate of return on those is less attractive. This pushes up stock market valuations. In the late 1990s, we saw good companies with PEG ratios over 2.0, and their stocks still did well over the following year or two. Conversely, during eras with high interest rates, expect the normal PEG ratios to trade well below 1.0. Thus, even this Foolish ratio cannot be viewed out of context.

The key point to take away, and the reason we share this ratio, is that for companies with profits (you can't calculate a P/E ratio for companies with no "E") you can get a pretty good gauge on how their stocks are being priced according to their growth rates. This is a critical bit of context that the Wise too often lack. Again, go back to the line that kicked off this section: "It has a P/E of 60! How overvalued!" Well, if the sustainable growth rate for the enterprise over the next five years is 60 percent or higher, we respectfully disagree.

Use the PEG ratio carefully. It's a shortcut that ultimately provides only an impression of a stock's valuation. It's then up to you to determine *why* the market has that impression.

24

BALANCE SHEETS AND CASH FLOW STATEMENTS

THE BALANCE SHEET

With the income statement covered, let's move on to the second financial statement that we watch: the balance sheet. Unlike the income statement, which reads like a top-down yearlong story of a business's progress, the balance sheet gives the reader a single snapshot of the company's books on the *last day* of the reporting period.

The statement comprises two sections: assets and liabilities (the latter of which is grouped with shareholders' equity). The balance sheet is so called because these two sections "balance" each other out in terms of value. Assets are balanced by liabilities, and when you run out of liabilities, everything else is considered "shareholders' equity," which is the basic net worth of the company. That's a pretty understandable concept, no? If you subtract liabilities from assets, you have the amount that belongs to the owners. Both the assets and the liabilities sections are further divided between "current" and "noncurrent" items, where the "currentness" of the item in question refers to how quickly it could be recouped, should the business be liquidated. Current items would be paid or collected within one year.

As we take our tour of the balance sheet, we'll again focus only on the items that matter to us. If you want all the gory details, well, you've picked the wrong book.

BALANCE SHEET (NUMBERS IN 000)	MESSNGR, INC.	
	2016	2015
Current Assets:		
Cash and cash equivalents	24,000	20,000
Accounts receivable	34,000	14,000
Inventory	20,000	10,000
Prepaid expenses	1,500	1,000
	79,500	45,000
Property & Equipment:		
Subtotal	12,000	6,000
Less accumulated depreciation	1,200	800
	10,800	5,200
	90,300	50,200
Liabilities:		
Current Liabilities:		
Accounts payable	6,500	3,200
Accrued expenses	18,000	10,000
	24,500	13,200
Long-Term Debt:	0	0
Stockholders' Equity:		
Common stock; $.01 par value	2,400	2,000
Additional paid-in capital	26,300	10,500

Retained earnings	37,100	24,500
	65,800	37,000
Total Liabilities and Stockholders' Equity	90,300	50,200

1. Cash: very, very likable.

The very first line of the balance sheet is always named, "Cash and cash equivalents," or some similar phrase. This is the amount of money a company has sitting in the bank. The "cash equivalents" part refers to the cash not needed for running the business—money that's currently earning a speck of short-term interest. (If a second line below it is labeled anything like "short-term investments," that line should be *combined* with the cash line; both serve similar functions and should be grouped together, for our purposes.)

We only have one real rule with company cash: we like to see lots of it.

Companies build up cash for several reasons. The first is the best: good operations generate cash. To review, operational cash flow is simply the dough that piles up as the company runs its business. We call businesses that take in more than they put out "cash generators," green machines cranking out seven- and eight-figure additions to this most-favored-status line of the balance sheet. Watching a cash generator do its thing can bring tears to a capitalist's eyes. Actually being invested in such a company can feel even sweeter.

But there are other ways to come by cash as well, including a share offering. We just ended the last section by mentioning companies that issue more shares of common stock in order to raise cash. When those offerings occur, the resultant cash comes right to this asset line.

Some analysts like to express the amount of cash a company has in per-share amounts. To get that, just divide the cash and cash equivalents figure by the total number of shares outstanding. For example, Messngr has built up an impressive $24 million in cash by the last day of 2016. With 12 million shares out, Messngr sports cash alone worth $2 per share. This means that no matter how many earthquakes shake the company's Reno headquarters, the stock won't drop below $2. (Stock prices *can* conceivably fall below a company's cash per share, but that generally happens only in the very rare case of a company burning through so much cash in its operations that the cash on its balance sheet likely won't stick around much longer.)

Cash means more than just a dependable rock-bottom stock price. It also represents the power to pay off debts, if a company has them. Or it could represent the potential to acquire complementary businesses or buy out a competitor. The best growth companies on the planet create future growth with their own cash. Develop a bias toward stocks backed by cash-generating businesses that have a wad of bills sitting in the bank gathering interest, ready to be deployed whenever a good opportunity presents itself.

2. Avoid too much debt.

The inverse to cash is long-term debt. Like people taking out thirty-year mortgages, many companies borrow to fund future opportunities. Companies routinely take on debt to fund acquisitions, new product developments, franchising expansion, etc. Consider a few examples. Disney assumed more than $10 billion in debt to buy out Capital Cities/ABC. The parent of Burger King borrowed $9 billon to acquire Canadian doughnut chain Tim Hortons (just counting the days until they combine menus and we finally get Whoppers sandwiched between glazed doughnuts). And Microsoft took on a chunk of debt to purchase LinkedIn for $26.2 billion (even though it has plenty of cash).

Debt is just one of the financing tools available to companies. It's not always horrible to expand rapidly using debt, but it's a dangerous game. We vastly prefer businesses that don't take on much debt, if any. We like them to be so profitable from operations and growing so rapidly that they don't need additional outside capital, or the risk of significant interest expenses, to thrive. They own their own financial condition. These will make for some of your very best investments, through good *and* bad economic periods. By the way, you'll find "long-term debt" (if the company has any) midway down the liability side of the balance sheet, just after current liabilities.

3. Make sure growth in accounts receivable and inventory approximates sales growth.

Accounts receivable and inventory both constitute assets—they represent money that the company would receive if it were liquidated. Accounts receivable measures the amount of money that a business is owed by its customers, not all of whom pay 100 percent cash up front for every product. Inventories are an asset because they represent finished or near-finished products that the company has not yet sold.

Both items are considered assets because they have monetary value to the company. But from an investor's point of view, they're more like liabilities. Through a Foolish lens, you can well see that both accounts receivable and inventories represent momentary failures on a company's part to convert its business into cash. Accounts receivable are what your loan sharks have failed to collect so far, and inventories are what your salesmen have not yet managed to unload.

Both these assets will always exist as inevitable components of running a business (unless you're a lightweight software company). As an investor, you need to track how the *growth* in accounts receivable and inventory tracks against overall sales growth. You'd like to see this growth rate decline in comparison to sales, but it's more realistic that the growth rates of accounts receivable, inventories, and sales will move roughly in sync. If that's the case, you have nothing to worry about.

When, on the other hand, accounts receivable and inventories rise far faster than sales, or demonstrate a huge one-quarter jump, consider very seriously whether that company is delivering for shareholders. We've seen many otherwise healthy small-cap stocks literally fall apart (losing 80 percent or more in a hurry) because they failed to collect what they were supposedly owed, creating a *huge* cash-flow drain. (We say "supposedly owed" because in some situations, the company might not actually have made the sales it claimed.)

Unless they have a lot of cash, small businesses *have* to maintain a tight control on growth in receivables and inventories. We can't overstate how important that is. Don't bother with any companies having problems in this arena. You can find too many better ones that aren't.

Incidentally, beyond just looking at the growth rates in accounts receivable, we also monitor the proportion of receivables to overall sales. This shows you how much of a company's sales are getting paid for right away. In the case of Messngr, we see 2016 receivables at $34 million, with 2016's sales being $97 million. That means that receivables are running at 35 percent of sales ($34 divided by $97), or, expressed in calendar terms, receivables take about 4.2 months (35 percent of a year) to pay off. Messngr fans, 35 percent is a discouragingly high figure. It gets even worse when put in the context of the previous year, in which sales were $50 million and receivables were $14 million. That's 28 percent, meaning our receivables-to-sales ratio is already high and *trending higher*. It appears that bakers are welching on their InfoCookie fees. A strong, well-managed business wouldn't permit this to happen.

Finally, note that the reverse equivalent of accounts receivable and inventories is accounts payable and accrued expenses: liabilities that a company *owes*, but which (paradoxically, again) a company should do its best to increase. The longer a company can string out its suppliers and creditors (while still ultimately paying), the more use the company will get out of the cash it keeps on hand (for operations or interest). That's smart cash management. However, in most strong small-cap growth companies, accounts receivable and inventories will still far exceed accounts payable and accrued expenses, making these latter balance sheet items less meaningful.

4. Do whatever ratios catch your fancy.

Some people go overboard analyzing the various ratios calculable from the data in a balance sheet. We don't find many of these terribly meaningful, but we'll share with you a couple of things you can learn.

The most common ratio associated with balance sheets is probably the *current ratio*. It gives investors a basic test of short-term liquidity, dividing the current assets (cash, receivables, inventories, etc.) by the current liabilities (accounts payable, accrued expenses, etc.). Ideally, this figure will fall somewhere above 2-to-1 for the typical American industrial company, tending toward higher ratios for small caps. The current ratio tells you how nimbly a company can act to take advantage of an unforeseen circumstance.

In reality, of course, even a high ratio may not help in times of trouble. Taken on its own, the current ratio doesn't tell you much about a company's liquidity, because it depends on the company's ability to convert its current assets into cash. That's not always possible. If, for example, TastiScrolls were found to cause mild decreases in the libidos of laboratory rats, one might think that Messngr would be far better prepared to deal with this potential crisis with a current ratio of 5 than with a ratio of 1. In the wake of the FDA investigation, however, Messngr is going to have to write off all its current inventory. What's more, some of its customers might decide that they aren't going to pay the money they owe Messngr, since they can't sell their Tasti-Scrolls, either. Messngr's inventory and accounts receivable balances won't add up to a pile of glucose in this situation.

For what it's worth, let's calculate Messngr's current ratio for 2016 and 2015:

		2016	2015
Current Assets		79,500	45,000
Current Liabilities	divided by	24,500	13,200
Current Ratio	=	3.2x	3.4x

Messngr's current ratio for 2016 was 3.2, which is certainly acceptable. Note that this is *down* from the previous year's 3.4.

You can apply the current ratio to any annual report you look at, though we've never let it make or break an investment decision for us. We like to see the ratio remain even or trend slightly higher, but you won't find us getting emotional on the subject. Still, a survey of the current ratio can be a useful way to discover potential new investment ideas among financially healthy mid caps.

A second ratio, very similar to the current ratio, is the *quick ratio*. The quick ratio is more "cash-centric"—it's the current assets minus inventories divided by the current liabilities. It gives you an even better read on how prepared a company might be to encounter unforeseen difficulties or opportunities, or just to meet current short-term debt obligations, so you want to see as high a number as possible.

		2016	2015
Current Assets		79,500	45,000
Inventory	minus	20,000	10,000
Current Liabilities	divided by	24,500	13,200
Quick Ratio	=	2.4x	2.7x

Messngr's quick ratio declined from a powerful 2.7 in 2015 down to a still-impressive 2.4 in 2016. Still, this drop may signal bad news.

Another fairly common ratio is the *debt-to-equity* ratio. As you know, companies issue bonds or shares of stock in order to raise money. One of the fundamental differences between debt (bank borrowings or bonds) and equity (stock) is that debt has to be repaid (at least, the lenders want their money back!). From a stockholder's point of view, therefore, the less debt, the better, unless the company can make far more money from that debt than it will have to pay out in interest. If a company maintains little debt, it retains the ability to go out to the capital markets and float a bond or convertible to raise cash, should the need arise.

To calculate the simple version of this ratio, find a company's long-term debt and its equity. Long-term debt sits in the liability portion (non-current) of the balance sheet. Equity appears in the stockholders' equity section of the balance sheet, below liabilities. In most online quote pages, like at Fool.com, you can find this called out as "Total Equity" or "Total Stockholder Equity." Then, just divide debt by equity. You want this figure to be as low as possible—preferably zero, in most cases. Messngr has no debt, and thus a debt-to-equity ratio of 0.

The final ratio we'll mention is perhaps the most important—but again, not one upon which we'd base any investment decisions. It's called the *return on equity ratio* (ROE), one additional measure of corporate profitability and management efficiency. To find it, divide the net income by the total stockholders' equity from the balance sheet. You're measuring the amount of profit a business generates relative to the amount of money shareholders have put into it.

In a low interest rate environment, the average American company's ROE is about 10 percent. So a respectable figure is 12 percent; a strong figure runs closer to 20 percent. As with most of these ratios, you want to see a high number that remains high over time, either by standing pat or increasing slightly. For outstandingly profitable emerging-growth companies, this number may start out ridiculously high (50 percent or even greater, in some cases) and trend down as the company grows. Don't count that against a stock.

		2016	2015
Net Income		12,600	7,400
Shareholders' Equity	divided by	65,800	37,000
Return on Equity	=	19.1%	20.0%

Messngr produced net income of $7.4 million in 2015, and a check of the balance sheet reveals total shareholders' equity at $37.0 million that year. Thus, the return on equity was 20.0 percent. The next year, as you might expect by now, was a tad worse: return on equity for 2016 came in at 19.1 percent.

One last note: corporate CFOs can inflate a company's ROE by carrying a lot of debt. In your analysis, you should pair a company's ROE with its debt-to-equity ratio, to make sure the former is based more on operating performance than on a debt-stuffed balance sheet.

◆　◆　◆

Having finished our Foolish discussion of the balance sheet, we'll conclude with the cash flow statement.

THE STATEMENT OF CASH FLOWS

We place great importance in a business's ability to create—not consume—cash. Your own portfolio should be filled with "cash generators."

Novices sometimes have difficulty conceiving of the cash-flow statement. If it's measuring income and expenses, how is it any different from the income statement?

The cash flow statement provides you a different way of looking at income and expenses. It's most akin to your monthly bank statement. There, you'll notice that the various income and expense items that show up are all accounted for *when paid*—when your employer deposits your paycheck, for instance, or when you pay your credit card bill.

On the other hand, the corporate income statement contains items (like sales, for instance) that have been recorded, but *not yet paid for*. This is perfectly legitimate accounting, but not the most useful way to reveal exactly when and what money is going out of a business, and when and what money is coming in. That's exactly what a cash flow statement shows, and why we watch this report.

As the saying goes, "Cash is king."

Now, the cash flow statement is actually three statements in one, because accountants organize all inflows and outflows in three categories:

1. operating activities (the most important one), or the company's businesses,
2. investing activities, generally expenditures on "hard assets" such as property and equipment, and
3. financing activities, typically inflows like common-share offerings and outflows like repayment of debt.

The cash flow adjustments coming out of these three separate categories are cumulative, and the bottom-line result of this statement is usually called "increase [or decrease] in cash and cash equivalents." As you might recall, that's the same top-line item in the asset side of the balance sheet. Here we have yet another example of how the income statement, balance sheet, and statement of cash flows commingle; financiers often link these things into a single spreadsheet, because when you change one figure on one statement, you'll often affect at least one other figure on one of the others. As investors, we like to see the "cash and cash equivalents" line increase over time; to understand why that is or isn't happening, look to the cash flow statement.

We typically don't spend much time looking at anything but the first section on operating cash flow. With that in mind, let's end this chapter with a look at the operational portion of Messngr's cash flow statement:

STATEMENT OF CASH FLOW (NUMBERS IN 000)	MESSNGR, INC.	
	2016	2015
Cash flows from operating activities:		
Net income	12,600	7,400
Adjustments to reconcile		
net income to net cash		
provided by operating activities:		
Depreciation	1,200	800
Effects of change in		
operating assets and liabilities:		
Accounts receivable	(20,000)	(5,000)
Inventory	(10,000)	(4,000)
Accounts payable	3,300	2,000
Accrued expenses	8,000	4,000
Net cash provided by operating activities	**(4,900)**	**5,200**

Determine the driving reasons behind a company's cash flow (or lack thereof).

In many cases, the top section of the statement of cash flow can give you the clearest picture of just how a company is managing or botching its finances.

The top line of "cash flows from operating activities," and generally the biggest cash-flow source, is net income. Just below that appears an addition in the form of "depreciation." It isn't critical to our investing, but basically, it's the allocation of the cost of fixed assets (plant and equipment) over their useful life.

We've learned about the balance sheet, having featured several items on it (like accounts receivable). The bottom section of "cash flows from operating activities" presents the changes of these items from the previous year to the current one, making each an adjustment to cash flow.

If you go back and review Messngr's balance sheet, you'll see that the company reported accounts receivable at $34 million and $14 million for 2016 and 2015, respectively. The difference between these figures is $20 million. That very figure, $20 million, appears as the 2016 change in receivables on the cash flow statement. The number is reported in parentheses, meaning it is accounted for as a deduction from cash flow. This makes sense, given that Messngr's customers now owe the company $20 million more than last year—a cash drag.

You can then fill out the rest of the bottom section by making similar adjustments for all other significant operating assets and liabilities. Of course, this isn't necessary, since the company's accountants have already done it for you. Deduct the resulting sum from net income and depreciation, and you get the operational cash flow.

For the first time, we can now see how clearly Messngr screwed up its 2016 cash situation. After showing a positive flow of $5.2 million in 2015, the company went cash-flow negative to the tune of $4.9 million in 2016. This partly explains floating another 2 million MESS shares in 2016; as it watched the business go cash-flow negative, management may have wanted more working capital on hand.

Our review of the cash flow statement helps us see the main reason behind Messngr's problems: a gigantic leap in accounts receivable from $5 million to $20 million, indicating that the company is having trouble collecting what it's owed from its customers. As an investor, you would want to focus on this primary issue going forward.

The cash flow statement gives you the opportunity to see what's going on in a company's bank account and to figure out what's working financially and what isn't.

Read the management discussion of "liquidity and capital resources."

Required by law to appear in annual reports and 10-Ks, this write-up makes for the best few paragraphs of substantive reading you'll get anywhere in a company's information packet. We're mentioning it in this section because the "liquidity and capital resources" text relates directly to the business's cash flow, to which you'll often read several overt references. Here you have the opportunity to hear straight from management how it will manage its cash and finances in the next year. You'll learn the size of any credit lines that your company has established at banks, and how far (if any) it has drawn off those lines. You'll sometimes get estimates of a company's capital expenditures over the next year and explanations of how the company will fund those expenditures ("from operating cash flows" is the best explanation). In short, this section provides you a nice read on a company's immediate financial future, in no-fluff talk.

♦ ♦ ♦

Okay, that's it: a brief accounting course and a list of items to look for in small-cap stocks. You now know much of what we look for in financial statements, and how—broadly speaking—these financial statements affect your companies and your financial future. We encourage you to dig deeper, if you want to increase your understanding of the financial inner workings of a business. Or you can leave it at that, content to know that a business is not a black box packed with mysterious equations and formulas designed to make your head hurt. But whether those past couple of chapters were pleasurable or painful, they will provide a bit more infrastructure to gird your investing strategy.

PART VIII

SOME ADVANCED TOPICS

25

THE ROAD TO OPTIONS

The information you've consumed for the past couple dozen chapters will take you a very long way as an individual investor. Truth be told, many an investor will happily stop here, comfortable with finding, analyzing, and buying shares of great companies and holding them for the long haul. But we're here to tell you there's something else. For the next several pages, we'll outline some other ways to invest, sharing with you the benefits and drawbacks of each of these roads less traveled.

USING MARGIN

When you open an account with a broker, you'll be asked on the application whether you want a cash or a margin account. If you choose the cash account (the more common of the two), then you can buy only stocks that you intend to pay for at the time you put in your "buy" order (or, in some rare cases, within a few days). Simple.

If you open a margin account, however, you're asking the brokerage to agree to lend you money from time to time, so that you may use it to invest more money than you have in your account. Pick your stocks well, and you can turn a profit using money that you don't even have. Margin is a secured loan, basically, where the collateral is the existing securities in your account. How much you can borrow is determined by how much is in your account, up to 50 percent of the purchase price of the stock you wish to buy. For some highly volatile stocks, certain brokerage firms allow much less than that.

For the borrowing privilege, you pay interest to the brokerage, just like any other loan. In fact, it's a lot easier to open a margin account than to apply for a bank loan! To quote online discount broker TD Ameritrade, "Having a margin account is like having a preapproved credit line with your broker." Are you gleefully imagining fat stacks of dollar bills at your disposal? Not so fast. Some aspects of margin credit differ dramatically from pure credit. We'll get to them in a bit. Even without addressing those differences, Fools know that credit is a tricky thing, best used carefully.

Just like with a credit card, margin accounts charge you interest for the privilege of using the firm's money. While the rates charged for margin are lower than the rates you'll pay to a credit card company, you should still remember that this isn't free money. (Margin rates *do* typically go down as you borrow more, but that doesn't exactly decrease your risk.)

There are some restrictions on margin use. Stocks under $5 per share are not marginable. Not that you'd want to invest in a penny stock anyway, right? (Let alone with borrowed money!) Initial public offerings (IPOs) are not marginable for a certain period after their debut. Now and then, you'll also find that other Nasdaq stocks are not marginable.

The Federal Reserve Board regulates the amount of credit brokerages are allowed to extend to their clients. As mentioned, the law says you can borrow up to 50 percent of the value of your marginable securities. So for stock purchases, you put up 50 percent of the price, and your broker puts up 50 percent. Let's walk through an example.

Suppose you have $10,000 in your margin-approved brokerage account. This allows you to purchase up to a total of $20,000 of marginable securities. Your ten grand gives you $20,000 worth of "buying power."

Suppose there is a marginable stock that costs $20 per share. You could, if you wanted, buy up to 1,000 shares of that stock. At the maximum, you'd put up 50 percent (or, $10,000) of the purchase price for those thousand shares, and your broker would put up the other 50 percent.

One thing to remember about margin is that the amount you can borrow is not a fixed number. In this respect, margin differs from the static credit limit given for your credit cards. Margin is tied to the value of the marginable securities in your portfolio. Therefore, your buying power changes daily, along with the changes in your stocks' prices. If your portfolio goes up, the amount you can borrow increases. We'll get to what happens when your portfolio goes down later.

HOW MARGIN WORKS

Margin has a magnifying effect on the gains and the losses in your portfolio. Let's look at the example above again to illustrate this key point.

Once you've opened your margin account and deposited your money, you're ready to go. Starting with $10,000, you want to buy 1,000 shares of a stock that costs $20. You will therefore borrow $10,000 from your broker at 7.68 percent. Say your order gets filled at exactly $20 a share and (to keep the numbers round) you pay no commissions on that trade. The total invested is $20,000 ($10,000 from you, and $10,000 from your broker, for 1,000 shares of a $20 stock).

Let's imagine that the stock goes up over the next year to $45 a share. The value of your total investment has gone from $20,000 to $45,000. If you then sold your shares, you'd pay back your broker's margin loan of $10,000 plus $800 interest, leaving you with $34,200. That's $24,200 profit, a *242 percent gain* off the $10,000 you chipped in initially. (After you pay your taxes, you've netted over $19,000.)

Suppose instead that you'd only bought what you could afford on your own: 500 shares at $20. The stock rises to $45. Without any margin from your broker, your investment is now worth $22,500, a 125 percent gain on your original investment, of which you'd have a net profit of $10,000 once you've paid your 20 percent capital gains tax (equivalent to $2,500).

By using margin, you made $19,000 after taxes on original assets of $10,000, as opposed to making $10,000 on that same $10,000.

And it all sounds just great, doesn't it? What could be more perfect? *Free money!* Just too easy. "Why doesn't everyone do this?" you may wonder.

Well, that's what your broker might like you to think. Margin loans make high-margin profits for brokerage firms. Most brokers would absolutely love it if right now all their clients lunged for the phone and blurted, "Harry, max out my margin and let's exploit all of this buying power! It's like a drug!"

A Fool, however, knows better. By now, we hope you know that what's good for your broker is not necessarily good for you. Brokers love to see clients sustainably use margin, because the interest they charge gives them a guaranteed revenue stream, backed by the holdings in your portfolio. Any broker telling you to use margin has a vested interest—literally—in the matter.

What happens when fortune *doesn't* smile on your investments? Imagine that your $20 stock falls to $15 over the next year.

In the margin situation, your $20,000 investment has fallen to $15,000. You sell the stock and pay back your broker's $10,000 loan, plus the same $800 interest. You're left with $4,200. Or, more likely, your broker will automatically sell $800 worth of another holding in your portfolio—and charge you commission to do it. Congratulations! You've managed to lose 58 percent of your original investment on a 25 percent drop in your stock!

If you hadn't used margin and had just purchased 500 shares of the stock at $20, after it fell to $15 you would have retained $7,500 of your original $10,000. A 25 percent loss is, for you, just that.

THE DREADED MARGIN CALL

What could be worse than margin-magnified losses? Meet the margin call (also sometimes referred to as a "maintenance call"), which occurs when the value of the collateral you put up for the loan (i.e., the marginable securities in your portfolio) falls below a predetermined minimum requirement. Usually, this requirement is about 30 percent of the loan, though it may run 50 percent for more volatile stocks.

That means that if the value of the stocks in your portfolio (the collateral for the margin) falls below 30 percent of the amount loaned to you by the broker, your broker will contact you to insist on more collateral. The equity in your account (that is, the market value of your securities, minus the amount loaned to you by your broker) must stay above this minimum requirement.

Let's use some numbers again to get a better handle on this. Taking our 1,000 shares of the $20 stock bought on margin, imagine the price falls to $13 a share. At this point, the $20,000 investment is worth $13,000. Remember, you and your broker each put up 50 percent of the money, but you have to pay back what you borrowed. So $10,000 of that $13,000 remains the broker's (plus interest).

Your measly $3,000 in equity is now 30 percent of the amount of the loan, about the level at which we earlier indicated you'll get a margin call. If this stock falls any more, you'll have to send additional collateral to fulfill the minimum requirement, either as cash or other fully marginable securities. Only a percentage of the market value of an added security can be used to meet your margin call, though.

Hmm. What if you can't meet your margin call because you don't have additional cash or other securities to send? Your brokerage will then sell the margined securities in your account to cover what it's owed. You gave them this right when you signed the agreement to open a margin account.

Adding insult to injury, after such an obviously unexpected and disappointing drop, you'll often find yourself exiting the stock (at your broker's insistence) at the worst possible time. You have few or no shares left yourself. You may even owe the brokerage some additional funds. And lookee there, your stock just recovered to $20—without you. Perhaps now, it's somewhat clearer how the risks of margin might outweigh the benefits.

Investing with margin isn't a complete no-no automatically for all people in all situations—just for many, in most. If you already have been investing for a few years and decide to use margin, you should limit your-self to borrowing no more than 20 percent (at the very maximum) of your portfolio's value. Thus, on a $20,000 portfolio, you'd be borrowing a few thousand more (up to $4,000), putting $21,000 to $24,000 to work for you. That's called leverage. A little of it can be a useful and not too risky thing, if invested Foolishly in great companies over the long term.

We wrote that last paragraph somewhat reluctantly, in fear that some less-experienced investors will think, "Okay, so I *do* get to borrow and invest. The Fools say so. Great!" and run out and go on margin. So again, if you *ever* use margin, do so with extreme caution and moderation, and only if you fully understand what you're doing. Don't use it indefinitely, either; those interest payments rack up. We would never advise anyone (experienced or otherwise) to max out on margin, borrowing 50 percent of the value of their portfolio, let alone for long periods of time.

Benjamin Franklin said, "Experience is a dear teacher, but fools will learn at no other." Small-*f* fools perhaps, Ben, but not Fools. Don't wait until margin burns you to conclude that you've been using too much of the stuff, or that you shouldn't have been using it at all. Many of the best and most experienced investors we know have always steered completely clear of it. As of this writing, none of the real-money portfolios in our investment services at Fool.com have used margin, and they're all doing just fine.

Of course, there is *one* reason why, even if you're not interested in buy-ing stocks on borrowed money, you still might want to open a margin ac-count . . .

26

SHORTING STOCKS

If you've ever elbowed up to a craps table and slapped down a few chips on the Pass Line, you were doing what most people at a craps table do: betting with the crowd.

Adjacent to the Pass Line, however, is a cheaper strip of real estate (usually a vacant lot) known as the "Don't Pass." It's virtually the opposite bet; you win when the Pass Line crowd loses and lose when it wins. The odds for Don't Pass are no worse than the Pass Line. (None of these are good odds, of course!) But because you're betting *against* the roller and most of the rest of the table, betting Don't Pass is considered bad form. Craps jargon for people like you is "wrong bettor." Many other bettors will actually dislike you for doing it, a feeling reinforced whenever you smile at dice rolls that make them frown.

The same goes for investors who habitually sell stock short.

A SHORT LESSON: HOW IT WORKS

When you short stocks, you profit not when they rise, but when they *fall*; it's a neat idea that not everyone realizes is even possible. Of those who do, most won't consider it. Some think it's un-American to profit off the failure of corporations and other investors, which gives short investors a Don't-Pass reputation. Many others have rightly heard that the stock market has been the best place to put your money since the start of the twentieth century. These people don't want to short stocks, because they fear that the market's tendency to rise will pull their short up with it.

Before we consider shorting's pros and cons, let's learn how it works.

For starters, to short stocks you'll need a margin account, covered last chapter. You initiate a short by first borrowing shares from a current shareholder. This may sound difficult, but it isn't. In fact, you'll never notice it happening, because your broker does this for you automatically. When you go to enter your order, you simply enter "sell short" or "sell to open" to begin the transaction, along with the stock ticker and the number of shares you want to short. Your broker will find shares to borrow, and in the very next breath, *sell* these borrowed shares at the current market price, or the price you stipulate with a limit order. Then, in the coming days and weeks, you sit and wait, rooting for the stock to spiral downward. When you're ready to cash out of your investment—whether for profit or for loss—you close out the position by buying the stock back, so that you can return your borrowed shares to the lender—another thing your broker does for you automatically. That's it. You "buy to close" or "buy to cover" the same number of shares you originally sold short, and your trade is done. You end with a profit if the stock had fallen, or a loss if you had to buy the shares back at a higher price than that which you sold.

Let's look at a couple of examples.

You decide to short 100 shares of a business you think is going nowhere, Overrated Technologies (Ticker: FALL), at $56.50. You click a few buttons at your online brokerage to sell short 100 shares of Overrated. The broker will borrow 100 shares for you and then sell them immediately at $56.50. Three months later, when the stock has dropped to $46.50, you want to cash out. You'll place an order to buy 100 shares of FALL at the market price ($46.50), returning these newly bought shares to the lender.

What have you made? Well, you sold 100 shares in the first place at $56.50, meaning your sale came to $5,650. Then, to close out, you bought 100 shares back at $46.50, or $4,650. Your profit was $1,000, minus commissions. Off the initial investment of $5,650, you've made $1,000, a three-month return of 18 percent. Snazzy.

Now let's reshuffle the cards and pretend things get ugly. You've sold your Overrated Tech shares short at $56.50 and alas, the stock begins to go up—$60, $65, $70. You keep holding, thinking, "The company is *so* over-valued now!" A year later, it has surpassed $75, and you can't stand it any longer. You want out. With the price at $76.50, you say "uncle."

What have you lost? You sold 100 shares short at $56.50 ($5,650). You eventually bought back those shares at $76.50, for which you had to come up with $7,650. You lost $2,000, or 35 percent—not counting the broker's commission.

Now on the face of it, the technique would seem to require no cash at all. You're borrowing shares and selling them, right? That creates cash, adding bucks to your account. When you then decide to buy back, you're just paying out of your cash to reacquire the borrowed shares. However, if you're buying the stock back at a *higher* price than that at which you sold (the second example above), you'll pay more than you initially received. In other words, you'll need additional money to cover your losing short position. For this reason, brokers require you to short the stock from a margin account, and to have enough cash and stocks on deposit to meet the margin requirements. You should always check with your broker first and make sure you understand the firm's policies for margin requirements and shorting.

In brief, shorting reverses the normal order of trading stocks: You sell first, *then* buy. Selling short is really no more difficult than that . . . except that the whole economic system and market is designed to foster rising prices over time, which means shorting is truly going against the long-term tide.

WHY BOTHER SHORTING?

In fine Foolish style, let's first examine why *not* to short. After all, you don't have to. Stocks *do* go up over time, after all, so most people will do fine just owning a "long" position in a good index fund. Why fight the tape *and* expend any additional time at all with your investing? In fact, if you don't follow the market closely (i.e., check your stocks at least once a week), then you definitely should *not* short at all. Shorting requires an almost daily attentiveness to the stock market. If you can't or won't watch your stocks that closely, don't attempt it.

Then there is the specter of the rising short. When a stock you short goes up, you have to fork over extra dollars to bail yourself out. It's the nature of the investment. You have what some people refer to as "unlimited upside risk." That sounds scary. You can lose 200 percent or 300 percent of your original investment, while your best possible result is only a 100 percent gain.

If this makes you uncomfortable, or if you are at all uncomfortable about anything you read in this chapter, stay away—but do at least familiarize yourself with shorting in this chapter. Shorting stocks is far less common than more traditional investing, which offers one good reason to at least take a look.

As you know by now, Fools like swimming against the tide. When most investors are trying to figure out how many more half-dollar gains they can squeeze out of their equities, we're looking the other way, assessing how far each might fall. This rare contrary view can be lucrative.

A WALK ON THE SHORT SIDE

Let's discuss why few in the "professional" investment community at large short stocks, and why in some cases they're openly hostile to shorting. Few brokers suggest short selling to their clients. Only a fraction of mutual funds do any shorting. Probably an even smaller percentage of banks and pension funds short. Furthermore, we live in a world in which Wall Street firms cannot even safely issue sell recommendations. How peculiar!

Not really, actually. Investment firms make millions by helping companies raise money to finance their growth, and rely on access to corporate insiders for equity research. Let's say you own a company, and you take a Wall Street analyst out to a cushy lunch to share your business outlook with her: all about next year's growth prospects for hot dogs, how misunderstood hot dogs are by the conventional dietary press, how resilient the hot dog is as a traditional player at deli stands. She then goes back to New York, and two weeks later she issues a sell recommendation on your stock, dropping it several points in the process. Suffice to say, you're probably not inviting her to lunch again anytime soon. Even more, you wouldn't share your business plan with her firm in the future, and you likely wouldn't consider employing her to help you raise capital or float a bond.

That's why Wall Street rarely says, "Sell." It only says "Buy" and "Hold"—and some would argue that "Hold" is really just a (fairly simplistic) code for "Sell."

Given what you've just read, you can now understand why the establishment rarely says, "Short." So pity Wall Street. In fact, do it one better: Take advantage of its constraints. Short stocks.

We're constantly coming across establishment ideologues on CNBC or in the *Wall Street Journal* who portray shorting stocks as incredibly risky. They love to play up this idea of "unlimited upside risk." The idea, again, is that if you short a stock and it goes up, and just keeps going up, you'll *have* to cover one day. The stock could theoretically cause you to have to cover at infinity—which, frankly, is more than we have.

But the fact is, we've yet to meet the investor who got victimized by "unlimited upside risk." Oh sure, we've met people who've lost money shorting . . . in some cases, *lots* of money. We've also met people who've lost lots of money investing in all sorts of things: stocks, real estate, options, currencies, futures, Beanie Babies, precious metals, even their own businesses. The world presents us hundreds of opportunities to lose money every day.

We use a very simple device to make sure that we won't lose a ton shorting. We set a "quitting price" whenever we short a stock, typically 20 percent above the price at which we shorted. If our short sale rises to its quitting price, we throw up our hands and wave the white hanky. Now, do we do this when we *buy* a stock? Nope. We have *no* downside sell rule with our purchases, and we've been known to lose more than 20 percent on many a once-loved investment. We have lost more money, historically, on our losing longs than on our losing shorts. (We have also made more money on our winning longs than on our winning shorts, for obvious reasons. That's what we mean by low-risk.)

You need not live in fear of shorting. If you don't have time for it, we understand. Or perhaps you've assessed the higher "switching costs" of this strategy, and decided it's not for you. After all, you'd be trading more frequently, and thus paying more in short-term capital gains taxes and commissions. All good considerations. But if you're steering clear simply because you've heard they're "dangerous," you might be missing out.

If we believe we can identify undervalued stocks, surely we can locate overvalued stocks as well. And once you've learned how to short, you can take advantage of these very situations to augment your bottom line.

We include shorting stocks in our Foolish investment approach as a way to profit on individual stocks we deem overvalued, and as a hedge. If the market as a whole is plummeting, shorts will help counterbalance your losses. But we short in moderation (no more than 20 percent of our portfolio), because although a good short seller will make consistent money on his shorts, he does well to keep the majority of his funds in traditional long investments. The primary direction of the stock market is up. Accordingly, most of the short positions you take should last only a few months. (It makes sense that "shorting" stock is best used as a "short-term" strategy.)

Because you can make money selling stocks short in almost any market environment, you should short stocks not because you think the market is going to crash, but simply because selling stocks short can lead to consistent profit. The whole idea is to make money both ways, simultaneously—long, as your growth stocks and the general market rise, *and* short, as the stocks you've identified as overpriced wither. When it works right, it's a thing of beauty.

THE REAL ISSUE: WHAT AND WHAT NOT TO SHORT

We use three primary tests to determine which stocks to short:

1. High debt-to-cash ratio combined with low cash flow.

If cash is the lifeblood of a company, debt is hemophilia: once the skin is breached, it's tough to stem the outflow. Some small- and mid-cap companies will assume a lot of debt to grow their businesses quickly. At first, results look great—revenue and income are rising quickly, thanks to the rapid expansion, and the company's stock price follows upward. If expansion isn't coming from the existing business, or if that core business slips up, growth through debt becomes unsustainable. Interest payments can cripple the overextended company in no time flat. The bleeding, once it starts, instantly attracts hungry scavengers.

Keep in mind that large companies often will carry a sizable debt load that exceeds current cash. But they can handle this, because they have deep credit lines and high cash flow from existing operations. You'll need to find situations where the debt itself, not cash flow, is funding the company's growth—or just keeping the company afloat.

2. Short "closed" situations; avoid "open" ones.

We like to draw a distinction between "open" and "closed" situations. We never short open (or open-ended) situations: companies that could create humongous surprises by crushing all expectations. Often, these companies have just introduced revolutionary products or services, have hit the groove of a tremendous growth period, or have industry peers who have recently reported consistently stellar earnings. Avoid shorting these companies, because they could easily catch the market by surprise. Consider Amazon, a consistently popular and *killing* short since its debut in 1997. The company proved that it could grow revenue year after year, adding product lines left and right, and defying skeptics by convincing enough investors that earnings would come later. Short sellers didn't buy that argument, and they got slashed and burned in the process.

With no online retailer in second place behind it, and with online retail still only representing a fraction of total retail sales, Amazon was (and is!) a classic open situation. It has so much more potential ahead that you'd be crazy to short it.

Closed situations are just the opposite: companies that have no real compelling product or service and little likelihood of dramatically surprising market expectations. They're typically in nothing-special industries, probably past the end of their maximum growth phase. Going back in our Foolish Time Machine, a good example here was Bed Bath & Beyond back in the mid-1990s, a fine enough company whose stock happened to be *way* beyond our expectations for its near-term corporate growth. (The company's motto at the time, "Beyond any store of its kind," fueled numerous wisecracks at Fool HQ.) For the few of you who don't get an unremitting flow of 20 percent off coupons in your mailbox, Bed Bath & Beyond operates national superstores that sell every color of household item imaginable, at bargain prices. Was this a compelling industry? Nope. Was Bed Bath's product unique, life-changing, and capable of seizing the imagination of an entire generation? No. Was Bed Bath blowing away all its earnings estimates? Not really; it was hitting its targets or exceeding them by a penny or two. This was a classic closed situation, and having shorted it right about $30 in mid-1993, we waited slightly more than a year for the stock to drop eventually to $18, following an unimpressive earnings report. At that point, we closed the short for a clean profit.

Returning to the present day, it's worth noting that Bed Bath & Beyond shares are up about 1,500 percent since we closed the short in 1993! Our hat is off to them. But really, this drives home our earlier points that short sales are best as *short-term* positions (we won with ours!), and the economy and market are set up to rise over time (don't fight it over the long term!). Even a fairly simple retail business can grow incredibly over a few decades. We should celebrate that. And we do.

But this doesn't change the argument that Bed Bath & Beyond is a closed situation, and Amazon is an open situation. Even with closed situations, short sellers need to stay on their toes and take gains where they can get them. And always steer clear of open situations.

3. Short stocks with low short interest; definitely avoid those with high short interest.

Having explained that you should short only closed-situation stocks, ideally with lots of debt and low cash flow, we have one more test left to apply before deciding to short. It's time to check the short interest.

Short interest is simply the total number of shares of a given security that have already been sold short. Among other places, this figure is reported in the *Wall Street Journal*, *Barron's*, and *Investor's Business Daily*, and in a company's profile at Yahoo! Finance (finance.yahoo.com), or at Nasdaq.com and other investment sites. Why do we bother checking it? Well, let's think about what it represents.

On the one hand, short interest signifies the amount of bearish sentiment in a stock. Imagine that *IBD* shows short interest of 4 million shares for Lunar Development Technologies (Ticker: NEVR). The company has only 16 million shares outstanding and a float of 12 million, meaning that 25 percent of its total shares outstanding and 33 percent of its float have been borrowed and ditched. Hordes of bears are obviously skeptical about the company's efforts to terraform our satellite neighbor.

On the other hand, however, short interest represents latent buying power. That's because in the short to intermediate term, almost every single share already sold short will be bought back. The irony is clear: while high short interest *looks* like a bearish sign, it actually can be a bullish indicator.

Knowing this, you should typically *avoid* Lunar Development Tech as a short, because too many others have already shorted before you. If the stock has resided at $18 to $19 per share for months, what's going to happen if it drops to $16 suddenly? "*Finally,*" many short sellers will say to themselves. And a fair number of those holders of 4 million in short interest will buy back impatiently to earn their long-awaited small profit. Result? The stock goes right back to $18 to $19 again. You'll have a hard time ever earning the 20 percent or greater profit you're shooting for.

Now, if Lunar Dev Tech happens to announce surprisingly good news—say, early indications that it has maintained plant life for more than four weeks in an airless atmosphere under a geodesic dome—*look out!* The stock suddenly jumps to $22 on the news and creates a panic among stunned short sellers. They start covering. The stock rises to $24 on volume of a million shares more, driven by fearful bears. That rise creates even more fear—wow, the thing's up over 30 percent in two days!—and so even more short sellers buy back at these higher prices, creating further upward spiraling in the share price. Ladies, gentlemen, and Fools, witness the "short squeeze."

As we've just demonstrated, stocks with high short interest are bad to short because: (1) they're less likely to drop significantly because short sellers are impatient to take profits, and (2) they're ripe for the dreaded short squeeze. Conversely, stocks with a *low* short interest are just fine to short. Little short selling has taken place so far, with the likelihood of more occurring if the stock remains overvalued. When your fellow investors move in and begin to short this unshorted stock, they'll create downward pressure, increasing your returns.

The best way to measure short interest is the "short interest ratio." Above, we looked at the percentage of a company's total shares outstanding that are short. That's one sort of short-interest ratio, and it's not bad. But we can go one better by comparing the stock's short interest to its *average daily volume*. This figure will reveal the number of days of normal trading volume that it would take short sellers to cover their positions completely. Blasting back off into outer space, we find that NEVR shareholders are trading 200,000 shares of this stock on an average day. So let's take short interest (4 million) and divide it by the average daily volume (200,000), giving us a short-interest ratio of twenty days to cover. That is, as you may have expected, very high. We almost never short any stock with more than ten days to cover. We prefer to short stocks whose short-interest ratios are five days or less, making them less likely to get squeezed. You should, too.

A FEW PITFALLS

All right, you're ready to take the plunge—and find a stock that will hopefully plunge with you. But before you do, we need to catalog five annoying little things that can work against you, as a short seller. Just so you'll be prepared.

First, you check your broker, and you find that the shares *aren't* available. It does happen sometimes with stocks that are either small caps, or recently popular shorts, or both. In these situations, you simply have to get on the waiting list and keep at it. Seems like a raw deal, since no waiting list exists for those who want to buy. But that's one of the limitations to shorting stocks, and we all live with it. Fortunately, it doesn't occur too often.

You also may be tripped up by a second minor and rare annoyance: the need to get an "uptick" before your short trade can go through on any stock that has already fallen 10 percent so far that day. In creating this rule, the SEC effectively said, "If you want to short a stock that has fallen 10 percent that day, and it trades at $34, you'll have to wait for a trade at $34.01 before you can carry out your order." This is a stumbling block put in place to prevent short sellers from piling onto a losing stock and sinking it even more. If a stock you want to short goes into sudden free fall after reporting bad earnings, and is down 10 percent already, you can't hop on the shorting bandwagon until some brave soul pushes the stock up a tick. This uptick rule only stays in effect that day—or any day a stock falls by 10 percent or more.

Third, sometimes your broker may be forced to "return" your shorted shares to the anonymous lender, usually because the lender wants to sell them and your broker can find no other shares to borrow. Forced into doing so, you may have to buy back the shares prematurely—whether you've made money or not. This happens most with very small stocks that have few shares outstanding and heavy short interest (the sort that you probably shouldn't have shorted in the first place). Should this happen to you, stay calm, take your lumps as your short is closed on you (you have no choice!), and take your time finding a more appropriate short. Or consider using options to bet against a stock next time (more on that in a bit!).

A fourth niggling little detail involves no additional interest paid to you on your short-sale-inflated account balance at many brokers. To review, when you sell a stock short, your account's cash balance rises (as it does with any sale) to reflect the liquidation of the stock. However, you'll find that most brokers won't pay you *any* interest on this additional money. This compares with the close-to-100-percent interest that institutional investors typically receive on money raised by short sales. This is yet another minor drawback to the small-time short seller, who can now number the government, Wall Street, and her broker as hostile parties to her short sales. Fighting back, our online readership joined together to poll a slew of deep-discount brokers to determine whether any would be willing to offer individual investors interest paid on short sales. As it turned out, we discovered that TD Ameritrade, the Omaha-based discounter, *did* pay this interest. Policies may change, but it's worth asking your broker if you plan to do a lot of short selling.

Here's a fifth bee in your bonnet: if a stock you've sold short pays a dividend, *you* pay that dividend. No way around it. This is, in a way, a form of recompense for your borrowing these shares from your anonymous, unsuspecting fellow investor. In most cases, however, the dividend amounts to less than 3 percent annually.

Despite this list of five lesser irritations, we still enjoy occasionally selling short. None of these hang-ups is terribly consequential, and even all five together don't much bother us. We just wanted you to know about them.

We'll close this section by urging you to follow your shorts carefully and respect the goals you set for them. If your stock dips 20 percent, for most of us, that's good enough to buy back and cash out. Don't get greedy! If your stock instead rises 20 percent, you're going to think, "Now, more than ever, it's *really* overvalued!" The last thing on earth you're ever going to want to do is to have to buy the darned thing back. But you should. You've timed your investment poorly, whether your research was good or bad. Just admit you've been wrong and move on, in case some surprising good news is poised to drive shares higher and bust your short.

A SHORT CONCLUSION

Is the Foolish way to short the *only* way to short? Of course not. Some people play sectors, concentrating their short selling in specific industries that they believe are either overhyped or in trouble. Others short with everything they have, eschewing the Foolish notion that only a minority of one's portfolio should ever be short. We haven't heard of people succeeding with this approach over the long term, but it represents another alternative, and these folks must make *some* money from time to time.

Understanding short selling is one way to separate the sophisticated investor from the novice, even though it's not terribly difficult to do or to understand. (Please note that not all sophisticates do much shorting, if any!) Believing that selling shares short is difficult and highly dangerous, some people pay oodles of money to enter "hedge funds," mutual fund partnerships whose managers are "hedged"—that is, they have long positions alongside short positions. Having read this far, you already know most of what these "pros" know.

Once your "Pass Line" friends find out you're shorting stocks, they may start to regard you as Darth Vader. That's the impression most people have of short sellers. If so, you might as well milk it—put on some dark clothes, sport a low visor, and breathe loudly. Especially if you're about to cross the *next* Rubicon in our motley book.

27

OPTIONS

If some view selling short as the workings of the Dark Side, then many view *options* as intergalactic chaos drifting to us from another solar system, overpowering our calm world of long-term stock investing. But like short selling, options can have a solid place in a long-term-minded, Foolish investor's stock portfolio. In fact, like short selling, options give you another tool—in this case, many tools—to hammer, saw, and drill your way to investing profits.

You see, options can make money when a stock goes nowhere, or when it falls, or, yes, as it rises. By using options, you can set up some positions in your long-term stock portfolio that will profit during the periods when stocks as a whole go nowhere or down. Sound cosmically good? We think so, too. Especially when you consider that you can use options to *reduce* your risk; many options strategies are *less* risky than buying a stock outright. Options can net you better prices on new shares, for example, or require much less capital than buying a stock.

In this section, we introduce you to options by outlining some of our most popular option strategies. If you're intrigued, head to Fool.com and its options services. We can teach you all you need to know to succeed with options, even as you remain a long-term investor with your stocks. Many Fools use options to generate steady income, target leveraged upside without going on margin, protect against declines, and more.

But first, what in the blazes *is* an option?

OPTIONS DEFINED

Used by investors as savvy as Warren Buffett, stock options have been listed and traded in a transparent, liquid market since their debut in 1973. An option gives its owner the right to buy or sell an underlying stock at a predetermined price (called the strike price) by a set date—the option's expiration date. An option is a contract between two parties—an option buyer and an option seller—that *could* lead to a stock transaction by the expiration.

The option contract has its own value (a fraction of the stock price) that is derived daily from the difference between the option's strike price and the current share price, along with some extra value on top of that in the option to account for future volatility. An option ends in a stock transaction if the trade price (or strike price) stipulated in the option contract is more attractive than the current stock price. In other words, the contract gives its owner the right to exercise the option into a stock transaction if he wishes. He would do so if the option is "in the money" at expiration, rather than "out of the money"—less attractive than the current share price.

Now take a deep breath. Read that paragraph again if you need to. It's not that tough. But there's more to follow. Ready?

Two types of stock options exist: calls and puts. A call option gives its owner the right to buy a stock at a set price, so the value of a call goes up as a stock rises. In contrast, a put option gives its owner the right to *sell* a stock at a predetermined price, so the value of a put option goes up when a stock *falls*. You might remember this by thinking of a making a telephone call. You call someone up. When you're finished, you put down the phone. (We're not saying you should put down the person you call up!) Call up, put down.

At any rate, it won't take you long to learn that call options appreciate with a rising stock, and put options appreciate when a stock falls.

Things *truly* get tricky in this next part: you can either buy an option at the start, or you can *sell it* at the start, called "sell to open." Remember our section on shorting? (Of course, you do. It was just a few pages ago.)

When you sell an option at the start, you are effectively *shorting* that option, getting paid its going price (called the premium) and taking on the potential obligation of the option (rather than owning the rights of the option). When we give examples of options strategies in a moment, you'll see how this works.

Other important factors to know: each option contract represents 100 shares of the underlying stock, so these vehicles offer you tremendous leverage. Since an option contract trades for a fraction of a typical stock price, yet controls 100 shares, you're getting stock exposure in spades for a sliver of the stock's cost. This is great leverage.

But you still need to be ready financially to buy or sell the 100 shares of stock for every option you use, *if* you ever want to let the option turn to stock, that is, also known as "get exercised." An option does not always end in a stock transaction. Instead, many investors just close the option contract toward the end, at the going price, and register a gain or loss compared to their starting price that way.

Now let's talk about that price for a moment. Every option has what is called "intrinsic value" and "time value."

Intrinsic value is the irrefutable value of the option. If a call option gives you the right to buy a stock at $10 per share, and the stock is trading at $11, that call option has intrinsic value of $1. It lets you buy the stock $1 below the current share price, so it carries that $1 value as its intrinsic value. If the stock rose to $12, the call's intrinsic value would double to $2.

It then also has some *additional* value, called "time value." This is the extra value an option holds to, in some tiny way, try to account for all the unknown volatility that will happen between now and the option's expiration. The contract has this value because it gives you the right to an asset at a set price, and the longer that contract has until expiration, the more unknowns exist, so the more time value will account for that. Options carry time value right up to expiration, even if it's dwindled from several dollars to just a nickel or dime at that point. US stock options can expire in a mere week, a month, or as far away as more than two years—you choose which expiration you want, based on the options offered on a specific stock you're targeting, your goals, and your strategy. To see the options available on any stock, you simply enter the stock ticker at your broker, then click to see its Option Chain. All the months and strike prices available will appear for you when you click to see "all." Not all stocks have options listed on them, but most liquid stocks do.

So you have intrinsic value and time value, which combined make for an option's price, or premium. You have calls and puts, each with various strike prices and expiration dates that you get to choose from. And you can buy or sell an option to open it, giving you the rights of the option as the buyer, or the obligation of the option when you're the seller.

Why would want you take on the obligation? In three words: *to get paid*. If you're the option *seller*, you get paid the option premium on day one, and that becomes income for you; that's the first strategy we'll talk about, because it's also our favorite.

First, just *one more thing*. Okay, a few more things. Before you can partake in options, you need to apply for options permission at your broker. You get the option approval form from your broker and fill it out. It really helps if you have a margin (or a traditional) account with a discount broker. We don't suggest using margin, but having a margin account makes it possible to *short* options, just as it makes shorting stocks a possibility. You can conduct many option strategies in an IRA, but it will require you to have ample cash in your account. Whether using a margin account or an IRA, a discount broker will help keep your commissions down. Commissions on options are typically a bit higher than on a stock trade.

The final consideration is your stock portfolio itself. We want you to have a full-fledged, long-term stock portfolio before you even *consider* adding options to it. Options and stocks complement one another. Options give you more ways to profit on stocks, but there's no question that stocks should provide you with the greatest gains over the years. Stocks that are allowed to compound are the lifeblood of a strong, life-changing portfolio, while options are an offshoot of that, one with growing possibilities as your stock value grows. For example, the more money you have in stock equity, the greater monthly income you can make with options—income you can draw out to live on, while leaving your stocks alone to appreciate! If that's not an incentive, what is?

Now, about that income . . .

SELLING PUTS FOR INCOME, OR A LOWER STOCK PURCHASE PRICE

Longtime Fool advisor Jeff Fischer started using our favorite option-based income strategy around the year 2000. It's called writing puts, or alternately, selling puts. In this strategy, you "sell to open" a put option that obligates you to buy shares of a chosen stock at your strike price, *if* the stock falls below that price by the option's expiration. You get paid for setting up this obligation, because you are basically selling an insurance policy—so *you* get the premium! This policy says that if the stock declines below the option's strike price by expiration, you will buy the stock at the strike price, no matter how far the stock has fallen. This insures another investor, who pays you for this insurance. It's best to see it in an example.

Assume shares of Peach Technologies (Ticker: PCHY) trade at $11. You would be happy to buy shares at $10 or lower, and you want to collect income while you wait. You would sell to open a put option with a $10 strike price, expiring in three months. You collect the option premium when you set up this position. Let's say you get paid $0.50 per share to sell the put. That's $50 per contract (because each contract represents 100 shares), and that's a 5 percent yield that you're collecting in just three months. Sure beats your savings account!

Your yield is measured against your potential $10 stock buy price (the premium you collect, divided by that $10, equals 5 percent). Then all you do is wait. Selling a put is like setting a limit order to buy 100 shares of a stock at a lower price, but getting paid while you wait to see whether your price hits.

In this example, you keep the $0.50 per share, and you wait. Simply wait. If Peach Technologies still trades above $10 at the option's expiration date in three months, the puts you sold to open expire unused. You made a 5 percent yield on cash you set aside to potentially buy the stock at $10, the option has expired, and you no longer have any potential obligation to buy shares—so you can sell to open another put for more income! You could keep doing this, getting paid each time, until you finally get shares of stock, assuming you do. If the stock runs up and never looks back, you won't get shares, only the put income. So if you're eager to own the stock, we often recommend that you straight-up buy a chunk of shares as well. We usually sell to open puts that expire in mere weeks to about three months, and look to repeat the process.

Now let's consider the other outcome. If Peach is trading *below* $10 per share at expiration, you—as the put seller—are on the hook to fulfill the put option by purchasing shares at $10. You still keep the $0.50-per-share premium the options originally paid you, so your net start price on the stock is $9.50 per share. The stock was $11 when you first considered it, and you're getting to buy shares at $9.50, or 13.6 percent lower. You can then keep those shares as long as you wish, just as with any other stock you own.

Selling to open a single put option is a way to buy 100 shares of a stock more cheaply if it declines, and get paid while you wait. If you want to buy 500 shares of a stock, you could sell to open five put options. And so forth.

But what if the stock falls below your strike price early, only to rise above your strike price again before expiration? In that case, you usually *will not* get to buy shares. What a stock does before an option's expiration *usually* does not matter—most options, even once they're in the money, are only exercised at expiration. One of the few times an option is exercised before expiration is when the stock moves so dramatically (say it falls to $6 in this case) that the option becomes very deep in the money, becoming like a proxy for the stock, since it no longer carries time value at that point, only intrinsic value. But for now, the key thing to know is that nearly all options will only be exercised at expiration, and not before. The stock can jump all over the place, making your option in the money and out of the money, but what matters is where the stock is at expiration. Any in-the-money option will be exercised at expiration, unless you close the option beforehand.

If all this has your head spinning, don't fret. Thousands of Fools who didn't know the difference between an option and an oven mitt have since invested successfully with them; it just takes time, and some simplification.

On that charge, we can simplify this strategy once and for all: You sell to open a put option when you are happy and willing to buy 100 shares or more of a stock at a lower price (your chosen strike price), if the stock declines below that price at expiration. You get paid the option premium when you sell this put contract to the market. Then you wait and see where the stock is at expiration, knowing you can buy to close the put option anytime along the way, if you prefer, at the going market price. We usually sell the put, collect the premium as income, and then simply wait. Either we end up with new shares at a price we like (a price made even lower by the income we were paid), or we just get the income, not the shares, which happens most of the time. But in either scenario, we should be happy with the outcome!

BUYING CALLS FOR UPSIDE LEVERAGE

Now, what about a strategy where you *buy* an option? That's called "buy to open," and we most often use it to buy long-term *call* options. To review, a call option appreciates in value as a stock appreciates. An option costs a fraction of the stock price, but represents 100 shares of stock, so you don't need a crystal ball to see that large stock gains turn into even larger call option gains. Since a call option gives you the right to purchase a stock at a fixed price, if the share price goes up and up, the value of the right to buy that stock goes up and up, too. Since a call option costs less than a stock and represents 100 shares, you can open a position with much less capital at risk than it would take to buy 100 shares. And your potential loss is only what you invest in the calls, no more.

Once again, it's example time. In this case, let's assume you're as bullish as an ice cream vendor in Central Park in August; you believe Peach Technologies is underpriced and that the stock is going to rise over the next few years. You could buy stock at $11 per share; 100 shares will cost you $1,100. Or, you could buy the call options expiring in two years with a strike price of $10. This call gives you the right to buy the stock at $10, no matter what, anytime between now and expiration. For this right, you might pay $2 per share. A studious Fool will now notice that this equates to a $12 per share all-in purchase price ($10 strike price plus $2 for the call leads to a $12 purchase price on shares if you exercise the options). That's $1 higher than the *current* share price. Why would you ever do that?

Well, because you get the benefit of only risking $200 for exposure to 100 shares (remember, each option represents 100 shares, so the $2 cost on this call option costs you $200), rather than $1,100 to buy 100 shares outright. You have much less capital at risk. And you get leveraged upside on this capital. If Peach stock were to rise from $11 to $14, it gains 27 percent. But your call options *double* in value. How? You paid $2 for a $10 call. With the stock now $14, the right to buy it at $10 is worth at least $4, so your call option has achieved a clean double in value. You could sell it for twice what you paid. Or you could keep owning it, and see if Peach keeps ripening. Ultimately, you can turn your calls into stock—exercising the option—and buy shares at $10 a year from now, even if the stock is $20, or any higher price, and then keep on owning the shares for the long haul if you want. You risked only $2 per share initially to get to know the company better with a call option, but now you can begin your long-term relationship to the stock if desired. That's one choice. Or you could, as always, just sell to close the option and take your gain that way.

Looking at the leverage in a call option a bit further, let's assume that Peach continues to rise. When the stock is $16, your $10 strike price call option is worth at least $6, for a 200 percent gain, while the stock is only up 45 percent. With the shares at $18, you have a 300 percent gain on your calls on a 64 percent gain in the stock. And so forth. Impressive, eh? But keep in mind that you usually invest less capital in a call option than you would in the stock, so you have to make up for that smaller investment base with greater percentage returns.

In the opposite scenario, let's say Peach Technologies hits a rough patch, and the stock slides from $11 to $6 by your option's expiration. The call you paid $2 for is worthless. Why? Because the call gives you the right to buy the stock at $10, and with shares now lower than that, your option has no value.

You can buy the stock cheaper on the open market, so nobody wants your $10 call option, not even you. The good news: you lost only $2 per share, because you bought a call rather than the stock (the stock is down $5); and now you could buy the stock at $6 if you wanted. Or, you can walk away, having kept your loss minimized, and give up on Peach.

We usually buy long-term call options (using the latest expiration date available) with a strike price 5 percent to 20 percent *below* the current share price. This is our way of paying less time value for the option, and more intrinsic (or realized) value instead. We aren't keen on taking a flier on a call option with a strike price far higher than the current share price—that situation requires the stock to soar just to assure you a profit in the end. We take the more conservative route of buying an in-the-money call and giving ourselves a long time for a stock to keep rising, adding value to our call. We buy calls on companies we know well and strongly believe in. Ideally, we want the possibility for at least a 100 percent return on our calls when the underlying stock gains about 20 percent or more, because we are risking a 100 percent loss on the option if the stock is below our strike price at expiration. There is no recourse in that case—except to buy the stock on the open market if you want and invest in a recovery. Or buy another call, if you prefer. But the point is, the calls you buy end up worthless if the stock is below your strike price at expiration. When you buy calls, only invest an amount you're comfortable losing.

BUYING PUTS TO PROFIT ON DOWNSIDE

Though we Fools don't use it all that often, one more option strategy you should know about is a protective, or bearish, approach, called *buying* puts. Remember our income strategy of *selling* puts, where you get paid to take on the obligation of potentially purchasing a stock if it declines to your chosen strike price by expiration? On the other side of that trade, someone has the right to *sell* that stock. Yes, the put buyer has that right. *Buying* puts gives you the right to *sell* a stock at the strike price, protecting the put buyer against a decline. You pay for this right by purchasing the option, and you can exercise the option anytime you want, though you normally would only at expiration. You can use a put you own to sell shares of a stock you own at the strike price of the option, thereby sidestepping any decline in the stock. Or, if you don't own the stock itself, you might buy put options simply to profit if a targeted stock falls, selling back the puts for a profit after the stock declines.

Take our trusty Peach Technologies again. Assume LowSlung Tech (Ticker: SLACK) is debuting a cheap competing product, and you expect Peach to take it on the chin. Peach trades at $11. You could "buy to open" the $10 put options on Peach expiring in a year, and then wait to see what happens. If you pay $1 for the puts, and Peach shares subsequently slide to $6, you've quadrupled your money in the puts. With the stock at $6, the right to sell Peach at $10 is now worth $4, so you can sell the puts you purchased for $1 for $4. Good work if you can get it. We rarely buy put options, though, because they're expensive, and because you need the underlying stock to fall *before* the puts expire, which is no easy task. Plus, you usually need the stock to fall sharply to get your puts into the green. In our example, our break-even price is $9 per share on the stock (we paid $1 for a $10 put), so at $11, Peach stock needs to fall 18 percent to $9 just for our puts to break even (still be worth $1) at expiration. Buying puts can be an expensive endeavor, especially if you have to buy them repeatedly while waiting for a stock to fall. It's only in really bearish situations, or when we want to protect an important stock we own, that we consider the practice of repeatedly buying puts.

Usually, once again, we are *selling* puts, not buying them—selling them again and again for income. But one out of every twenty times, you might see a reason to buy a put to profit on a decline or to protect a stock you own with a guaranteed sell price if you come to need it.

OPTIONS DONE FOOLISHLY

We sincerely hope this section on options whetted your appetite without mushing your brain. The key things to remember are that calls appreciate when their stocks rise, and puts appreciate when their stocks fall. You can either buy or sell an option to open the position. The buyer purchases the

rights of the option, and the seller gets paid to take on the potential obligation of the option. We sell to open options more often than we buy them,
generating income.

But buying long-term options is a great way to leverage your returns
and risk less cash in the process. Options work alongside your long-term
stock portfolio. Don't think, fellow Fool, that you should have an option
portfolio separate from your stock portfolio. Options are another way to
express a belief in a stock, and in some cases, options will be exercised into
stock. Use them in your stock portfolio as a complementary tool.

Finally, realize that options have tax consequences in a taxable account.
Any option you sell to open is considered a short. It gets short-term tax
treatment, and any gains get taxed as income. Any option you buy and hold
for more than one year can get long-term tax treatment. Many other options strategies exist beyond the three we outlined, so if your interest is
piqued, check out our options offerings on Fool.com. Many investors have
expanded their financial results by adding income from options, leveraging
upside, hedging, and more. Options can let you profit even when stocks are
going nowhere. When used in smart moderation and with defined purpose,
options are less like Darth Vader, and more like a stock investor's best friend.

PART IX

PUTTING IT ALL TOGETHER

28

WHY INVEST?

If you sat down at your desk and looked at the hard numbers based on any average one-year investment performance, you might conclude that there's no reason to put your money into the stock market. Consider this: If you have $10,000 to put away in stocks, the average market year (10 percent) will reward you with profits of $1,000, one-fifth of which you'd have to pay to the federal government in taxes if you sold at the end of that year. The hassle of pulling together the money, transferring it to a discount broker or moving it into an index fund, monitoring your monthly statements, and sending the documentation over to your accountant at year's end—all that effort and what do you get? Profits in the neighborhood of $800 a year. Divided out, in an oversimplified fashion, that would be about $67 a month, or $2.19 per day.

That's hardly inspiring. Take that same amount and run it out ten years, and you'll have made a mere $8,000 on your initial $10,000 investment.

Eighty percent growth per decade should have you asking yourself why you paid anything for this useless book. There simply must be better ways to put your savings to work for you.

How true all of the above would be—if there weren't one great flaw to the analysis. Can you spot it? If your portfolio grows at an after-tax rate of 8 percent per year, you don't actually make $67 a month. The percentage growth might remain the same, but the dollar growth will *increase* each month. After all, 8 percent of $10,000 is less than 8 percent of $11,000. And in those numbers lies the simple beauty of compounded growth. Time builds wealth. You'll make more in the second month than in the first, and you'll make more still in month 12. By the tenth year, you'll effectively be realizing nearly $148 in pure after-tax profit per month, and this assumes that you don't put away any additional money between now and then—an assumption that we hope is very wrong.

But maybe $148 a month on a $10,000 investment ten years later doesn't inspire you, either. For those with extra zeroes to their name, that's equivalent to $1,480 a month in pure profit off a $100,000 starting kitty, and $14,800 a month off a $1 million personal bank. And the key is that when you build a Foolish investment portfolio, compounded growth carries your savings forward generationally, by investing in other people's efforts. Your capital grows without any Herculean effort on your part, particularly as—in the least challenging strategy—you'll just be loading it into an index fund. Let the scientists at Johnson & Johnson, the salespeople at Costco, the analysts at PayPal, the technologists at Google, and the bankers at Bank of America turn profits for you, as they will if you invest in an S&P 500 index fund. By letting others build up your savings, you'll have more time to devote to the nonfinancial things that matter to you.

Put your money into an index fund, and $10,000 will turn into $20,750—even after Uncle Sam takes his cut—at the end of a decade. And again, those numbers suppose that you won't be putting additional savings away between now and then (though of course you will!). You can see that the initial dollar amounts don't mean much compared to the basic principle of compounded growth: you'll generate greater and greater returns with time. Investors who focus on that longer-term perspective, who can hammer together a vision of what their life will be like ten, twenty, thirty years down the road, and who recognize how much sweeter it'll be to have a larger and larger portfolio generating higher and higher dollar profits, *these* are the true Fools. Save, invest the dollars intelligently in stocks, and watch the portfolio grow.

Allow us to share the (unsolicited) thoughts of one of our members on the celebration of his twelfth anniversary as a member of *Stock Advisor*, which sums the whole journey up so well. Over the past twelve years, he writes, "our Foolish portfolio has been chugging along without a ton of effort on my part. I've had a bunch of loser stocks in my portfolio, but yet it has delivered ten-year returns of 12.7 percent versus 6.7 percent for the S&P. The winners in my portfolio have brought great returns, and the losers, well, they have become less important in the scheme of things. All this happened while we were trying to get through this thing called life," wrote the father of two. "We don't know what next year will bring, but I am confident that we can make decisions to live and work where we want for the next part of our journey. The gains we have made through investing with the Fool have allowed us this flexibility, and that is priceless."

BLENDING YOUR INVESTMENTS TOGETHER

It is precisely this awesome potential for long-term profitability as part owners of businesses that encourages Fools to seek out extra percentage points of compounded annual returns. Remember our discussion earlier about every extra percentage point of annualized gains? Each of these points is lucrative. On your path to attempting to land those points, you'll need to build a Foolish portfolio, one that is ideally constructed on the shoulders of giants, and use additional holdings in promising high-growth stocks to see further than the market's returns. Over the past decade, investors have seen players like Apple, Tesla, Amazon, Netflix, Google, Chipotle, Under Armour, and dozens of other smaller or mid-cap companies break away to all-star status in their respective industries. All of these companies have made their long-term shareholders extraordinarily happy, and all of them were sitting there right under growth-stock investors' noses, waiting to be scooped up.

Of course, while you'll hear all sorts of talk about great growth stocks—quite a bit of it in these pages, since growth stocks have given us our greatest investment successes—you need to understand how to evaluate them. An ill-chosen small company's volatility will be your bane, not your boon. We hope our chapters explaining how to think about and select growth stocks of all sizes went a long way toward helping you make your own decisions in this field, rather than relying on fund managers to charge you for generally mediocre performance.

But remember that selecting your stocks isn't always easy, and it's never an idle process. Skipping the deeper analysis, even "just this once," is often the lead-in to a story on the My Dumbest Investment discussion board on Fool.com. We live in an age of tremendous access to information. If you want to learn what customers think of a restaurant you're considering as an investment, head to Yelp and get the full story straight from the tables. If you want to know whether your CEO inspires confidence in her employees, Glassdoor has up-to-date ratings. There are plenty of reputable websites that offer (ideally, independent) analysis of stocks. The Motley Fool alone produces more than a hundred free articles every day, covering everything from micro caps to blue chips to macroeconomic trends. Our teams of analysts pore over the management teams and financial forecasts of hundreds of companies to find the elite ones worthy of recommendation to the members of our premium services. None of these should replace your judgment or decision making; rather, they are all tools you can use to inform your thinking, calling out red flags or accentuating further advantages that reinforce your opinions.

And now you're armed with the tools to dig into a company's numbers on your own. One of the beauties of the US market is that by law, publicly traded companies have to lay out their performance four times a year for everyone to see. By dedicating a handful of hours each year to review quarterly financials for the companies you own or are considering owning, you're giving yourself an important—and potentially lucrative—leg up on other investors, those who are blithely buying companies based on a "hot tip" that they dug out of the spam filter or overheard in the steam room of their health club. If you take the time to gain a sense of management's philosophy, understand the company's products and services, examine the cash situation, and consider where it fits within its industry as well as the addressable market it could pursue, you will have a considerable advantage in determining whether a company might outperform in the years ahead.

Prudent investors will look at businesses that make the rules in their industries. Companies that have already proven that they have what it takes to dominate will continue to do so. And you'll want to watch for the companies that are blazing their own trails, leading new and important industries, and learning to rule them. Consider using a portion of your portfolio to take some chances on tomorrow's Coca-Cola, the future Google, the emerging Pfizer. Following the criteria presented in this book will lead you to some dogs, but the winners you find will carry you well beyond the index fund's horizon.

Picking long-term market-beating stocks isn't a great mystery. It isn't a random-walk process. It isn't only for the wealthy. And it isn't something only MBA graduates can do. Quite the opposite, actually. It's a wealth-building opportunity for anyone who has a little money to invest, the patience and temperament to profit from other investors' short-term thinking, and the desire to enjoy the freedom that comes with financial success.

If you're going to invest in individual stocks, you must aim to outperform index funds. If you can pull it off, twenty years from now you won't be worrying about your financial position, no matter how much money you've put away for investing today. And remember, always track your performance against the indices. If you aren't beating them, guess where you should reinvest your money? (Hint: Two words. The first begins with an "i." The second is "fund.")

Given that we spend so much of our time focusing on the long-term ramifications of investing in the stock market, be advised that we think you should enter stocks cautiously. There's no rush. Consider starting with an index fund or some blue-chip stocks exclusively in your first year. While you find your footing, you can simulate growth-stock investing by getting a free CAPS account to test-drive your strategy. When you're convinced you can outdo index-fund investing, and you're confident you have the timeline and temperament to stick with it even when things don't go your way, explore the worlds of Rule Breakers, small-cap stocks, and other corners of the market that might appeal to you. Find your edge, and then over time, push your edge to the edge.

29

BEING YOUR BEST INVESTING SELF

This above all: To thine own self be true.

—William Shakespeare, *Hamlet*

THE HOME STRETCH

Just as with any business, higher returns open up new worlds for investors. Whether that means a new career; extended travel abroad; a chance to buy some time for more creative, less profitable ventures; more hours to spend with the family; the opportunity to pursue charitable works; or just a chance to buy something fun, prosperity leads to opportunity, and opportunity, prosperity.

The stock market, while volatile, has provided and will continue to provide the best annual returns of any investment vehicle, by a large margin. That's because it will always offer investors the best, most liquid opportunities to capitalize on the greatest business growth opportunities available in the known galaxy. Taking advantage of these situations, and committing yourself to long-term prosperity, no matter what happens in the near term, will contribute to the great financial and emotional rewards associated with forsaking Wisdom.

You might not know it, but you're incredibly lucky: There has never been a better time to be an individual investor in stocks. From access to information to improvements in technology to a broader range of options from which to choose, this is truly a golden age for savvy investors. But it's also easier than ever to make mistakes that could cost you big—after all, an ill-considered purchase or an untimely sale of a stock is now just one imprudent click away.

As a parting gift, we offer longtime Foolish writer Morgan Housel's compilation of lessons he's learned—advice that might help you avoid the most common mistakes and gain a healthy perspective along your path as an investor.

WORDS OF WISDOM

Investment fees are falling, but investment costs are not.

Index fund fees now round to zero. That's a big win for investors. But the emotional cost of investing is as high as it's ever been. The massive increase in financial media is great, but it has a downside: we are bombarded with headlines that feed on greed, fear, and doubt, making it easier than ever to get sidetracked by excitement, confusion, and pessimism. Everything that's valuable has a cost. The biggest cost in investing is the emotions of being uncomfortable, not knowing what the future will bring, and wondering whether you're doing the right thing. These costs are orders of magnitudes larger than fees paid to advisors, and their currency is stress hormones, rather than dollars. A lot of investors realize they can't afford these costs and quit. But paying them, for those who can, is as worthwhile as it's ever been.

Most investing success boils down to avoiding catastrophic mistakes.

Few "good" decisions are needed to do well over time. This is a new development in the investing world. In the past, successful investing meant being on the inside, with access to the products and information required to do well. Today, every tool needed for success is available to every investor, no matter how small. Low-cost funds, news, disclosures, tracking software. They're all there for everyone to use. All you have to do is keep your head on straight and not screw it up. That's the most valuable skill an investor can possess.

Most investing mistakes and frustrations come from trying to run a marathon in an hour.

Diversified investing is simple. Companies earn profits, and over a long period, those profits accrue to shareholders. If you leave it at that—and you should—investing is a basic game that doesn't require much action. But instead of letting profits accrue over time, much of the investment industry attempts to speed up the process by front-loading gains into shorter periods. This is done by guessing what other investors will do next and trying to get ahead of them. It's exponentially harder than true investing, and it's the cause of most investment mistakes.

Progress happens too slowly to notice; setbacks happen too quickly to ignore.

The market quickly lost 38 percent in 2008, and it was huge deal. Books were written about it, and congressional hearings were held. Investors will long remember how it affected them. The market then slowly tripled from 2009 to 2015, and barely anyone flinched. You had to sit down and show people the numbers to get them to believe you. This is common: recessions take place over months; recoveries take place over years. It can take decades for companies to become valuable, but bankruptcies happen overnight. Pain hurts more than the same level of gain feels good, but the duration differences between progress and setbacks help explain why there are so many pessimists amid a backdrop of things getting better over time.

Few things are more valuable than room for error.

Having a big gap between what could happen and what you need to have happen to meet your goals is priceless. Long-term success has more to do with the ability to shrug your shoulders at the world's unpredictability than it does constantly being right.

"Don't do anything" is the best advice for most people most of the time, but it's not intellectually stimulating enough for many people to take seriously.

Most fields have a positive correlation between effort and results. Investing is one of few where the correlation is negative, especially for amateurs. The higher your IQ is, the harder it is to accept this.

No one is smarter than the collective intelligence of millions of other investors. Some, however, are a little more patient and less emotional. That's where the potential for "edge" is found.

Thirty years ago, investing was mostly an analytical game, because information was scarce and computers weren't scouring the world for mispriced assets. That's changed. Most analytical opportunity has now been fully exploited. But there's still huge opportunity to gain an edge over most investors through patience and good behavior.

There has never been a better time to be an investor.

Ever, in history. More people have access to first-class services than ever before. It's so important, and we don't spend enough time realizing how good it is.

30

A FOOLISH FAREWELL

Even bad books are books and therefore sacred.

—Günter Grass

The Motley Fool Investment Guide has, from start to finish, shared the same aim of all our online financial undertakings: to educate, amuse, and enrich. We've spent more than two decades designing and evolving our investment approach, and we're thrilled to share it with you. It's all a part of our mission to help the world invest . . . better. For some, that means taking a smarter view of analyzing companies, building a successful portfolio, and taking advantage of more advanced strategies. For others, that means simply getting started, because the sooner you start putting your money to work, the sooner you benefit from the snowball effect of compounding returns.

Before we send you on your way, we're going to run through our Absolute Essentials one last time.

MANAGE YOUR OWN MONEY

Be a Fool: manage your own money and beat the market and the experts without spending your every waking hour worrying about the investments somebody else picked for you that you know nothing about. You can be confident that at every step, you'll have your best interests at heart. Furthermore, if you can ignore the siren calls of hype stocks and the impassioned offerings of the "Have I got a stock for you" brokers, and look instead to the examples of Philip Fisher, Warren Buffett, and Peter Lynch, you can see that the task is not impossible. Using a few simple principles that anyone with discipline can duplicate, each of these paragons has crushed the stock market on an annualized basis.

Find the companies and the leaders you trust. Explore the businesses that are changing the landscape of their industry. See if you can uncover a small-cap hidden gem, then watch as it blossoms into a major player. Take advantage of all the research tools at your disposal—both the obvious ones (like financial statements) and unexpected ones (like online videos)—to get the fullest possible picture of whether this is a company that's earned a spot in your portfolio. And then hold on for the long term, ignoring the noise as best you can. And if you find you're not beating the S&P 500 on a regular basis, or your investment decisions are keeping you up at night, there's no shame in rolling your money into a low-cost index fund. The Foolish aim with stocks is to beat the market as soundly as we can with as little time and effort as possible—and make sure we're enjoying the hunt.

BE AGGRESSIVE, TOO

You're not going to make a million overnight. The investment strategies you've found here are for those willing to look to the future and wait while their money and the market do the work. The most attractive aspect of the long-term approach to investing in stocks is that it eliminates day-to-day risk and worry. If you're generating more than the market's annual growth on disposable income, sleeping peaceably, and reflexively saving money, you can *and should* constantly open up your model, challenging yourself to do better. Far too much of our nation's financial psyche is weighted down with thoughts merely of spending and saving, like a dieter who forgets that exercise is the key to staying in shape. Be aggressive in investing your money once you've learned how to run the numbers, how to weed out fabricated growth, how to account for your returns against the market overall, and how to be patient and disciplined.

We certainly don't think that 15 percent annualized growth is out of the realm of possibility for the individual investor. That's a few percentage points above the average annual returns of an index fund, a method that demands none of your time. The question, of course, is how much time it would take to achieve 15 percent gains, and how much it's worth to you.

Permit us then to run some numbers one last time. Let's take $25,000 as our nest egg. To that, we'll add $2,500 in new savings per year. And we'll compound out 15 percent in annual growth. How long until that initial $25,000 has turned into $1 million? Twenty-three years.

So, where are you going to be in 2040?

ONE LAST THING

You know, the market could tank this year. And you'd better believe that our analysts will locate some new undiscovered winners. In either of these cases, the book you hold in your hands does not offer the *latest* help you can get. But until you've mastered what's in here, the latest help wouldn't be much help at all. Let this book serve as your textbook, with Fool.com and all the other day-to-day offerings as your life's continuing education. Keep the knowledge that you've gleaned over the past chapters at your disposal, but understand that the world is gonna change.

But being Foolish is not just about being prepared for change. It also means sticking to your guns. Even if the market bombs altogether this year or next, we'll be there buying right into the bottom, knowing that the market will always come back, and our stocks will return stronger with it. And as the markets continue their steady climb higher over the decades, we'll be finding new industries to analyze, new investing strategies to explore, new criteria to examine in our search for the businesses we want to own. In bad times and in good, we are Foolish investors. And we hope you'll be along for the ride with us.

Fool on!

DG/TG

ACKNOWLEDGMENTS

This book represents a process that has spanned decades and involved dozens of Fools, at least eight of whom we're certain to overlook. Apologies to the neglected ones. The original edition of the book, published back when we had to encourage our readers to get online, owes thanks to Susan Jensen, then our assistant agent, who "discovered" us. Suzanne Gluck represented us with humor and aplomb as our agent. Bob Mecoy was our patient and easygoing editor at Simon & Schuster the first time through, and he was admirably assisted by Brian McSharry, Isolde C. Sauer, and Patty Romanowski who together, as we wrote in the acknowledgments of the original book, "explored [with us] the limits of modern facsimile and electronic mail technology."

We thank so many early members of our team, such as Erik Rydholm, Dwight Gibbs, Todd Etter, Mary Arnold, Gary Hill, and a bunch of others who helped set the tone for so much Foolishness.

Building on the solid foundation of a book constructed back in the 1990s proved a bigger task than expected—who knew so much had changed?—and we owe great appreciation to many. Thanks to our agent, Howard Yoon, for restarting the conversation and serving as our advocate. Our editor at Simon & Schuster, Amar Deol, was truly our partner in the process, all the way to the final deadline (which we made!). And a second thanks to Isolde for another great round of edits.

Thank you, thank you to everyone at Fool HQ in Alexandria, Virginia, who make us proud every day as you live our corporate purpose to help the world invest better. Thanks, in particular, to the team of Fools who carried the book into modern times. Andy Cross and Jeff Fischer have spanned the gap between the books, and it's been a pleasure to work alongside them on our journey. Ron Gross and Amanda Kish were tireless and thankless researchers and contributors for the book you now hold. James Royal, Ilan Moscovitz, Sara Hov, Dan Caplinger, Robert Brokamp, Morgan Housel, and Chris Harris chipped in their expertise. Brian Richards and Nathan Alderman helped smooth out the rough edges. Robyn Gearey got the party started. And many thanks to Roger Friedman for quarterbacking this project all the way through.

And finally (almost), we thank our families: the one that got us started—thank you, Dad, and we miss you, Mom—and the ones that surround and support us today.

And finally (truly), to our readers, members, listeners, and friends of the Fool, thank you for teaching us more than we ever taught you. Fool on!

APPENDIX A: STOCKS 101

A PRIMER FOR THOSE WHO'LL ADMIT THEY NEED IT

So you've decided to do more than invest in your company's 401(k), venture beyond your mutual funds, strike out on your own, and buy some stocks. But what do you do *next*? There are hundreds of talking heads on TV and Twitter and self-proclaimed financial gurus who fill your inbox telling you *what* stocks to buy, *why* to buy them, and always *when* to buy them (which often is right after they do). But these mavens rarely, if ever, tell you just *how* you might go about buying stocks.

Many investors plunge right into the stock market, using the first brokerage firm recommended to them or the one with the catchiest ad. Taking the time to think about boring stuff like tax-deferred investment vehicles and commission schedules might seem dull. And it is. But if you take time to familiarize yourself with some of these concepts, you may end up saving time, money, and heartache.

WHAT *IS* A SHARE OF STOCK?

Funny how common it is for individual investors to jump into the equities markets without understanding why and how businesses are built, why they issue stock, and how they grow.

Growth: that's the first matter at hand. Whether they're seeking to maximize their revenue or change the world for good (or both), businesses start out expecting to grow. Tomorrow's profits will allow for higher salaries, more employees, increased opportunity, prosperity at work and at home—all the good news we hope for. Of course, there are loads of other reasons that businesses blossom: some aspire to serve customers, others to exploit them, others to serve a larger corporation, others to fund a higher calling. But one thing's true of 99 percent of them: they aim to expand.

How? Sometimes a company has a great new product, like a car that drives itself. Other times it's recognized a niche for the provision of a great new service, like cloud storage or data mining. But often, whatever the driving force is—products, services, or whatever—the company lacks the money to drive the operation forward.

Let's examine FlubSoft, the brand-new virus-protection software company that you and we just started together. Kicking off this new operation is expensive: we need office space, phone services, networked computers, health insurance, salaries, and more. It's no wonder that the vast majority of start-up businesses go belly-up within five years.

To survive these initial costs, FlubSoft has two traditional sources for funding. First, it can head down to the nearest bank, lay out its financial statements and projections, and plead for a loan. It's possible we'll get the funds, but the less established the company, the less likely a bank is to lend it money. And even when loans do come through, they can do more damage than good. Risky loans demand higher interest rates, and the higher the rate, the greater the possibility that our company won't be able to pay it down. Never a borrower be, some say.

FlubSoft could instead sell chunks of itself—"equity"—to investors willing to take a shot at a big payout down the road. Conveniently, this path would help us avoid costly debt financing, while now sporting business partners who are cheering for our virus detection and defense software.

The best of start-up companies—and we wouldn't have started this business, you and the Fool, if we didn't aspire to superiority—can generate millions of dollars by selling 30 percent to 40 percent of their equity to venture capitalists. In this situation, we'd create shares of ownership in our company and sell them off. We could pick a number and declare that 100 shares of stock make up FlubSoft in its entirety. (The number is insignificant; the percentage of the company's total value is what matters.) If we sold 40 percent of our company to VentYour Capital for $1 million, we'd keep 60 shares, and VentYour would take 40 shares. Our company wouldn't be listed on any of the US exchanges, but we would enjoy the same sort of "shares of ownership" as Microsoft, Wal-Mart, or General Electric. Equity financing helps FlubSoft avoid potentially backbreaking high-interest loans from a traditional bank—but the original owners have to share the spoils with the new investors.

Now, how do we get from being anonymous little FlubSoft with a dozen employees, a decent infrastructure, and impressive sales growth, to gargantuan FlubSoft with five hundred employees, a square block of office space, national and international distribution, and tens of millions in annual sales? *We go public*, again selling more ownership in our company. This time, however, we'll be selling shares to a base of millions of investors, and taking our spot on one of the US exchanges.

THE PUBLIC COMPANY

There are three main ways that shares of ownership in American corporations wind up in the hands of former nonowners. The first is the initial public offering (or IPO). Companies aiming to go public work through a brokerage that focuses on investment banking to sell their first batch of shares to investors. They become, for the first time, a publicly owned entity that trades every day on a stock exchange.

The second way is for those public companies that have already had an IPO to acquire *more* capital to fuel future growth, in what's known as a secondary offering. No matter how many more times a company offers shares, the sale will be called a secondary offering. Issuing more shares dilutes the existing value of the shares held by the previous owners by creating more units of control, but for a growing company, this is often not a problem. If we at FlubSoft need another $5 million to finance a new venture into entertainment software, we could sell another load of ownership, believing that the growth from our new project would far outweigh the share dilution. Most of the companies with a couple of hundred million shares started out with only a few million. They kept going back to the well for more cash.

The final way that stocks get issued is directly to employees, whether they're officers of the corporation or rank-and-file workers, through various profit-sharing and compensation plans. The board of directors, which represents the shareholders, figures that paying the company's officers in stock *and* salary gives those people a little extra impetus to improve the company and, as a result, the stock price. As a bonus, companies are able to lower their salary overhead by partially compensating employees with stock.

SPLITS

Companies increase the number of shares available through what is called a stock split. It simply involves a company altering the number of its shares outstanding and proportionally adjusting the share price to compensate. This in *no way* affects the intrinsic value or past performance of your investment, if you happen to own shares that are splitting.

A typical example is a 2-for-1 stock split. A company will announce that it's splitting its stock 2-for-1 in one month. One month from that date, the company's shares (having traded the day before at, say, $30) will now be trading at half the price from the previous day (so they'll open at $15). The company, which had 10 million shares outstanding, now has 20 million shares outstanding. The price has been halved to accommodate a doubling of the share total.

Why would a company do this? Excellent question. First, as a stock price skyrockets, some people will be psychologically unwilling to pay that "high price," so a stock split brings the shares down to a more "attractive" level. To be very clear again, the intrinsic value *has not changed*, but the psychological effects may help the stock. Second, a stock split generally occurs in the face of new highs for the stock. Thus, it's an event dripping with positive connotations and associations . . . suddenly each owner has "twice as many shares" as he or she started with. And lastly, with lower-priced shares, a stock's liquidity increases, making it easier—and in some cases less costly—to trade.

THE PRINCIPAL MARKETS

Public stocks are traded in public markets, organizations that create outlets for trading equities. Each market has various requirements that a company must meet before it can be listed—minimum asset value, minimum annual sales, maximum management ownership limitations—all designed to prevent manipulation of a stock's price.

Once upon a time, there were only three markets in the United States: the New York Stock Exchange (NYSE), the Nasdaq Stock Market (Nasdaq), and the former American Stock Exchange (AMEX), now known as NYSE MKT LLC (catchy!). Recent years have seen significant changes in the field, as old giants have been consolidated and new exchanges have taken significant market share. There are now more than twenty national exchanges, including the NYSE, Bats, NASDAQ, IEX, and many others, representing most every type of investor and most every letter in the alphabet.

The New York is the oldest exchange, and it has the strictest requirements for listing. Its typical member is a more established company—the giants that have been in business for decades. In 2007, the NYSE merged with Euronext to form NYSE Euronext. On November 13, 2013, nearly two centuries after it was officially created, the New York Stock Exchange (along with other assets of NYSE Euronext) was acquired by a company that had been in existence for less than two *decades*. The purchaser, Intercontinental Exchange, was founded in 1997 and launched in 2000 as an electronic trading platform for energy products.

The next largest exchange is even younger than Intercontinental Exchange. With its headquarters in Kansas and its fully digital exchange, Bats

Global Markets has rapidly grown from a tiny operation founded in 2005 to the second-largest exchange by volume. Bats is known for its fast response times, making it a preferred exchange for many algorithmic traders. A fully digital exchange—unlike the NYSE, where physical humans exchange shares—Bats has no central location, but rather is a network of brokerages that move stocks to one another via a computer system. The brokerages that participate are called "market makers." They sign up to fulfill orders for individual companies. Thus, a certain brokerage might "make a market" in Microsoft, but not in Intel, which means that if you want to buy some shares of Microsoft, they'll find the shares in *their* inventory, but if you want to buy some Intel, they'll have to reach out to another firm and borrow the shares. This has absolutely no effect on you as an investor; you'll probably never know who makes the market in your stocks.

Market makers on each market make money from the bid-ask spread, or the difference in the prices at which individual investors can buy or sell a stock. They'll quote you one price to buy and another price for someone else to sell, and pocket the difference. Spreads have come down over time, largely as a result of our improved technology and the exchanges switching to a decimal system, versus the old days when stocks were quoted in eighths of a dollar.

The Nasdaq was around in those days. It has historically been known for offering fast-growing technology companies, although it lists stocks in every industry. The Nasdaq was the first fully digital exchange, eschewing the then-traditional "trading pit" for a system of connected computers. While this might seem commonplace now, in 1971 it was viewed as a risky endeavor.

The NYSE MKT was formerly the AMEX, and was acquired in 2008 by NYSE Euronext. Most trading here involves smaller companies, exchange-traded funds (ETFs), and derivatives.

One of the newer exchanges, having been approved by the SEC in 2016, is the Investors Exchange, or the IEX. Unlike other exchanges, which have built their brands around historical cachet (the NYSE) or speed of execution (NASDAQ and Bats), the IEX is designed to fill trades *more slowly* than other exchanges. As computers do more trading, and increasingly rely on speed of execution to make trades slightly (we're talking milliseconds) before humans or other computers, the IEX slows trades down, so that no market participant (human or otherwise) can trade before another.

Whether we watch that platform take a bigger share of market volume, we stick with old standbys, or we develop an entirely new technological vehicle (the Blink to Buy Exchange, coming soon?), it seems certain that our markets will continue to evolve to meet the needs of businesses and investors.

THE TRADITIONAL BROKERAGE

Now that we have an idea of what stock is, how companies go about issuing it, and how exchanges work, we can talk about how you purchase shares of your own. The most common way is through a brokerage—an institution licensed by state and federal authorities to buy and sell securities (a fancy word for stocks). Brokerages join the various exchanges and are policed by them as well as by the Securities and Exchange Commission (SEC). Knowing a little bit about how brokerages work can help a Fool pick the "right" one.

Although they might stress their uniqueness, the largest, most renowned *full-service* brokerages are largely similar. The traditional big-name brokerage has a retail division, a research division, and an investment banking division. These firms also have a "back office" that does the number-crunching for customer accounts and a "trading desk" that processes and communicates customer orders to the various stock exchanges.

The retail part has all those salesmen (brokers) and investment advisors who call individuals or institutional clients, trying to get them to buy or sell the firm's recommended stocks. They make money for themselves and their firms by generating commissions off trades. It's a little-known fact that most big-name brokerages actually *lose* money in their retail operations. "What?" you say. "Why have them at all?" We'll make that clear in a bit.

The research side comprises all the analysts and assistants writing reports that evaluate individual companies. The firm recommends them as a "buy," a "hold," a "market performer," et al. You'll rarely see a firm labeling a stock a "sell." As we noted earlier in the book, research firms rely on their relationships with every company they follow; they don't want to jeopardize those ties by motivating investors to sell. As a result, *hold* in analyst-ese usually means *sell*.

The investment banking side of a brokerage is the most important for the big firms. This is where they make the bulk of their money. When companies want to make IPOs or companies want to issue more shares as an alternative to borrowing money, the investment banking people do the multimillion-dollar deals.

The brokerage firm will leverage its alternate businesses to its own favor when it brings companies public. How? Read on.

CONFLICTS OF INTEREST AT A TRADITIONAL BROKERAGE

As we noted, brokerage firms are loath to jeopardize their very lucrative investment banking relationships with the companies they cover. This relationship has a profound effect on a brokerage's retail and research divisions. Firms keep their retail operations—even if they're ostensibly losing money—to serve as a sales channel to push IPOs and secondary offerings. When Eventual Taxi Service (Ticker: LATE) issues 2.5 million additional shares, the firm that helped with the offering often puts LATE on its Hot Weekly Buy List. Then legions of brokers call their clients, asking whether they want in on this cost-cutting operation. (Slogan: "When you absolutely, positively need to be there . . . at some point.") So keep in mind that when a broker recommends a stock, it's not always because he thinks it really is a great buy. Sometimes the firm needs him to sell it.

DISCOUNT BROKERAGES: A REVOLUTION ON WALL STREET

Before the days of lightning-fast electronic communication, full-service brokerages and the brokers they employed were a fairly vital link between individual investors and Wall Street. When you needed to tell someone down on a stock exchange trading floor which stocks you wanted to buy or sell, you needed an agent. That's how the commission system, on which most brokers' pay is still based, evolved. Commissions are the fees that you pay to a broker to fulfill your request to buy or sell a stock. Because of the time and trouble that it took to place an order—sending a runner to the exchange to communicate to the brokerage's agent on the trading floor— compensation was pretty substantial.

But with changes in technology, Wall Street has lost the stranglehold it once held on investors. Now that the internet has changed everything, the balance of investing power has shifted toward Main Street. It's now as easy for an individual investor in Anchorage, Alaska, to send in an order to buy or sell a security as it is for a well-paid broker in the Big Apple. Yet the oldest brokerage firms on Wall Street still do business in much the same way they did one hundred years ago, charging substantial commissions.

What specifically happened to break the control that the traditional brokerages held over the investment world? The watershed moment occurred in May 1975—"May Day," as it's known—when the SEC, the federal agency that has been charged with policing the investment world, decreed that the traditional fixed system of commissions would be repealed, and brokerages could charge whatever they wanted, within certain guidelines. Thus, with pricing variables, the price wars began, and the so-called discount brokerage business was born.

A discount brokerage is designed to serve the individual investor. The "discount" label means that the brokerage doesn't act as an investment bank. It doesn't launch IPOs, and it generally doesn't have any in-house analysts. All it does is buy and sell stocks. Discount brokers also don't offer individualized service, and you typically don't have a relationship with any specific broker. Instead, the discount broker allows investors to place trades online for a discounted commission.

The hodgepodge of discount brokers offers varying fee schedules, benefits, and account minimums. The two main kinds of discount brokerages are a normal discount brokerage, which does some of the same retail-side stuff as a traditional brokerage—providing news, some research materials, and a few perks at low cost—and a "deep discount" brokerage, which is essentially there only to take your order and execute it with the fewest possible frills.

It's difficult to generalize about "deep discounters," though, since each offers a different combination of services and features, including cheap commissions, services, locations, and hours. Some try to undercut the discount brokerages by offering very cheap—or even free—trades.

Some people believe that discount brokerages are riskier than regular brokerages and might fold in a stock market crash, but that's mainly just full-service industry scare tactics. To the extent that they offer the same minimum account insurance that full-service brokers offer, discounters are just as secure. The government-sponsored Securities Investor Protection Corporation (SIPC) insures accounts up to $500,000, which includes a $250,000 limit for cash. (Obviously, double-check that your prospective broker is SIPC insured.) If your account is larger than $500,000, ask your discount broker how you can go about insuring it further.

SO, WHICH BROKERAGE?

The first major decision you need to make when investing is what kind of brokerage you want to use. The use of full-service brokers must be considered, under most circumstances, quite un-Foolish. If you choose that route and send your money to the houses of Merrill, or UBS, or Morgan Stanley, you are saying, "Do it for me, Jack [or Janice, or Jiang, or whatever your full-service broker's name might be]. I think you can manage my money especially well, and I'm going to pay you extra to do it for me. I'm going to pay you a premium for *every* trade you make on my account, since you're going to be coming up with virtually all my investment ideas, and/ or I'm going to pay you an annual management fee for the fine job you're doing for me."

Some investors, because of time constraints and a fear of going it completely alone, find having their own broker helpful when starting out. The assistance that the right, dedicated broker or investment advisor provides can be a valuable commodity. The idea of having someone whose everyday duty is to watch the stocks in your account and call you whenever there is any news about them can be a real comfort to many a fledgling investor. Also, for busy people who have neither the time nor the inclination to do their own research, the notion of a broker giving you advice that comes from the firm's professional analysts can be downright exciting.

Typically, having a full-service brokerage means having a broker through whom you make all of your trades. This broker is supposed to know about you and your goals, and to advise you about what stocks and funds may or may not be appropriate. He or she will supply you with scads of research, newsletters, and model portfolios developed by the brokerage in order to give you ideas about potential investments. In theory, it's quite comforting.

Most investors, however, mistakenly think that all this activity will lead to market outperformance. If you're going to use a full-service broker initially, be sure to stack her returns against the S&P 500—the no-research approach to the stock market. If she can't beat the S&P—after deducting *all* commission and research costs—you won't be needing her assistance.

CAUTIOUS OR CONFIDENT?

Depending on the amount of money you have, how often you plan to buy stocks, and how much of your own research you plan to do, you'll make a choice somewhere on the continuum between price and service when picking a brokerage. And there are two typical roles that a Fool plays at the start: cautious or confident.

If you're a cautious beginner who's concerned about going it alone and would like to start slow, you can find a lot of ways to do this without relying on the big-name, high-priced firms. Though it's not without flaws, generally the most satisfactory option is a regional or boutique brokerage, which can offer you competitive commissions, low account minimums, solid advice, and accountability. The less involved they are with investment banking, the better. Remember, if you're going to go this route, you should expect your broker to outperform the S&P 500 by enough to make it worth your while. Setting expectations right from the start with your broker is essential.

Always remember: any broker who gives advice is basically a salesman shopping around his brokerage house's stock or fund picks, and getting paid a percentage (the commission) for every sale he makes. How good the salesman is should matter less to you than the quality of his wares. Do the ideas your broker is selling you make good money or not? If you have a good full-service broker who is driving your account to market-beating returns, then clearly this person is earning you additional dollars. If your broker, after reckoning fees and taxes, beats what you could do on your own, celebrate him, deify him, and maybe pay for his Thanksgiving turkey.

THE CONFIDENT INVESTOR

Fools are most at ease when they can demonstrate their expertise by making their own investment decisions, using only a discount brokerage. However, even when you've decided that you need no advice from brokers or analysts' reports, you should keep in mind that there are still plenty of options left to you.

The larger discount brokerages can provide a number of premium services, including checking accounts, credit cards, and even some one-on-one guidance. Although you might pay a little more per trade, sometimes these perks are enough to make an investor choose Charles Schwab or Fidelity Investments over, say, Robinhood.

Over the years, commission prices have come way down, sometimes even to zero. Now, you'll want to shop for a broker based not just on commissions, but on what services you'd like the broker to provide. It may be high interest rates on money market accounts, free IRAs, checking and ATM availability, low fees for transfers and stock certificate issuance, etc., etc. Figure out what services you want, and look for them.

FINDING YOUR DISCOUNT BROKER

1. Advertisements, whether in print, online, or on TV, can be misleading. When you read about an incredibly cheap rate to trade stocks, read the fine print. Often, you'll be reading only a sample detailing *one* sort of trade, or the low price may be for a limited time with restrictions. Read the brokerage agreement carefully.
2. Commission schedules can vary considerably, depending on the brokerage firm or the type of trade. Make sure to have a good

understanding of what you'll be paying for the types of investing you'll be doing most of the time.

3. If you trade foreign stocks, make sure your discounter is set up to trade them. That's because some deep-discount brokers, particularly those offering the least services, are poorly equipped for handling such transactions. You'll be sorely disappointed if you've just transferred your account to an outfit that can't meet your needs.

4. If you want to use a margin account, which allows you to buy stocks with money borrowed from the brokerage, you're in luck, because discounters sometimes offer cheaper margin rates than full-service brokers. Make sure you inquire about the current margin rate of interest charged by each of your prospects. Keep in mind that this rate fluctuates from time to time and will probably be based on how much you're borrowing (the more money you borrow, the lower your margin rate). That said, remember that the Fool recommends staying away from margin. Borrowing to make investments can get you into all sorts of trouble that just isn't necessary.

5. Whatever you do, keep score! We highly recommend that you set up an online portfolio on Fool.com or Yahoo! or Google, where you can practice various strategies and follow the daily happenings in your holdings. One nice feature of our Motley Fool scorecards (scorecard.fool.com) is that we automatically track you against the market indices, so you can always see how you're doing with each individual holding, and overall. And if you happen to own an Amazon Echo device or any of the other voice-recognition platforms that are popping up, you can set up a watch list of the stocks you care about at the Fool and keep track by simply saying, "Alexa, ask the Fool how my stocks are doing."

TAX DEFERMENT: IRAS AND 401(K)S

Individual Retirement Accounts (IRAs) and 401(k)s are accounts that you can set up and trade on without paying any taxes until you're old enough (currently, age fifty-nine and a half) to withdraw and use the money. If you're fascinated by the topic, entire books have been written about the vagaries of tax-deferred retirement vehicles. If that sounds like a form of mild torture—or at least a cure for insomnia—we can offer some quick advice.

First, always try to avoid penalties for early withdrawal. These devices are great options to help you secure your financial future down the road— even more so if your employer will match your contributions. But if you want to stuff money in an IRA, make sure it's money you are not going to need until you are fifty-nine and a half years old. All the tax deferment in the world does not help you if you have to remove the money early and pay a penalty. The IRS has a fixed 10 percent penalty on all money withdrawn from tax-deferred accounts before retirement age, whether from annuities, IRAs, or 401(k)s. The law provides exemptions on withdrawals for the purpose of paying for death or disability, higher education expenses, or buying a first house. Before you tuck your money into a tax-advantaged account, think about whether you'll need that cash for anything other than one of these purposes before you hit sixty.

Incidentally, tax-deferred is not the same as tax-free. Tax-deferred investments allow you to pay the taxes on your investments at some future point, letting them grow without taxation until your retirement. This deferment can be a very powerful tool, especially if you continue to add more money on a regular basis. However, do not add anything beyond the stated limits to your IRA or other tax-deferred retirement account, or you'll have a nasty 6 percent excise tax taken off the top. And of course, if you have an IRA, don't think you have to fill it with mutual funds. A self-directed IRA allows you to invest directly in stocks, making changes whenever you like. Almost all brokerages will set these up for you, some for free, some for an annual fee between $20 and $50 per year. These days, there's no good reason to pay an IRA fee. Find a broker that will handle your account for free.

As we touched on, if your employer offers to match your contributions to a 401(k) or 403(b) plan, by all means take the guaranteed 100 percent return. There's no reason to pass up free money. And don't worry if you switch jobs—you can always simply roll over your 401(k) into a self-directed IRA at a brokerage firm and use that money to invest in common stocks as well through the tax-deferred instrument.

Finally, if you decide to open an IRA (and we hope you do!) consider carefully which benefits you more, the Roth IRA or the traditional IRA. The basic difference is that the money you put into a Roth is taxed up-front, but after that, you don't pay *any more taxes whatsoever* on any gains your account incurs. (When you cash out, it all comes to you at face value.) On the other hand, any funds you put in a traditional IRA are *pre-tax*, so that you pay less in taxes now and can reinvest that money, letting it compound until your retirement. Then, however, you pay taxes on the IRA distributions. That means you'll have to decide whether your tax rate is most likely higher now than it will be in retirement, or vice versa. Also, the younger you are, the more you should tend to open a Roth. Paying taxes now in order to rack up decades' worth of compounded returns, then eventually withdrawing *all* of it . . . that's a sweetheart deal. If you have more questions on this, check on Fool.com. In addition, several financial sites, including investor.vanguard.com, offer great explanations and advice to help you calculate which method is best for you. Give them a try before making your decision.

INVESTING ON A LIMITED BUDGET: THE DIVIDEND REINVESTMENT PLAN

For investors who don't have a lot of money and don't want to open a brokerage account, there's still an alternative to your average underperforming mutual fund. Direct purchase programs are almost always offered as a feature of a company's dividend reinvestment plan (DRIP). These gems provide shareholders with a simple and cheap way to purchase stock without incurring brokerage costs. You just buy stock directly from the company.

DRIPs arose for two reasons. First, most companies have employee stock purchase programs. Since these companies have already undertaken the necessary steps to sell stock in-house, they figured they might as well offer it for the benefit of shareholders (the nominal owners of the company) as well. The second reason was an attempt to decrease the volatility of the stock. If investors own shares in their name, rather than having brokers hold their shares, these investors have to jump through some hoops in order to sell.

The structure of DRIP investing promotes long-term holding, very much in the companies' best interest . . . and in our minds, often very much in the interest of the individual investor, who ought to buy quality companies and hold on to them tight.

With direct purchase programs, you can put small amounts of money into the common stocks of companies that you believe are superior long-term investments. Many Fortune 500 companies have these plans, and many of them have excellent long-term prospects. Nearly every high-yielding Dow stock has a DRIP plan. For a complete, up-to-date list, check out dripdatabase.com. Read the terms of each DRIP plan carefully, since they vary wildly from one to the next.

It can be a little complicated to enroll in a DRIP plan. For many, you'll have to register a share of stock in your name before you can open a DRIP account. That means that your broker will have to send you one of your shares. Some brokers will charge you a pretty penny for this privilege, so make sure you check what fees will be involved. A good alternative that bypasses this process is to open a low-commission account with an online discount broker that will let you buy small lots and reinvest dividends much more cheaply than a normal brokerage.

◆   ◆   ◆

And that's it. It's never been easier to become an individual investor, purchasing shares of the world's greatest companies and those that are on their way to joining those ranks. Thanks to regulations and technology, the gates have been flung open, so that anyone with internet access and even just a couple hundred investible dollars can have easy and affordable access to the markets. Time to get started!

APPENDIX B: APRIL FOOLS!

The fool doth think he is wise, but the wise man knows himself to be a fool.
—William Shakespeare, *As You Like It*

The financial world is full of costly nonsense. From overpriced products to folly to outright scams, the cost to investors and society is colossal. Parody, it seems to us, is the best way to deflate Wall Street's respectable humbug.

And so, every April 1, The Motley Fool orchestrates an April Fool's stunt. We go all out to share the next "big thing" . . . then share the truth and the lesson we want our readers to carry away from the joke. Whimsical, incompetent, and vaguely nefarious, our hoaxes illuminate and debunk the many farces of finance.

Here is a collection of those jokes, the lessons they embody, and the funniest reader emails we received in response (some from readers who clearly got the joke, others not so much). We hope you enjoy!

2016: MOTLEY FOOLS RUSH IN

Looking for a new way to invest in hot start-ups before they come public? Try *Motley Fools Rush In*. Our matchmaking software makes investing quick and thoughtless: swipe right or click the heart to invest in start-ups like Mary Jay (a marijuana multilevel marketing firm), Ironic Detachment Brands (overpriced stuff for hipster millennials), and The Big Hedge (a plan to build a wall around Wall Street). You can even use *Fools Rush In* to pitch your own start-up to investors!

The lesson? Don't invest—especially in risky or non-public companies—without deliberation. If you're going to invest in a young growth company, look for the six signs of a rule breaker.

Our Favorite Reader Emails

I'm curious why a quick Google search for Park Slope Pizza, Sheboygan WI returns no results.

Who doesn't want to get into a Pyramid scheme at the beginning?

What exactly is your business?

Direct Selling Works. People want marijuana. What I want to know is if the stuff will be organic.

It's like Chipotle, but for buying dogs.

2015: THE KIDDIE CARD™

The Motley Fool is proud to finally offer a credit card for children. The Kiddie Card™ is easy-to-use, lucrative, and teaches your child to *learn early* by helping them to *spend early*. Plus, it's affordable: your child's interest rate is only 7 percent plus her age!

The lesson? Beware of credit card tricks and hidden fees, and teach your kids how to use cards responsibly.

Our Favorite Reader Emails

I really need, I mean he really needs it, to work in more international locations, especially the Caribbean.

I want Virtual pet bucks. I should be able to purchase a virtual house, food, toys, clothes, and pet sitter for Fluffy.

The $10,000 limit is way low. Tack on some zeroes, and make all infants heroes!

2014: MOTLEY FOOLCOIN™

Digital currencies are all the rage. But a series of high-profile disasters have undermined trust in Bitcoin. FoolCoin, by contrast, only lets trustworthy people use it. Designed by the genius Mandelbrot twins, FoolCoin is built to increase in value. Ride your FoolCoin to the top for guaranteed profits or spend it on our sponsored financial products.

The lesson? Currency speculation—especially in cryptocurrencies— might be popular, but it's a risky game. If a financial scheme appears to be extremely complicated and unsafe, it probably is.

Our Favorite Reader Emails

As a trustworthy reader, I would appreciate a FoolCoin & would like the Hedge Fund Savant Beta™.

I am mostly trustworthy.

It's just so difficult to choose a favorite between those two iconic, charismatic twins. I'd have to go with the one who so tastefully lets his chest hair rage out of his shirt.

I hate you. But I hate myself even more for falling for this joke.

2013: SPECIAL ALERT! THE HUGEST BUBBLE
IN HISTORY SET TO EXPLODE

Our secret Swiss source forecasts the market will collapse on April 17. But there's no need to fear—we can squeeze profits from the upcoming tragedy together. From our 3D-Printed Market Goggles™, to the ShadowFear Index™, to rare earth metals, the opportunities are endless.

The lesson? People have forever been trying to predict the future with little consistent success. You can ignore most market forecasts—trying to time the market is a fool's errand.

Our Favorite Reader Emails

What??????????

What in the hell are you guys talking about ??????????

Invest heavily in toilet paper . . . and shovels . . .

I want two (2) pairs [of Market Goggles™].

I want green and blue.

One stock I am interested in to play the bubble is Johnson & Johnson (JNJ).

Wait, is that a prominently featured bottle of Macallan?

Aw yeah.

2012: THE MOTLEY FOOL IS GOING PUBLIC

That's right, you can now buy shares in The Motley Fool. Just don't pay too close attention to the fine print . . . Our fake financial filing revealed conflicts of interest, overpaid executives, nepotism, poorly thought-out business models, dodgy accounting, and meaningless jargon.

The lesson: Look before you leap—even into your favorite companies.

Readers Respond

Over eighteen thousand people emailed to express interest in buying shares. Four people applied for our "Creative Accountant" job posting.

2011: ZIPPYTRADE 2000

WikiLeaks outs The Motley Fool as secret day traders and incompetent jerks. In the name of transparency, we smoothly make amends by letting you buy the consumer edition of our internal day-trading software.

The lesson? Timeline and temperament are what separate investors from speculators. Buy stock in solid businesses, don't time the market, and buy to hold.

Our Favorite Reader Response

Dear Motley Fools: Yuck. You sound like what you are, which is a bunch of liars and cheaters caught in the act. In summary, [expletive redacted] you.

2010: MOTLEY FOOL LONG-TERM MORTGAGE MANAGEMENT

Looking to make billions while profiting from the housing crisis? Our mortgage-backed security investment scheme will save America and make us all rich.

The lesson? Don't buy what you can't afford. Don't buy what you can't understand. And don't buy Wall Street's too-big-to-fail status quo.

2009: THE MOTLEY FOOL GETS A BAILOUT

A loophole allows us to pilfer $25 million in government bailout funds. We blow $24 million on personal extravagances and let you vote for which struggling investment banker we should donate the final $1 million to.

The lesson? Our lavish spending mirrored how some Wall Street firms spent their final days. Merrill Lynch bought ornate office upholstery for its

CEO, while AIG wasted billions on bonuses. Bailouts may have been a fact of life for resolving the 2008–9 financial crisis, but we at least demanded the process involve transparency, rationality, and common sense.

A Typical Reader Email

This is what is wrong with this country. I hope you choke on the money.

2008: NOW'S THE TIME TO STOP BUYING STOCKS

Wall Street has been on a roller-coaster ride lately, and frankly, we are sick and tired of watching, analyzing, and writing about the day-to-day movements of the stock market. So, in keeping with our long-term investing philosophy, The Motley Fool will not be covering stocks or writing investment-related content of any kind for the next six months. Get ready for our new focus on whimsical and exotic topics.

The lessons? Don't panic—accept that market downturns are a fact of investing. Moreover, down markets can offer long-term investors the opportunity to pick up stocks that have gotten cheap.

Our Favorite Reader Response

While I'm sure there will be great value in your spatulas guide, you just haven't convinced me this is your forte.

2007: THE CEO BILL OF RIGHTS ACT OF 2007

It seems you can't go anywhere these days without some activist ninny ranting hysterically in the business media about overpaid executives. But policing CEO pay only hurts innocent shareholders. We've drafted legislation to protect America's business leaders, but we need your help to pass it!

The lesson? While CEOs fulfill very important roles, they should remember that they are employees, too. They must answer to shareholders and society, instead of their own greed and hubris.

Our Favorite Reader Emails

> How about respect for your readership?? Common sense?? Integrity?? . . . Rather than waste any more time with The Motley Fool, I will concentrate my efforts on making others aware of this nonsense.

> Since when does the "underappreciated 100 times the average worker" CEO need your help? Are you serious?

2006: THE MOTLEY FOOL SUES THE FEDERAL GOVERNMENT

The media is portraying Enron as a story of corporate mismanagement and greed. But in truth, Enron was brought down by a smear campaign of whistleblowers and prosecutors; its maligned executives had worked tirelessly and creatively to save customers money and drive up the value of shareholders' stock. On behalf of Enron's investors (and anyone else who considered buying Enron shares), we're launching a class-action lawsuit against the US government.

The lesson? Enron's management really was guilty as heck. And Enron's bankruptcy demonstrates how arrogant, cynical, and selfish management can be so dangerous.

Our Favorite Reader Responses

> You should be ashamed. I think I just spent my last day at Fool.com.

> The idea of a $100 billion lawsuit against the federal government by the hundred million Americans who were scared away from the stock market is frankly, kindergarten hour.

> My first thought was the whole [thing] is a dumb parody/satire or bad joke or something. My second thought was (and is)—if these guys are so whacked out to file such a stupid and inane lawsuit, why should I listen to anything they have to say about investing?

> You are nuts.

2005: MOTLEY FOOLOTTERY!®

For years, we've been stern critics of state lotteries, which prey upon the poor and ignorant. Today, we're running state lotteries out of business. FOOLottery offers larger purses, 110 percent odds, instant winnings, "Play now, pay later" technology, and a "You'll have fun" guarantee.

The lesson? Lotteries are a blight on society. Players get hammered by a 50 percent loss of capital on every ticket, every day of the year. (That means $20 million wagered daily in the state lottery would turn into fewer than two cents within thirty days.) The net result for 99.99 percent of players is mounting losses, which can demolish hopes of a comfortable financial life.

Our Favorite Reader Responses

I never received my BUDDIBonus tickets. What a ripoff!

I couldn't believe it when I read about the incredibly unprofessional manner in which the lottery drawing was held. Hand-drawn characters on Ping-Pong balls? Can't tell the difference between an "o" and a "0"? Are you kidding? I thought you guys were different, but I now believe that I was wrong about you.

In response to your fool lottery, I can't believe you would risk your brand image with such a ridiculous stunt . . . Though I had considered subscribing to one of your services or newsletters on Fool.com in the past, I can say now that won't happen. This stunt shows that your company is inept at the very least, and at most corrupt and fraudulent.

I was unable to find out the price of the tickets. What are the methods available to pay? How is this legal? I thought only states were allowed to run lotteries. Is this run offshore?

2004: WARREN BUFFETT BUYS KRISPY KREME

Legendary value investor Warren Buffett was spotted purchasing a doughnut at a discount to its intrinsic value.

No discernable lesson here.

Our Favorite Reader Responses

Another coup for Warren!

I think Krispy Kreme is a well-run organization and makes great donuts.

2003: MOTLEY FOOL PENNY PAL

Yeah, we know. A penny stock newsletter sounds a little contrary to what we've preached in the past. But if you're a longtime Fool, you've seen our stock-selection strategies evolve over the years. This is simply the next step.

The lessons? Look for high-quality companies. Don't trust hype. Understand a company's financials. And don't rely on newsletters that are paid by a company to recommend its stock.

Our Favorite Reader Responses

THIS IS A TOTAL SCAM! "Fools" BEWARE! Also, those fools who do fall for this scheme should consider jointly taking legal action against Dave and Tom Gardner. Make no mistake about it, what they are doing here is absolutely immoral and unethical and will likely cost many fools their life savings. I am disgusted that the Gardners would stoop so low. I guess they're willing to sell their souls for a buck.

I don't know how the Fool missed this company. Left Sock Industries (LFSI) is trading at $0.09. They collect all the socks that go missing in the world and strive to pair them up with other socks and resell them.

2002: LOVE.FOOL.COM

Did you know that according to recent studies, 70 percent of all relationships end because of money?

Yet every online dating service relies on the same failed principle: matching people based on their personalities and interests. We believe that financial compatibility is the foundation of every healthy relationship, which is why Love.Fool.com matches people based on financial criteria—as opposed to love, emotion, mutual interests, or anything else.

2000: SHAKESPEARE'S PORTFOLIO DISCOVERED

Newly found documents reveal that Shakespeare owned a stock portfolio. What makes us especially proud is that this entire investigation, and the unearthing of Shakespeare's bones, was initiated largely because of the efforts of one graduate student working full-time as an intern at The Motley Fool UK. Early estimates report that Shakespeare probably invested the equivalent of 60 cents in 1585 and generated 6 percent annual returns, bringing the value of his holdings to $18.7 billion!

The lesson? Time and compounding interest grow wealth—dramatically. So start now and keep investing!

Our Favorite Reader Responses

Alas, poor capital, I knew you well, is this a mutual fund I see before me. Forsooth, what wit is there contained amidst the foolish community, and such a motley crew as this shouldst claim merriment at expense of those too too gullible to notice 'twas the very awakening of the fourth month.

The Fool has fooled and foiled, that revenge is never far but twixt those who plot shouldst beware the wit of those befooled.

1999: EMERINGUE.COM

The IPO market is hot. But unless you are an insider, it's impossible to buy shares before their first-day pop. That's why *we're* getting in on the inside by cooking up our first-ever IPO: eMeringue—the number one meringue delivery service on the internet. Buy really early, and sell before the bad news hits.

The lessons? Never buy a stock just because someone else does. Beware of IPOs—they can be full of conflicts of interest, and only insiders can get in on the initial offering price. And remember that not all hot internet stocks will be winners.

Our Favorite Reader Responses

My first reaction to The Motley Fool's underwriting an IPO was one of betrayal. How could these lying, conniving, bunch of scoundrels cash in on the community WE HELPED TO BUILD . . . So, I decided to do some snooping . . . As it turns out, the domain name is registered to The Motley Fool! . . . They have broken SEC regulations . . . Looks like Dave and Tom will be trading in bell caps for prison garb. I'll give you an update after I contact the SEC.

I specifically asked that my Pepsi-flavored meringue recipe be included on the website in time for the IPO. With a company the size of Pepsi behind your product, the stock is bound to go through the roof.

Hi there, I just got off the phone with the CoB of eMeringue, and he told me they are thinking about a stock split. The next BoD meeting is in April, and a split is on the table!

It is too late. Those shares are going to split 6 ways from Sunday tomorrow morning,

Down to about $20! This doesn't look good for the Gardners. My wife would've killed me if I had got caught up in this.

This is crazier than Priceline.com! People are jumping on this, and *I don't even think they realize that you still have to bake a [expletive] pie.* A lot of people are going to have egg on their faces.

Correct me if I'm wrong: *Don't you still have to bake the [expletive] pie? They just sell the meringue, right?* I'm at a loss to see that this has much promise.

Even more ominous, they have had over a year to fix it, but the eggulator on their website still can't do baker's dozen calculations.

1998: WE WERE WRONG: ACTIVELY MANAGED
MUTUAL FUNDS ARE GREAT!

The Motley Fool has long used a simple, devastating statistic to blast Wall Street: 91 percent of all managed mutual funds lose to the market. But one of our interns (subsequently taunted and fired) noticed a little mistake—we've been looking at the graph upside down. It turns out that 91 percent of mutual funds *outperform* the market.

The lesson? Sorry, Wall Street, the vast majority of your mutual funds actually do lose to the market. High fees and a herd mentality—buying stocks as the market rises and selling as it falls—will do that to you. An individual investor who wants to invest in funds will usually be better off simply owning low-cost index funds.

Our Favorite Reader Emails

You are complete idiots, not Fools. Pack it up.

It is perfectly obvious that you have discredited yourself completely. Upside down indeed!

WHY . . . underscore WHY, would you announce this on April Fool's Day?

I am impressed that you have not tried to avoid the issue, gloss over it, or blame others.

I have seldom heard the words "We were Wrong" or "We are sorry." Never in financial matters. It gives me comfort to know that you are honorable men who will own up when you discover an error.

What you should do is get out of the business. To be wrong is one thing—to be wrong for 4 years is another. To demonstrate the arrogance of firing an apprentice for being brighter than you is unforgivable. You have no place in our culture . . . You should follow the Japan culture of rectifying your mistakes with Hari-Kari. You are all losers.

Good luck with the lawsuits, if you need some legal representation, call me.

We hope you've enjoyed this April Fool's Day collection. Until next April 1 . . . Fool On!

INDEX

mutual funds (*cont.*)
   fees/expenses for, 33, 34–35, 36, 46,
      47–48, 64, 274
   growth of, 31–32, 47
   index funds compared with, 46,
      274
   and investing styles, 34, 36–37
   large families of, 32
   loaded, 5–6, 35, 46, 64
   and long-term wealth, 33, 37
   losses in, 4
   and manager tenure, 33–34
   manager's investments in, 36
   and market indexes, 38–39, 40–41
   moving out of, 69–77
   need for understanding, 49
   new, 33–34
   number of, 31
   and obstacles to investing in
      stocks, 7
   and offerings of The Motley Fool, 5
   passively managed, 45–46, 68
   performance of, 35, 36–37, 45–48,
      49, 50–51, 53, 64, 68, 70, 101,
      273–74
   points to consider about, 33–37
   primer about, 32–37
   reservations about, 63–64
   and risk, 34, 40, 44, 49
   and security, 23, 63
   as shareholder-friendly, 36
   and small-cap stocks, 93–95
   as specialty funds, 34, 37
   stocks compared with, 58–59
   "survivorship bias" of, 45
   target date funds as, 37–39
   and taxes, 45–46, 260
   as too big, 40
   and trends, 37
   turnover in, 46
   value of, 31
   volatility of, 39–42

   "window dressing" for, 48
   and Wise, 5–6
My Dumbest Investment (Fool.com),
   17–19, 236

Nasdaq
   and finding small-cap stocks, 167
   Goldman Sachs study of, 178
   IPOs on, 94
   listings on, 89, 252
   and margin accounts, 202
   as principal market, 251
   and shorting stocks, 215
   and tracking your portfolio, 46
Netflix, 66–67, 114, 137, 145, 147, 149,
   153, 235
New Horizons, 94
New York Stock Exchange (NYSE), 89,
   167, 251, 252
New York Times, 164
New Yorker magazine, 9
niche businesses, 117, 146, 158, 170. *See
   also* specialty businesses
Nike, 41, 48
nonpublic companies: April Fool's jokes
   about, 264
numbers game: and Rule Breakers, 141,
   142
NYSE MKT LLC. *See* American Stock
   Exchange

older people
   and pursuit of security, 22–23
   See also age; retirement accounts;
      target date funds
One Up on Wall Street (Lynch), 17, 95
Onion, 31, 115
online brokers, 26–27, 73, 262. *See
   also* discount brokers; *specific
   broker*
"open" situations, 213–15
operating costs, 167–68